AN
EDIBLE JOURNEY

Exploring the islands'
fine food, farms and vineyards

ELIZABETH LEVINSON

TOUCHWOOD EDITIONS
VICTORIA • VANCOUVER • CALGARY

TouchWood Editions
#108 – 17665 66A Avenue
Surrey, BC V3S 2A7
www.touchwoodeditions.com

Library and Archives Canada Cataloguing in Publication
Levinson, Elizabeth, 1958–
      An edible journey: exploring the islands' fine food, farms and vineyards /
Elizabeth Levinson. — 2nd ed.

ISBN 1-894898-18-4

      1. Natural foods — British Columbia — Vancouver Island. 2. Natural
foods — British Columbia — Gulf Islands. 3. Natural food restaurants — British
Columbia — Vancouver Island — Guidebooks. 4. Natural food restaurants — British
Columbia — Gulf Islands — Guidebooks. 5. Vancouver Island (B.C.) — Guidebooks.
6. Gulf Islands (B.C.) — Guidebooks. 7. Cookery (Natural foods) I. Title.

TX369.L47 2005   641.3'02'097112   C2005-901723-6

Front-cover painting by Grant Leier
Cover design by Pat McCallum and Christine Toller
Interior design by Retta Moorman
Maps by Katherine Hale
Edited by Marlyn Horsdal

Printed in Canada

TouchWood Editions acknowledges the financial support for its publishing program from the Government of Canada through the Book Publishing Industry Development Program (BPIDP), Canada Council for the Arts, and the British Columbia Arts Council.

The Canada Council | Le Conseil des Arts
for the Arts | du Canada

BRITISH COLUMBIA
ARTS COUNCIL
Supported by the Province of British Columbia

DEDICATION

For my mother, June, who has lovingly shown me the secret of happiness: family and food, preferably together.

ACKNOWLEDGMENTS

Heartfelt thanks to my publisher, Pat Touchie, for supporting this stimulating project; to my editor, Marlyn Horsdal, for her good-natured advice throughout; to Sinclair Philip and Michael Ableman, for their thought-provoking forewords; to Grant Leier, for so vividly reflecting the flavour of my journey in his painting; to Duddy, for reading the manuscript; to Chris Tyrrell, for his expert recipe testing; to Phyllis Remple, for baking up a storm; to Deirdre Campbell of Tartan PR, for taking such an interest; to Tom Ryan of Tourism BC, for sharing his love of Vancouver Island; to Frances Sidhe and Daniel Beiles, for making wine tasting less mysterious and more fun; to Daniela Kraemer, Thomas Render, Cynthia Eyton, Leyland Cecco and those members of the Macey-Brown-Levinson clan who cheerfully accompanied me on parts of this incredible edible journey. Unfortunately, some excellent establishments did not respond to me in time for inclusion in the second edition.

Special thanks to my dear husband, Clive, for his true love and support.

CAVEAT

The selection of "best food experiences" was made by the author. It was not intended to be exhaustive; rather, the choices were made to introduce readers to a wide variety of organic farmers, artisan food producers and restaurants on Vancouver Island and the Gulf Islands. No financial support was solicited or accepted from any person or business included herein. Every attempt has been made to ensure the accuracy of all data presented. The author and publisher assume no legal responsibility for the completeness or accuracy of the contents of this book.

Contents

CONTENTS

Recipes

Starters and Sides

Entrées

Sweets

Beverages

Condiments

Forewords

As a farmer and lover of land and good food I always dreamed that there was some place that embodied the right combination of climate, soils and attitudes to establish an agrarian renaissance. California once held that promise for me, with its ideal growing climate, deep alluvial soils and history of progressive thinkers. But after 30 years of farming there, watching populations surge and rich farmland give way to real estate development, I decided to look elsewhere.

While I resigned myself to the fact that apples and pears would have to replace avocados and citrus, Vancouver Island and the Gulf Islands have many of the elements for the revival I have been seeking. Far from ideal, with much of the food still being imported from the mainland, and full-time farmers only a fraction of the population, this region does have a committed group of growers, chefs and activists working hard to create a shift in how fresh food is being valued, produced, prepared and consumed. I have always believed that real change will only take place when media, whether books or articles or film, replace the harangue, the constant drumbeat of all that is wrong, with positive and hopeful models, and focus on placing those models firmly into people's minds.

Elizabeth's book does just that. It introduces us to those individuals who are forging a new way and provides us with an intimate view into their lives, their land, their kitchens and the food that they so lovingly bring to our tables. It is a celebration of the best culinary experiences that the islands have to offer, without the stuffiness and exclusivity that is too often associated with such works.

This book also accomplishes something else very important to me. It recognizes and honours farmers as highly skilled artisans and craftsmen, and places them at the heart and the centre of a movement that is restoring food as the gathering point for our families and our communities.

Michael Ableman, Madrona Valley Farm, Saltspring Island,
author of From the Good Earth *and* On Good Land

If healthy, ethical and pleasurable dining is your focus, Elizabeth Levinson will help make your food purchases and restaurant choices easy and fun. For the first edition of this book, Elizabeth received the highly coveted Cuisine Canada Gold Medal Award for Canadian Food and Culture; it will provide you with a delicious introduction to the foods of our region and also with insights into the worthy people behind this wonderful food. *An Edible Journey* is an excellent guide to one of the world's promising, emerging culinary regions — Vancouver Island and the Canadian Gulf Islands.

The world needs to discover regions such as ours to understand the promise of bringing pleasure and health back into our daily lives. The planet is riddled with increasingly unsafe, unhealthy and unsatisfying food choices and is polluted with globalist food litter that is destroying our health, our environment and the lives of many of the workers who provide us with this so-called food. Through this book, Elizabeth nourishes us all with delicious, satisfying and soul-enriching alternatives. She is an active Slow Food member and offers us what the International Slow Food Movement promotes: eco-gastronomic pleasure. She is clearly an authority on the best places to unearth ingredients, where to buy the best regional wines and where to dine on our remote island reaches. Her recommendations are always underscored by an altruistic and generous desire to share ethically produced and natural foods with her readers and friends. Elizabeth has become an important advocate for the natural and organic food movement and is familiar with all of our best markets, food suppliers and restaurants, from the most elegant temples of gastronomy to cafés steeped in counterculture.

If we frequent the restaurants, markets and suppliers recommended in this book, we support a community of local producers as well as the preservation of agricultural land. Eating local foods will bring more good foods to our area. Through the descriptions of the restaurants in this book and her introductions to their local suppliers, Elizabeth gives us a chance to reconnect with the foods we eat and familiarize ourselves with the stewards of our land and sea.

Over the last few years, *Travel and Leisure* magazine has portrayed Vancouver Island as one of the best tourist destinations in the world. As this book attests, our restaurants, foods and wines have improved tremendously over the past 25 years and Elizabeth's book will lead you to the doorstep of many of our culinary treasures.

Sinclair Philip, Sooke Harbour House, Sooke,
Canadian Representative to the
International Slow Food Council

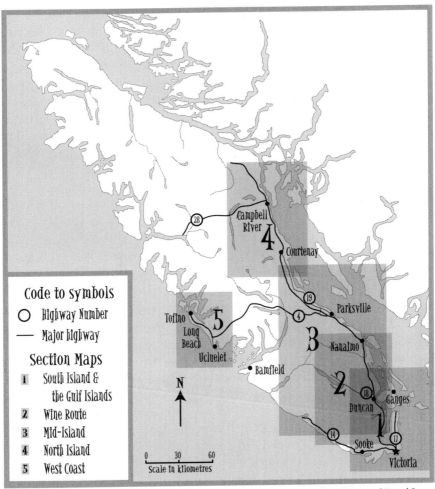

Code to symbols
○ Highway Number
— Major highway

Section Maps
1 South Island &
 the Gulf Islands
2 Wine Route
3 Mid-Island
4 North Island
5 West Coast

N

0   30   60
Scale in kilometres

Travel and Leisure *magazine has rated Vancouver Island "the best island destination in the continental United States and Canada" two years in a row. Its natural beauty and outdoor activities offer the ideal backdrop to gastronomic journeys. This book is roughly divided into four geographic areas plus a wine route, but the possibilities for combining them or mapping one's own trail are endless.*

Introduction

The pursuit of good food has become a keen interest (some say an obsession) for me. Even before the food scares — salmonella, E. coli, BSE, listeria, et al. — I always wanted to know where my food came from and how fresh it was. Once I began connecting with the local growers and food producers, I discovered an exciting community of people who felt the same way. And these people aren't just consumers like me; they are putting their livelihoods on the line by producing food devotedly, simply and in small batches, to ensure quality and freshness.

The increased availability of fresh, local produce, humanely reared meat, and lovingly crafted cheeses, breads and specialty foods fulfills my desires to eat well and support the local economy. My inherent need to "share" has prompted me to write it all down.

Sorry to ruin anyone's fast-food lunch, but in this globalized society, eating has become a sad state of "garbage in." The homogenization of our city centres, where restaurants and shops are standardized across the country, and the rapid construction of big-box grocery stores, their shelves lined with highly processed, GMO foods, has made it a challenge to find or fix a decent, nutritious meal. Or has it?

From a formaggi in Victoria to a home-based chocolate factory on Denman Island, from an oyster grower in Clayoquot Sound to a beekeeper in Sooke, from a balsamic vinegary in the Cowichan Valley to a nutritional-greens farm in Nanoose Bay and a chèvre maker high in the hills near Ucluelet, come the unmistakable signs of hope. Good food does exist on Vancouver Island. One just has to know where to find it.

Determined to find the best food experiences and then pass them along, I packed up the car in Victoria and headed north. Taking my notebook and only my appetite and curiosity to recommend me, I went in search of the growers, the small, artisanal food producers, the innovative chefs and the grocers who are making a difference and offering an alternative. When I returned home, I couldn't write fast enough to tell you about it.

This is a book about the doors that opened, the food I ate and, most importantly, the passionate people I met — the independents — who are putting fresh, local, seasonal eating back in the centre of our plates.

So, journey forth, and do as I do: enjoy every mouthful.

Elizabeth Levinson, Victoria

South Island

Galiano Island

Mayne Island

Ganges

Saltspring Island

Pender Islands

Saturna Island

18

Swartz Bay

1

17

Sooke

14

Metchosin

Victoria

N

& the Gulf Islands

When I write about the southern part of Vancouver Island, I am writing about my home turf, which is essentially the urban side of the plate. I emphasize "urban" because my hunting-and-gathering habits in the city are different than they are, say, on a remote Gulf Island. I eat out more, do "the coffee thing" more and do less farmgate shopping because the fresh, local produce is so readily available at my grocer, farmers' market or delivered to my door.

The journey ahead is one I take in whole or in part every week. In Victoria, I make a regular run for just-baked organic whole spelt and fig-anise bread from Wild Fire Bakery's wood-fired oven, French baguette and challah on Fridays from the great Alberto Pozzolo at the Italian Bakery, French and Quebecois cheeses from Ottavio Italian Bakery & Delicatessen, Cowichan Bay Farm's pastured chicken from Market on Yates, and 100% organic produce and all other necessities from Planet Organic.

In summer, I live for the original, organic Moss Street Market on Saturdays and the Metchosin Farmers' Market on Sundays, and make a special trip to Sooke for Tugwell Creek honey, Outer Coast seaweed and a visit with Josephine Hill at her Ragley Farm market. When it's a particularly grey day, I love receiving inspirational produce boxes from Share Organics, or grazing the farmgates on the Saanich Peninsula's country roads. When I've had enough of my own cooking, it's a treat to eat at Brasserie L'École or Zambri's or enjoy a takeout from Feys & Hobbs or the luxury of a meal cooked in my home by personal chef Jenny Cameron.

Coffee is the pause that restores me: at Mirage Coffee Shop, where Percy Bojanich's rendition of a cappuccino is artwork, at Chinatown's Cucina, where owner Mirjana brews a restorative stovetop black java that I sip from a bowl, at Caffé Fantastico for a straight-up Americano or, when food is also important, at Pure Vanilla Bakery and Café, where coffee and a chocolate banana muffin are often all it takes to restore authorial purpose.

Victoria

Brasserie L'École

Sean Brennan is contemplating a future herb-and-vegetable garden in the perfect little enclave behind Brasserie L'École. He knows how well suited the hideaway is, because he had a garden there in a previous incarnation: the brasserie moved in where The Met Bistro used to be, and Sean did a stint in its kitchen. "Over there," he shows me, "were the tomatoes, and all along the wall here — thyme and arugula." His plan is to restore the garden, both for its bounty and as a backdrop to al fresco dining. It has such appeal, tucked in behind this historic building in Victoria's Chinatown, that I encourage him, and look forward to booking a table in summer.

I've come to the back door because I want to see behind the scenes of what quickly became, and then, more importantly, stayed, the hottest table in town. In 2002, Brasserie L'École was named the third-best new restaurant in Canada by *enRoute* magazine. The magazine's reviewer, Amy Rosen, was looking for restaurants that "had to blow your mind." Says Marc Morrison, Sean's partner and the restaurant's congenial host and sommelier: "The rating came out on a Thursday, and after that, every night has been a Saturday night." Sean calls it a "happy craziness" that was further bolstered in 2004 with *Times Colonist* food writer Pam Grant's glowing review.

How do they handle the popularity? As far as I can see, like pros. Both have impressive restaurant backgrounds (Sean cooked at Vancouver's Raintree and Victoria's Vin Santo, among others, before making his mark in Cafe Brio's

"A meal without wine is like a day without sunshine."

— on the chalkboard at Brasserie L'École

3

Chef and co-owner Sean Brennan strikes a pose in the kitchen at Brasserie L'École.

kitchen in Victoria; Marc is a bike racer turned sommelier who also worked at Vin Santo and Cafe Brio). Front and back of house are well choreographed, and the wait staff are first class (including the exemplary and charming Lesley Vaughan, formerly of Sooke Harbour House). There's a warm conviviality in the restaurant, and table-hopping is often part of the scene. It's not unusual to go on a Saturday night and have everyone in the place know each other. Even a special cheese and dessert-wine tasting I attended mid-week turned out to be one of the year's best parties.

Like any mind-blowing restaurant, it all starts in the kitchen. Sean has just received a delivery from Josephine Hill of Sooke's Ragley Farm: large buckets of mesclun — surprisingly prolific for the middle of January — hearty mustard greens and arugula. Earlier, oysters arrived from Cortes Island — large, meaty Steller Bay oysters and the small, sweet Kusshi variety — and FAS Seafood dropped off sides of high-end sablefish that were processed at sea ("to retain the natural oils," Sean tells me). I welcome a tour of the walk-in, one of the most immaculate I've ever seen (the word is local health inspectors show trainees around the place so they can see what restaurant kitchens should look like).

There are inviting stacks of cheese, an increasingly popular course here. Sean buys his cheese from Andrew Moyer at Ottavio every Friday. Andrew often calls excitedly during the week to tell him about "something you have to try." The brasserie serves pasteurized

4

Rabbit Braised with Picholine Olives

SEAN BRENNAN, BRASSERIE L'ÉCOLE

Serves 9. Mother developed her taste for rabbit during the war when little else was available. Rabbit's mild gaminess takes on a deep Mediterranean flavour in Sean's recipe, which Mother says is the best she's eaten.

2	rabbits, cut into 9 pieces total	2
3	onions, diced	3
5	large tomatoes, seeded, peeled and diced	5
1	small bunch of sage	1
1	small branch of fresh rosemary, chopped	1
5	cloves garlic, crushed	5
1 1/2 c	picholine olives*	360 ml
2	bay leaves	2
3	tbsp flour	45 ml
1 btl	dry white wine	1 btl
	salt and pepper	
	olive oil	

Season the rabbit pieces and brown well in olive oil over medium-high heat. This will need to be done in batches. Remove the rabbit to a plate. In the same pan, add the onions and garlic and cook until translucent. Add the tomatoes, herbs and olives and cook for two minutes. Sprinkle the flour over and stir for three to five minutes to cook the flour. Add the wine, stir to combine, scraping the bottom of the pan to dissolve the brown bits. Add the rabbit pieces, cover and braise in 300°F oven until very tender — 1 1/2 to 2 hours. Season to taste and serve over noodles.
OPTION: Add cooked white beans, such as Great White Northerns, to the sauce.
*Provençal green olives

and unpasteurized cheeses from France, Quebec and Saltspring Island. Sean is keen that people order their cheese course before the meal to ensure proper serving temperature and eventually hopes to have a temperature-controlled display case on the floor. It's all about making sure patrons have the best possible culinary experience.

While Sean begins to prepare a pistou broth with soisson beans for the lamb shank, I ask him about the evening's menu. It is, as always, small and select, with the emphasis on fresh, local ingredients cooked to order. What

5

could be finer? There are half a dozen starters from soupe à l'oignon gratinée to Sean's famous confit of duck leg with braised red cabbage. One of my favourites is the endive salad with mustard wine dressing, apple slices and freshly picked hazelnuts. Mains include the hugely popular steak frites, mountain trout with bacon, chard, dried tomato and

Sommelier and co-owner Marc Morrison enjoys a rare relaxed moment at Brasserie L'École.

mushroom-potato hash and albacore tuna with onion marmalade and Jerusalem artichokes. It's always a stellar night when my husband finds braised buffalo or ostrich on the menu.

As former president of the Island Chefs Collaborative, which promotes local food, Sean says if he can't get something locally, he seriously considers the food miles attached to other products. He's concerned about depletion of the wild fish stocks and clearly does his bit supporting the local growers and food producers. As he says himself: "I am very comfortable with what I do." Sean says they want to be known for having "a very good, well-rounded restaurant, with the focus on the food, service, wine and ambiance." I say he can stop wanting; he and Marc have all that and more. Still, Sean tells me he "will like the place even more in a few years. It will look better when it's worn in a bit."

Cafe Brio

If dinner could begin appropriately with dessert, I'd always start with the white chocolate angel food cake topped with mascarpone sorbet and drizzled with cranberry confit at Cafe Brio. It fits every requirement I have for a great dessert: it's light and therefore couldn't possibly be caloric; it looks pretty on the plate without being fussy; it isn't overly sweet; it includes fruit, which must make it healthy; and it fulfils a nostalgic yearning for things my mother used to make as special treats. For this ultimate food-from-the-fifties, I am forever grateful to the café's pastry chef, Kalyn Sarkany.

Of course, there are many more aspects to Cafe Brio that have firmly entrenched it in Victoria's restaurant scene. The dining room itself, with its deep Tuscan yellow and rust walls laden with paintings, its surprisingly wide choice of seating — from private booths, deuces in cosy corners, and see-and-be-seen tables for 12 in the centre of the room to relaxed dining on the patio — and its friendly, central bar is immediately warm and inviting. The place is family-run, which gives a comfortable sense of dining in someone's home, and, though centrally located, it has an appealing hideaway quality. The food of chef Chris Dignan is the other important part of the equation; it can be sublime.

One is warmly greeted at the door with a "Hi, you two" by owner and bon vivant Greg Hays, a man whose food-industry experience spans the Herald Street Caffé and The Marina restaurant. He and his partner, Sylvia Marcolini, have hit on a concept that combines her Italian heritage with the couple's interest in featuring quality, local ingredients, and the rest, as they say, is happy culinary history.

I was invited into the kitchen just as service began for dinner one evening. My first impression was how large a space it is, and how well organized (I was reminded of my visit to Rob Feenie's first kitchen at Lumière in Vancouver, surely the smallest in the world for so renowned a restaurant). Former chef Sean Brennan (now co-owner of Brasserie L'École) set the high standards, always using the freshest ingredients.

Seasonality is the byword, and the restaurant is a strong supporter of our regional producers, including Engeler Farm, Saanich Organics, Gavin's Greens, Kildara Farms, Metchosin's Chris Mohr, Saltspring's Michael Ableman, Cowichan Bay Farm, Satellite Fish, Saltspring Island Cheese Company and Two Wings Farm. In fact, Cafe Brio has always been a restaurant that walks the walk when it comes to putting local, seasonal and primarily organic produce on its dinner plates.

The orders start coming in, and the kitchen heats up. Greg is showing a lively party of 12 from Washington's R. H. Phillips winery to their table. Their wines had been delivered earlier in the week to suit a special menu that will be served this evening to some local wine experts. The bartender is uncorking the first bottle of vino.

I retreat to a private booth with Kathy McAree, owner of Travel with Taste culinary tours. I've recently returned from Slow Food's Salone del Gusto in Turin, Italy, and she is just off the plane from

Enter with an appetite — Cafe Brio.

"doing the wineries" in the Hunter Valley, Australia, so there is a lot to catch up on and what better place to do it?

We order vermouth (Cafe Brio is known for martinis that roar, but I'm still in Italian mode) and peruse the menu. I'm delighted to see that Cafe Brio, like many restaurants, has come back to an à la carte format, although Chef Dignan is "always happy to do a tasting menu if folks will just call and ask ahead of time." Also, the appetizers are now presented as a series of "small plates," several of which can make a superb, self-selected tasting menu.

My pumpkin and acorn-squash soup with brown butter and spiced crème fraiche is deeply satisfying on this winter evening, as is Kathy's ricotta gnocchi with forest mushrooms and mushroom consommé. We all have different checkpoints when judging cooking. For me, it's often a soup or broth that will speak to the chef's abilities. Chef Dignan and Chef Andrew Springett of Tofino's Wickaninnish Inn are tops in my book for coaxing full, true flavour and aromatics from their ingredients and producing silky purees and clear, nourishing broths. Of course, Chris Dignan's house-made charcuterie and hand-fashioned pasta, which matches the best I've eaten in

Italy, challenge my choice of soup as a checkpoint for excellence, but that's another dinner.

With so much to chat about, Kathy and I happily accept the menu's wine-pairing suggestions to drink with our starters. In fact, at Cafe Brio, where there are 150 wines by the bottle and at least 30 by the glass — all carefully chosen by award-winning expert Greg Hays — it's impossible to go wrong with these suggestions. Vancouver Island wineries are well represented here: Vigneti Zanatta, Venturi Schulze, Newton Ridge, Chalet Estate, Blue Grouse and Alderlea.

For mains, I choose a fresh and lovely pan-roasted halibut with potato and garlic galette, wilted spinach and bourride paired with Quail's Gate Fume Blanc, and Kathy raves about her plump, roasted Cowichan Bay Farm chicken breast served with thyme-roasted fingerling potatoes with pancetta, sautéed Brussels sprouts and mustard sauce. We eat heartily; we drink wisely (as the menu thoughtfully recommends); and we discuss the exciting culinary scene on Vancouver Island and how we all fit into the food chain here. With respect to the regional ingredients and wines found on Cafe Brio's menu, Kathy regularly takes visitors to meet their producers and I frequently write about them, but we decide that our favourite role is as consumers, where we can both enjoy the skill and artistry that Chef Dignan brings to preparing and presenting them.

When we come near the end of the meal, one of the wine experts at the next table sends over two British Columbia dessert wines for our edification: Pinot Noir Ice Wine 2000 from Domaine Combret and Heritage Hearth from Alderlea Vineyards. And finally, we can order the angel food, which really takes the cake for me.

Caffé Fantastico

There's no question that Caffé Fantastico is the serious coffee drinkers' haunt. Most people come alone, order their "regular," then sit and savour it. As I sit on the faded couch sipping my own regular (an Americano half-caf), I am always impressed by the characters who drop in, some on foot, some with wheels. One day, a very fancy Mercedes stopped at the curb. A gentleman stepped out, ordered up and stepped back inside the car. Lovely little vignette there. Who was he? Does he come every day at the same time?

Owner Ryan Taylor is as discreet as they come about his customers but open and highly knowledgeable about his product. Having spent 10 years in the business, he insists on the best beans, properly roasted and freshly prepared for each order.

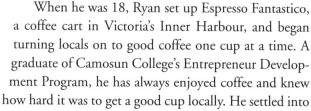

When he was 18, Ryan set up Espresso Fantastico, a coffee cart in Victoria's Inner Harbour, and began turning locals on to good coffee one cup at a time. A graduate of Camosun College's Entrepreneur Development Program, he has always enjoyed coffee and knew how hard it was to get a good cup locally. He settled into his current "off-Broadway" location five years ago, never advertised, and serious coffee drinkers somehow instantly found him. In the last year, he has been joined by Kristy, who tells me: "I was originally a customer who thought Ryan was making those hearts on top of lattes just for me!" In fact, he *was* making special hearts on her lattes; they are now married and have recently become parents.

For Ryan, quality is the number-one factor in choosing coffee beans. He is firmly entrenched in the specialty-coffee niche, which represents just 10 percent of the coffee market (the other 90 percent is Nescafé, Folger's, et al. — not to drop names). So, all the beans he considers are naturally high grade, shade grown and fairly traded. From that coffee niche, he wants the best. And, dealing with a seasonal commodity, he knows that crops will fluctuate, so he has to be very hands-on.

Ryan has a good broker, but he also travels to plantations himself and participates in cuppings (systematic tastings from small-grind samples of beans to evaluate the product). He is a member of the North American Roasters Guild and subscribes to the recommendations of the international Cup of Excellence, the Brazilian competition that rates coffees and then sends its winners to auction. Ryan has bought a couple of the COE winners for Caffé Fantastico, and is now training to be a judge for that prestigious competition.

Ryan says he is very concerned about the workers on coffee plantations and advocates fair wages and working conditions. He says it's important that these workers, who take great pride in what they're producing, are well treated. He says: "The environment [of the plantations] must be of the best quality for both the coffee and the workers." He agrees with Cup of Excellence quality consultant George Howell, who says the competition is truly "the ladder out of anonymity" for the growers and is pleased to see their efforts recognized and rewarded.

Caffé Fantastico offers freshly roasted, typically organic, specialty coffee, lovingly prepared by barista Derek Allen. Derek said he came to work at the café because he "had heard they were brewing coffee properly." Others who agree that Ryan and Kristy are getting it very right are the restaurants which serve their coffee: Zambri's, Sooke Harbour House, Wild Fire Bakery, Feys & Hobbs Catering Company, and The Mint and Black Coffee cafés. A second Caffé Fantastico opened in 2003 in Cook Street Village.

Cucina

For me, the sun rises and sets on Victoria's tiniest restaurant, Cucina. Located in Chinatown's Dragon Alley, it's right in the city, yet away from the madding crowds; the menu demands nothing of me, i.e., you get what you get; the food is fresh-that-day and expertly prepared; and its dynamic owner lacks every pretense known in the restaurant business.

Mirjana is a hunter-gatherer after my own heart. She tells me that "walking and talking" enable her to familiarize herself with her surroundings, to seek out the best ingredients for her cooking and the freshest blooms for the single, elegant floral arrangement in her restaurant. "The more I walk and talk," she says, "the better gatherer I become." Being located in the heart of Chinatown gives her an endless supply of exotic fruits and vegetables to incorporate in her cooking.

On Valentine's Day, I dined with friends on roasted beet and yam cannelloni in a sauce of ginger, orange, Bric and cream, decorated with pomegranate seeds and red grapes; braised lamb shank finished with quince, shallots, fresh herbs and chocolate (the secret ingredient is out, Mirjana!) on polenta; and a true artist's rendering of chocolate pâté with a flourish of cream and a glimmer of

The entry to Dragon Alley in Chinatown leads to Victoria's smallest restaurant, Cucina.

gold leaf. At the end of that exquisite meal, Mirjana joined us to drink her strong, black stovetop coffee and talk of many things.

Mirjana is an interesting woman: the proud mother of two international, human-rights lawyers (Deborah-Miji works for the UN in Split, Croatia, and Elizabeth works in London); political activist (having lived through war and lost family to war, she often shares her views on Cucina's chalkboard); and famous cook (her Saltspring Island restaurant, Pomodoro, was widely praised in reviews from *Vancouver Magazine* to *Vanity Fair*). Her progression, from "starving artist" in London to restaurant owner in Victoria, has been filled with great experiences. When she was in London, friends suggested she become a personal chef in order to make ends meet. That turned into "a real upstairs, downstairs position" when Mirjana became the cook in a large household and was sent off to get her Cordon Bleu diploma in Marylebone Lane. "I was the only student who arrived on foot," she tells me. "Everyone else pulled up in Bentleys."

With her certification in hand, Mirjana came to Canada. Here, she decided to take a break from cooking and became a gatherer of another sort. She worked in food, fashion and interior design styling for the advertising business. Three years later, Mirjana opened the 100-seat Pomodoro, which she operated for four years.

Her new venture, Cucina, finally feels like the right fit for Mirjana. A life-long proponent of fresh, organic food, she always chooses quality over quantity. Her mother told her: "You're not rich enough to buy cheap things," and she carries that adage with her as she gathers superior ingredients for her cooking. Though her roots are in Mediterranean cuisine, Mirjana's style is decidedly fresh and innovative. She tells me: "Food, politics and life are all one thing," and I'm telling you: that heady combination sings on the plates at Cucina.

Feys & Hobbs Catered Arts

The best way to see what a caterer does is to follow him around — if you can keep up with him, that is! When David Feys, Victoria taste-maker and *Special Events Magazine* finalist for "Best Off-premise Catered Event 2004," suggested I accompany him on his rounds one Saturday night, I leapt at the chance. What I didn't expect was that my stamina would give out after three of the nine parties his company, Feys & Hobbs Catered Arts, was responsible for that evening — whereas Feys glided calmly through.

Granted, he is younger and fitter than I am, but otherwise how does he do it? Says Feys, rolling his eyes and smiling knowingly: "I plan, plan, plan — and then deal with it!" He explains that the dealing-with-it part is "the myriad of things that can and will go wrong" before party guests arrive.

We meet at Victoria Estate Winery (VEW) at 5:00 P.M., where Feys and his staff are setting up its great room for a corporate wine tasting and dinner for 90 people. At first glance, it is a picture of calmness, with cooks prepping *hors d'oeuvres* in the open kitchen and servers inspecting and then setting out layers of wine glasses at each place on the elegant, linen-draped dining tables. Feys is simultaneously on his cell phone and BlackBerry™, which I soon realize are his indispensable links to what's happening at the eight other party venues.

He greets me warmly and, without missing a beat, clears away a box of Chinese lanterns that has tipped over and remarks graciously but firmly to a staff member that the catering truck parked at the front door needs to be moved. As I "shadow" him, Feys checks in with each member of his staff, tests the sound system, reviews the evening's liquor licence and confers with VEW's Doug Mutch about the pre-dinner wine tasting. Finally, hundreds of votive candles are lit, making the whole room shimmer in anticipation of a wonderful party. The guests begin to arrive and I exit quietly with Feys, each of us carrying a tray of wine glasses to his car.

Feys' SUV is his office on wheels, and it's where his mates, Australian sheepdogs Fynn and King Ozymandias, hang out during appointments (the dogs have succeeded the company's namesake, Mr. Hobbs, who recently passed on to catering canine heaven). Our next stop is just a stop. We park outside an elegant townhome at which a dinner buffet for 16 is being staged and enter through the garage, which has been transformed into a bussing station.

The food has already been delivered on rolling racks from Feys' Vic West prep kitchens, and his employee is busy slicing chicken breasts and gently heating mushrooms for the warm mushroom salad starter. We deposit the two trays of wine glasses, which were a last-minute request when the host decided it would be easier for the caterer to look after the bar as well. Feys surveys the preparations and compliments his staff before we head out to the next venue.

En route, when Feys' cell phone stops ringing ("We're getting to the point in the evening where nothing else can go wrong," he tells me), I ask how he got started in the catering business. He'd worked as a chef at Sooke Harbour House for five years, then had to take time out for surgery. In 1995 he "needed to make myself a job in order to stay in Victoria," and the catering company was born.

Miso and Sake Marinated Black Cod Pouches
David Feys, Feys & Hobbs Catered Arts

Serves 4. Says David: "Alaskan black cod or sablefish, as it is also known, is a delicious, moist, large-flake fish high in fatty acids. It is very forgiving to cook due to the high oil content. We love it marinated and smoked, baked or grilled. Choose the portion size that suits your menu — smaller for a first course, or multi-course menu, larger for an entrée." I had the good fortune to eat what David Feys was cooking at the annual FolkFest World Food Stage in Victoria and just had to have this recipe!

	16 to 24 oz trimmed sablefish fillets, cut into 4 portions	454 to 680 g
1/2 c	brown rice miso	113 g
1/2 c	granulated sugar	113 g
1/4 c	sake	60 mL
16	shiitake mushrooms	16
16	sugar peas, strings removed	16
	fresh ground pepper, to taste	

Trim the fish into equal portions and place in a non-reactive dish or tray. In a small mixing bowl, whisk together the miso, sugar and sake. Pour this over the fish and turn the fish over a few times to coat well. Marinate for up to 3 hours. Meanwhile, trim the woody stems from the mushrooms and discard; slice the caps. Cut parchment paper into 13" x 8" pieces. To assemble, place a piece of parchment in front of you with the widest part going side to side. Place a piece of marinated fish just to the right of centre with 2 tbsp of the marinade. Sprinkle ¼ of the sliced mushrooms and 4 peas on top of the fish and season with a twist of black pepper. Fold the parchment paper over to cover the fish and, starting from one end, crimp the paper to seal the contents all the way around to make a package. Continue with the other three portions. Place on a baking tray. (This may be prepped up to a couple of hours in advance. Keep refrigerated until just before baking.) Bake the pouches on the tray in a preheated 400°F oven for 12 to 15 minutes until the parchment is lightly browned and puffy. Transfer the pouches to warmed plates and serve immediately. Snip holes in the paper to allow steam and aroma out, and guests can eat right from the package.

He says it's really the culmination of his life's work, from toiling in a flower shop in Toronto to cheffing and designing special events at Sooke Harbour House. His reputation in catering has been built on personal service and uncompromising standards in his kitchen (with everything made from scratch, no farmed fish or endangered species and always an organic option).

Given the large number of parties Feys caters, it's amazing that catering is really only part of his business. Cracker production (his Multigrain Diamond Crisps and Zesty Roast Garlic and Chipotle Crisps are sensational); the provision of all food services at the Victoria Estate Winery; and a thriving retail side selling his delectable chutneys, jams and those sinfully good Drunken Sicilian Olives make up the rest of his busy but highly organized days.

Of all he does, Feys says "making parties and making people happy" are paramount, and he has a soft spot for the many brides whose weddings he's planned. Whatever the occasion, he's always had the ability to transform his clients' dreams into a grand party: from a film-festival cocktail party held in his state-of-the art catering kitchen to an Asian-inspired lunch to send someone off to a new job in China and the full-on Halloween party for 100 that included couriered invitations directing guests to a special party website, custom costumes and makeup, and dinner in a "graveyard," for which he was recognized by America's prestigious *Special Events Magazine*. Feys tells me: "Every great party starts with a picture in my head and the trust of my clients."

We arrive at the final venue (final for me, that is), a waterfront property where 60 guests will gather for an after-concert cocktail party. Feys lets his dogs out in the yard to frolic with the homeowner's pooch (their long-time friend), and grabs a bag of fresh nutmegs from his car. We head to the kitchen where one employee is preparing trays of bite-sized tourtieres for the oven and another is mixing up a huge vat of eggnog for the bar. Feys tastes the eggnog and quickly goes to work on it with incremental doses of rum, orange juice and freshly grated nutmeg. He moves purposefully across the kitchen to garnish lemon tarts with lime zest, then asks someone to place them on the dining table "where they can sit and get gooey and lovely."

Next, this tireless party planner heads to the reception rooms to select the background music and light the fireplaces. He quickly replaces a vase of flowers that had been serving as the dining table's centrepiece with a fanciful cookie house made by the hostess. The switch was just right and something that only a caterer who fully understands his client's unnecessary modesty could make.

After quickly but thoroughly briefing his bartender on the wines to be poured ("This is fresh and fruity; this is big and chewy; this blend has some chardonnay to round out the pinot blanc"), and instructing another staff member to clean out the hall closet for the guests' coats and change into her uniform, he is ready to move on.

For me, spending four hours with a man of obvious taste, quick wit and the ability to "deal with it" has been a treat. I make a mental note to call on him and those "pictures in his head" long before I start fretting about my next party.

Fourways Meat Market

The location may be challenging, but Fourways Meat Market has operated from the same spot for 56 years, and business is booming. Not only will you get used to turning in there, but you also will find somewhere to park and the best selection of non-medicated meat in the city.

A sign of quality assurance at Fourways Meat Market.

My friend Chris Tyrrell remembers the place in the 1950s when his father worked there. There was sawdust on the floor and a big butcher block in the centre of the shop, and, he tells me: "I was always fascinated with the yards and yards of link sausage being made."

Today, even though new owner Dave Robinson has made a few changes, the look and feel of the shop haven't changed. He wanted to "keep the old style," and give customers the kind of meat he has always "taken home for his own family: free-run, non-medicated, vegetarian-fed."

He said when he took over the business seven years ago, he lost some customers who were motivated primarily by price, but in the last few years, he's mainly won them back on quality. "Business has grown 100 percent every year," he tells me, evidence that he's doing things right.

Dave was a chef for 20 years, working at local spots like the Oak Bay Beach Hotel as well as in Barbados. He then worked six years as a butcher for Island View Freezers before jumping at the opportunity to have his own shop. His wife, Linda, was raised on a farm in Alberta, and they are both adamant about selling humanely raised meat.

With no government-inspected abattoir on the island, he doesn't want to wait for local meat to be shipped to Vancouver and back for inspection. He buys poultry (600 chickens a week!) from the Fraser Valley, beef from Mennonite and Amish breeders in Alberta and Saskatchewan, and pork from Port Alberni. His customers come from all over Vancouver Island. Every two months, a group of people from the west coast comes down to pick up their order, and he has been known to ship hams and salami to Alaska.

Hernande'z and Toro

It's one of those rare cold nights in Victoria with snow on the ground and few people braving the city sidewalks. Latin music lures us down a side street and into the tiny restaurant, Hernande'z, where we are immediately offered big cups of hot chocolate and the warmth of genuine El Salvadorean hospitality. The restaurant is glowing with lights from candles, large and small, placed on the tables and around the room. On the small counter stands a simple arrangement of dried branches, flamingo-pink calendulas and one perfect orange lily, surrounded by white porcelain bowls of peppers, bunches of cilantro, vine-ripened tomatoes and many heads of garlic.

"Food," says co-owner Jerson Hernande'z, "is more than a commodity. It is a cultural thing." He and his wife, Tamara Koltermann, have started offering leisurely Saturday evening suppers to show, as Tamara says, "what we always wanted Hernande'z to be in our dreams." During the week, the couple offer quick lunch service from Toro, a small kiosk in the Yates Street Parkade (remember they used to sell bumpers in there?). For just a few dollars, you can pick up a Burrito Pinto or a Burrito Verde, both chock-full of rice and beans and other good things. Enjoy either with the house-made salsa or sour cream and you're set until dinner time. This is delicious, nutritious "street food" such as you might find in South America, and it's become a popular addition to Victoria's downtown lunch trade.

On Saturday evenings, the pressure of the busy week is off. The candles burn slowly and dinner can last three hours, as Jerson prepares the specialties of his homeland. I ask how he and Tamara have come to this place in their lives. For years, they have cooked dinner at the restaurant several nights a week. They always make everything from scratch, and work began to intrude on family time with their three young children. Jerson believes strongly that "the future of our children is now," so they decided to switch to a more manageable schedule of weekdays in the kiosk and one special weekend night in the restaurant.

Jerson says: "It's hard, when you live in a fast-paced society, to find time to make slow foods like mole and tamale. Making anything that is not industrialized doesn't seem to fit the mold." On Saturday nights, they are determined to not fit the mold. The hot chocolate is Jerson's grandmother, Mama Nico's, special recipe. Tamara starts by sprinkling dried chile in our cups, then she slowly stirs the big jug of hot chocolate before pouring it in and grating organic cinnamon over top. It is a secret recipe, but best-quality dark chocolate is definitely a key ingredient!

Tamara describes Mama Nico, who raised Jerson, as "very Mayan, very grounded in her spirit and approach to life."

As we enjoy our drinks, Tamara sets a bowl of *chimole* on the table. This rough-cut salsa with peppers, tomatoes, lime juice, serano chile and cilantro is clean, fresh and alive — the ideal accompaniment to some of the black-bean-based appetizers that follow. The meal's starter is a spectacular presentation of *chile relleno*, a dry-roasted pomplamo pepper filled with basmati rice, red "flame" raisins and *queso anejo* (aged cheese) and topped with walnut cream sauce and glistening ruby pomegranate seeds.

Triangular slices of tacos with black beans and *queso anejo* and open-faced *coronada* (little crowns) topped with black beans and sour cream follow. The latter are particularly delicious with dollops of the *chimole*. Tamara has made one of her delightful non-alcoholic drinks to accompany these appetizers. A combination of hibiscus petals and freshly squeezed lime juice, these mocktails provide the perfect palate cleanser.

As Jerson cooks away happily, I notice that the windows have started to steam up and a cosy, home-away-from-home feel permeates the room. We begin to chat to the couple at the next table and discover we have mutual friends. When Jerson appears with the main course — wild coho salmon fillet baked in a banana leaf with coconut milk and serano chile, served with rice and black beans — it is as though he is feeding an extended family. Someone suggests Latin dancing after dinner.

For dessert, baked mashed bananas with fresh strawberries are brought to the table on a banana leaf, flambéed in rum. The contrasting primary colours are magical: green leaf, yellow banana, red strawberries and the dancing blue flames. Says Jerson: "In life and art, you have to apply dark colours to show the light." I see this reflected in my dessert, in the paintings of Victoria artist Luis Mereno that hang on the walls and in the personal story of Jerson himself, who "grew up in a Seventh Day Adventist household in a Catholic country," and ended up leaving El Salvador because of the civil war.

Coming to Canada "with only my food and my music," Jerson worked as a dishwasher. He found his light in Tamara, who was just completing her first degree in geography at the University of Victoria. Jerson found it difficult to work in North American restaurants and "eventually the philosophy of food from my home" drove him and Tamara to open their own restaurant. They are

Ensalada de Frijoles

JERSON HERNANDE'Z, HERNANDE'Z AND TORO

Equal amounts of dried black turtle beans and dried white navy beans (beans will double when cooked, so portion accordingly, allowing approximately 3/4 c to 1 c of cooked beans per serving). Portion all amounts of the following ingredients according to the number of servings and taste. (Says Tamara of the dressing: "You don't want the beans swimming in it, but you do want them well coated.")

sweet red bell peppers
fresh cilantro
balsamic vinegar
olive oil
freshly squeezed lime juice
coarse sea salt
butter lettuce

Rinse and sort separately the turtle beans and white beans. Boil the beans separately until tender. While the beans are cooking, wash the peppers and core and cut into 1" strips. Heat a cast iron ("It's very important to use cast iron! Do not attempt this with teflon!") pan to high and dry-roast the pepper slices. Wash the cilantro, chop off the stalks and dice with a very sharp knife. Add the cilantro to the beans, but do not mix. When the beans are cooked, rinse with cold water and put the black and white beans together in a non-reactive mixing bowl. Add the balsamic vinegar, olive oil, lime juice and coarse sea salt to the beans and cilantro. Mix gently to distribute flavours, taking care not to crush the beans. Wash the butter lettuce, gently open each head and form the leaves into crowns on each plate. Gently place the bean mixture inside and garnish with the roasted pepper slices and fresh cilantro sprigs.

determined to do things the way they believe is right, "working around what's in season and what's in our own garden." They use organic flour for their tacos and only pasture-raised or wild meat and fish — always taking a look at the farm before buying.

The story of Jerson and Tamara and their three beautiful children is a story of happiness and optimism and, says Jerson, "above all, fun." They are certainly showing Victoria how important culture is to food, one tasty tamale at a time.

Italian Bakery

I really began to understand Italian Bakery owner Alberto Pozzolo when he told me about the cauliflower. He had picked it from his garden and taken it directly to the kitchen, washed and chopped it, leaves, long stalk and all, then steamed it. He set the steamed vegetable outside to cool somewhat, then drizzled olive oil, salt and pepper over it to make a salad. "It was amazing," he tells me. "So fresh and flavourful, even that stalk." Ah, I am thinking. Here is a baker who connects to the earth, to the

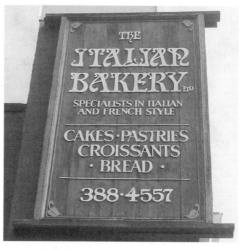

The venerable Italian Bakery.

terroir. He reaps what he grows, and his customers benefit from his own appreciation of food, plain and simple.

Plain and simple may not be the way to describe raspberry chantilly and lemon buttercream cakes, elaborate croquembouche and tiramisu, but these desserts represent only a small part of his, and his wife, Janet Cochrane's, business. The essential products are the breads, among them whole wheat, rye, Italian and French baguettes and the best challah in the world. And those buttery croissants, cinnamon buns and chocolate brioches that my 10-year-old shopping companions, Lizzie and Oliver, proclaim "five star." There is also a range of Italian pastries and cookies including cornetti and ovidi that were created by Alberto's grandfather in the family's original Pasticceria Piana in Turin in 1921.

I drop in on a Friday just as the baker, Marino, takes my challah order out of the oven. That massive oven was brought to Canada 25 years ago by Alberto's father, Michele, and it's still going strong. Alberto and I are kibitzing in the kitchen while his talented team makes magic around us: Jerry, originally from Prague, rolls out the dough for cinnamon buns, Leonardo from Albania is concentrating on chocolate biscotti and Caley, who has worked here for six years, since he was in high school, is gilding a dozen cakes with lemon buttercream. Alberto says he has "spent more time in this bakery than in any house I've lived in," and I can see he is at home here, working diligently to recreate the tastes of his childhood.

Alberto and Janet have recently expanded the business to include La Piola, a food emporium and cafe next door to the bakery. There, you can stop in for a quick espresso or gelato or enjoy a leisurely lunch of pizza or pasta. Shopping for everything from house-made lasagne and sauces (pizzaiola, puttanesca and al pomodoro), local fireweed honey and chestnut purée to organic chicken, rabbit, turkey and young goats meat and Italian cheeses is pure bliss. Alberto's full American and Italian breakfasts on weekends provide, as he suggests, "an opportunity for people to slow down and enjoy their food." Alberto and Janet have recently added bi-monthly evening cooking classes, which attract a significant following.

Mirage Coffee

It's all about the crema, baby, and according to Percy Bojanich, I make a very nice crema — that thick, foamy layer on the top of an espresso. I've been invited to don an apron and stand in the barista's shoes at Mirage Coffee, Percy's fabulously popular coffee shop in downtown Victoria. Having been trained by this master barista, I can safely report that he will always be the master. Getting those artful leaf or heart motifs on the top of a cappuccino takes real craftsmanship and, while my effort tasted pretty good, the design looked like an abstract of an abstract!

The care that Percy takes to prepare coffee is reflected in the taste, texture, temperature and design of each and every cup. The first step is roasting the beans, which Percy does daily in his in-house roasting room (that room, located on the café's mezzanine level, is open to the public by invitation only, as the roasting is a delicate process that suffers from interruptions).

Next, the freshly roasted beans are freshly ground. Each time a coffee is ordered at Mirage, beans are custom ground for that one cup! I try my hand at grinding and tamping, a step that requires more skill than meets the eye in order to achieve the perfect crema later in the process. I grind and tamp, grind and tamp, and eventually Percy approves the compacted grounds in my coffee basket for insertion into the espresso machine. With a flick of the switch (that part I did master!), a perfect espresso is extracted into a cup. At this stage, perfection is achieved through the use of fresh coffee properly ground and tampered. Stale coffee simply won't achieve the same quality crema.

The next step is steaming of the milk, and Percy gives me a few practice runs with the steam wand before declaring my efforts worthy of adding to the espresso. He tells me

21

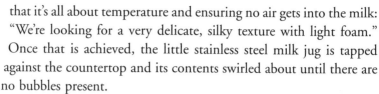

that it's all about temperature and ensuring no air gets into the milk: "We're looking for a very delicate, silky texture with light foam." Once that is achieved, the little stainless steel milk jug is tapped against the countertop and its contents swirled about until there are no bubbles present.

Then, with a quick flourish, the milk can be poured into the espresso. The trick is to pour slowly into the centre of the cup and jiggle the milk jug at just the right moment to achieve an artistic design. It's certainly easier said than done, though, so I was pleasantly surprised when Percy declared: "You're hired!" My adrenalin sure was running, and that was before I'd drunk the beauteous cappuccino.

Percy says it's true that caffeine is the fuel for a modern society, telling me: "Some of our customers really do need their coffee in order to perform their jobs, but I'm trying to achieve a company where the coffee is not just seen as a product to de-stress somebody or make them think clearly. I want people to sit down and enjoy their coffee in the way they do in my country." (He hails from Lima, Peru.)

With that civilized daily ritual in mind, Percy opened Mirage in May 2003, putting "the little money I had into the machines to make a good cup of coffee." I remember those early days, when the shop was half the size it is today and there were only four chairs to sit on. My husband and I were among the first customers, drawn to the shop by its unique coffee machines, which we glimpsed from the sidewalk, and the sense that something special was unfolding within.

Percy was working as a guest services supervisor at The Aerie Resort when he began to think about creating a *Kaffeehaus* closely akin to the European model. He tells me it was his fascination with the hardware (those Italian Elektra coffee machines are practically works of art) and the coffee-making process itself that inspired him to open a coffee shop and "achieve the perfect cup of coffee." Those perfect cups of coffee are all about "ambiance, place and taste," says Percy, whose now larger and more comfortable café "reflects diversity and foreign influences." Roman arches painted on the walls, Spanish ironwork, paintings from his homeland and clever use of lighting and mirrors all add to the *genius loci*.

This is a little shop that grew, from an owner who always had big plans. The evolution of Mirage has taken it from "just being a coffee maker to becoming a full coffee production company where we control the quality from the raw beans to the finished beverage." This coffee production model really kicked in when Percy took delivery of his shiny red Diedrich drum roaster. It roasts 50 pounds of coffee an hour and allows him to "create new blends and new experiences" for his customers. The roaster has enabled Percy to develop a busy wholesale arm that supplies Mirage blends to select restaurants in the area.

Percy imports organic, fair trade coffees from Kenya, Sumatra, Peru and Colombia and says his ultimate goal is to own a plantation in Peru. In the meantime, he is looking forward to having his older brother join him in the business, which will allow him to open a second shop in Victoria and another in Vancouver.

I'm reluctant to turn in my apron, as the barista experience has me hooked, but this is a shop where artistic ability is as important as creating the most delicious, aromatic coffee. I know that my true calling is as a customer on the other side of the counter.

Moss Street Market

Victoria's flagship organic farmers' market has just celebrated 13 years of success. Started by a small group of dedicated organic growers including Mary Alice Johnson of Sooke's ALM Organic Farm, the market offers produce from Umi Nami Farm, Eisenhawer Organic Produce, Rebecca Jehn's Organic Garden, as well as from noted growers Tina Fraser, R. J. Fisher and Robin Tunnicliffe.

Once the bell rings at ten o'clock (every Saturday, May through October) you can shop for top produce, cheese, flowers, preserves, sausages and delicious, freshly made bite-sized doughnuts.

Ottavio Italian Bakery & Delicatessen

I'm not the only hapless hostess who has gone knocking on the door of Ottavio's to find out how to put a cheese tray together, nor the only day-tripper wanting some morsels to pack in the picnic hamper. What surprised me was how un-intimidating it was, how inspiringly and humorously things were explained, and particularly, how much fun I had with owners, Monica Pozzolo and Andrew Moyer.

They certainly have come by their business honestly. Monica's grandparents operated the family bakery in Turin in 1921. When her mother, Ubalda, married her father, Michele Pozzolo, they immigrated to Canada and opened the Italian Bakery, now run by Monica's brother, Alberto, and his wife, Janet Cochrane. Andrew was a soccer buddy of Alberto's. He and Monica opened Ottavio's in 1997, and so the legend continues.

While Ottavio's has many gastronomic offerings, from breads and baked goods to the city's finest range of olive oils, homemade lasagne, soups and pasta,

Andrew and Monica have developed a stellar reputation as purveyors of quality cheese.

If you love cheese, it is a treat to spend time in the company of these passionate cheese merchants, to hear them wax poetic about a raw-milk Nectaire they found on a recent journey through the Loire Valley, and to share Andrew's excitement as he demonstrates his new double-handled cheese knife from Dehillerin, the famed cooks' supply shop in Paris. They describe an impromptu feast they had of cheese, half a chicken, some good bread and a bottle of wine from an incredible fromagerie at the side of the road. Ah, the glorious journeys one can have en route to great meals.

Monica and Andrew carry over 200 cheeses in their sunny Oak Bay gastronomia, with at least 150 in stock at any one time. They range from soft to hard types, made from cow's milk to sheep's milk, from French, Italian and Spanish origins to cheeses from Quebec, Ontario and a good showing from

Monica Pozzolo and Andrew Moyer proudly display their baking at Ottavio Italian Bakery & Delicatessen.

Saltspring Island. In short, they have the makings of many delectable cheese courses for both the uninitiated and the educated palate.

Andrew suggests I choose three or four cheeses for a basic cheese course; more, he warns, and "your taste buds might get lost." He says the key is to let texture and flavour guide my selection. As he speaks, he sets out on a thick piece of grey slate the follow-ing beauties: Vieille Mimolette, the aged, unpasteurized, hard cheese made from cow's milk, with a deep orange colour, smooth but firm texture and mild taste; Blossom's Blue, the organic, pasteurized, cow's-milk blue cheese from Saltspring Island's Moonstruck Cheese Company, that is both sweet and has a bite similar to Stilton; St. Albray, the soft, pasteurized cow's-milk Brie that's made at the foot of the Pyrenees; and finally, Valençay, which he describes as "the stinky cheese that's not as scary as it looks." Legend has it that this ash-crusted, unpasteurized, goats-milk cheese with its meltingly smooth white interior was first served to Napoleon when he returned to France from heavy losses in Egypt. The cheese looked too much like a pyramid for the general's liking, so he lopped off its top. (By the way, that vegetable ash is a tasteless coating that's simply used to age the cheese; historically, it kept the bugs off!)

The cheese tray that Andrew has composed seemingly without effort sits before me as an evocative balance of texture, taste and colour. Of course, there's nothing effortless about the years he and Monica have spent researching, tasting and reading about cheese. Their depth of knowledge is a great resource, not only to customers in the shop, but also to the many local chefs who buy Ottavio cheeses for their restaurants' cheese courses: Brasserie L'École, Zambri's, Matisse, Cafe Brio, Fire and Water at the Marriott Hotel, Feys & Hobbs, Vista 18 and Temple, to name a few.

Back to the tray in front of me: there is soft cheese, hard cheese, blue cheese and the proverbial stinky or pungent cheese for your more adventurous guests. The variations and permutations are, of course, endless. You can focus on a country or a region, or all cow's-milk or all sheep's-milk cheeses. Monica says her family's cheese course always includes one or two goat or sheep cheeses for those who are lactose intolerant.

The choice of accompaniments is equally infinite. Andrew suggests steering clear of acidic condiments like olives at the end of a meal. He and Monica agree that texture plays a big role in successful ac-companiments: roasted or caramelized hazelnuts or almonds, sea-sonal berries, dates or figs, a drizzle of honey, a piece of quince paste or panforte (that divine concoction of figs, dates, raisins and toasted nuts), savoury biscotti (particularly good with creamy chèvre), or sweet biscotti. Monica loves cheese with rusks or plain baguette. Neither she nor Andrew favours flavoured cheeses or fancy breads, preferring to let the cheese quality speak for itself.

Presentation is important too and also fun. Monica suggests that this is the time to show off a special plate, piece of slate, cutting board or small straw mat (she found hers in Chinatown). Choose a vibrantly coloured surface, as most cheeses are light in colour. A plainer surface can be decorated with grape or chestnut leaves or edible flowers before arranging the cheese.

The Personal Chef

You may already have a personal trainer, a house cleaner and someone to walk your dog, but somehow the idea of a personal chef seems extravagant. If anyone is going to change your mind, it will probably be Jenny Cameron and her fresh, wholesome cooking.

Warm, talented and extremely capable in any kitchen, Jenny is also a pleasure to be around. When we met to discuss her profession in detail, it was over latte at her favourite Victoria coffee bar, Caffé Fantastico.

Ever curious, I want to know how she came to be a personal chef, food stylist (for magazines such as *Chatelaine, Sunset* and *Boulevard*) and cookbook author (she co-authored *Herbal Celebrations* with her mother, Noël Richardson). It started early, she tells me. By her late teens, she had written to La Varenne, the famed cooking school, to seek a place in their program. They very kindly suggested that she first improve her French.

She decided "it would make more sense" to travel around Europe, cooking as she went, and then attend Dubrulle cooking school in Vancouver. She worked for catering companies in London and then returned to Vancouver to teach in the Granville Island Market kitchen where she became known for her theme demonstrations: from northern Italian and Asian fusion to basics and grilling. After a stint at the Deep Cove Chalet near Victoria, she took the plunge into her own personal cheffing business.

Jenny has always enjoyed taking on the full responsibility of organizing and cooking for dinners and cocktail parties. Through word of mouth, she has built up a base of clients who rely on her good taste and efficiency, and she loves the challenge of putting it all together.

"There's no set arrangement," she tells me. Sometimes her clients ask her to plan, shop, cook and serve a meal from soup to nuts. Other times, they may have something particular in mind to serve, or "the husband may have just caught a fish, and they want it incorporated into the menu."

As a hostess, I know that the best arrangement is when Jenny arrives around lunchtime with all the groceries and her Swiss Victorinox knives, and takes over the kitchen. By four o'clock, a helper arrives and by seven o'clock, they're passing around the *hors d'oeuvres* and the hostess can enjoy her own party.

Spanish Potato Garlic Tortilla

JENNY CAMERON, PERSONAL CHEF

Serves 6 to 8. Jenny learned this dish from a Spanish friend, who made it "very garlicy and with lots of olive oil." Jenny's version uses less fat and more fresh herbs, which vary with the seasons. It's a brunch or lunch dish to make again and again, and serve with a big, mixed-greens salad.

3 or 4	medium potatoes, peeled and thinly sliced	3 or 4
3 or 4	cloves garlic, finely chopped	3 or 4
4	large brown eggs, beaten well in a large bowl	4
1 c	of mixed, coarsely chopped greens (arugula, mustard greens, spinach leaves, watercress, cilantro, basil — any combination is fine)	240 ml
	olive oil	
	salt and freshly ground pepper to taste	

Heat a large, well-seasoned, oven-proof frying pan over medium heat for 3-4 minutes. Add 2-3 tablespoons (30-45 ml) olive oil and the sliced potatoes. After about 5 minutes add the garlic, and sauté until crispy golden, a little soft, and almost cooked, about 10 minutes. Transfer the potatoes to the bowl of eggs and combine well, add the mixed greens, and season. Transfer back to the frying pan, and evenly distribute the potatoes. Cook over medium-low heat until three-quarters cooked (the top should be a little wet). Transfer to the broiler, and briefly cook the top to a light golden brown. (Note: you may add grated cheese to the top before putting it under the broiler.) Transfer to a serving plate, golden side up, and cut into pie-like wedges. Serve warm, or room temperature for a picnic, brunch or supper. It is also delicious with aïoli or pesto on the side.

Personal chef Jenny Cameron prepares her winning Spanish Potato Garlic Tortilla.

Jenny says hosts and guests often ask questions about the food. More and more, people are interested in where she buys her ingredients. Fresh is most important to her, and she is a big supporter of local growers, particularly her family's legendary Ravenhill Herb Farm where she lives with her mother and stepfather (master gardener Andrew Yeoman), husband and young daughter. She cooks for all special dietary requests, from low-fat to vegan.

Jenny has cooked everything from an extravagant New Year's Eve dinner for two (vol-au-vents with shrimp, orange-tarragon soup, roast Cornish game hens and Pouilly-Fuissé), to an outdoor, waterfront luncheon for 200 (she had to have the host's kitchen re-wired to accommodate a second fridge that day) and just about everything in between. Generally, she likes to serve up to 60 for a drinks party, up to 40 for a buffet dinner and up to 20 for a sit-down dinner.

Planet Organic

My mother and I shop at Planet Organic grocery store every Tuesday morning, and may it always be so. We love that when we walk in the door, the floor gleams, the 100% organic produce looks and feels like it has just been picked, and the staff responds to our food queries with genuine interest and knowledge. We appreciate that the store supports many local growers and producers. We enjoy the homey atmosphere combined with good service and efficiency.

When I meet the new owner, Diane Shaskin, I can see why Planet Organic is in a galaxy all its own. Above all, she is passionate about food. She and her husband, Mark Craft, are experienced grocers. She is committed to — no, adamant about — stocking only organic produce. She listens to her customers.

In the early 1990s in Edmonton, Diane was a producer for CBC Television; Mark built energy-efficient homes. She knew she wanted to be involved with food, so, when a natural-foods store came up for sale, the couple bought it. At that time, they had no experience with food or retail, but they welcomed

Maple Pecan Cookies

DIANE SHASKIN, PLANET ORGANIC

Makes 24 to 32 cookies, depending on desired size.
Mother and I agree: this is the perfect cookie to serve
with morning coffee.

1 c	pecans	240 ml
1 1/4 c	rolled oats	300 ml
1 c	whole-grain cake and pastry flour	240 ml
1 tsp	aluminum-free baking powder	5 ml
1/4 tsp	salt	1.2 ml
1/2 c	butter	120 ml
1/2 c	honey	120 ml
3 tbsp	maple syrup	45 ml
12-16	whole pecans, split in two (for cookie topping)	12-16

Preheat the oven to 350°F.

Pulverize the pecans in a blender or food processor. Blend the nuts until some of them are flour-like and some are still chunky. Reserve them. Then grind the oats until they are like flour. Combine the blended pecans, blended oats, pastry flour, baking powder and salt in a mixing bowl. In another bowl, cream the butter. When it's smooth, cream in the honey and maple syrup. Add the dry ingredients to the creamed butter mixture; it will be sticky. Spoon the cookie dough onto ungreased cookie sheets with a teaspoon (use a larger spoon if you prefer larger cookies). Use a small glass to press the cookies into uniform size. Use your fingers to form into a uniform shape. Place half a pecan atop each cookie. Bake 16 to 20 minutes. Let cool several minutes on the cookie sheet before removing to a cooling rack.

the learning curve. Within a year, they had transformed the business. Terra Natural Food Market, with its distinctive Italian-country-grocer look and feel, took off running.

Says Diane: "Initially, we offered organic and some conventional foods, but quickly found that organics outsold conventional even when the price was higher." She made the decision early on to focus on organics. A slow-food proponent, she "doesn't like the idea of doing what's convenient." Even though "only 15 percent of the population shops at health-food stores," she is fully committed to her market.

Diane and Mark ran Terra for seven years, then looked at expansion options. With help from Darren Krissie, they went public. In the style of the U.S. company Wild Oats, which owns Capers, they are looking to "consolidate the health-food industry" in Canada. The company now owns four Planet Organic stores (Edmonton, Calgary, Lower Mainland and Victoria), the Great Ocean Natural Food Market in Halifax and Sangsters, a chain of natural health stores across Canada. While the structure is corporate, the real mission, says Diane, is "to provide the highest quality organic and natural foods while emphasizing customer service, employee satisfaction and community involvement."

It's evident to me that supporting local food producers is the foundation of their business. I often run into growers I know dropping off their wares, and one day, I shopped for produce while *EAT* magazine's Gary Hynes merrily snapped photos in the aisle. Planet Organic veggies were about to make the magazine's list of 50 Great Things to Eat in 2003.

Pure Vanilla Bakery and Café

The ultimate urban bakery café does exist this side of Manhattan — a perfect perch for the café-society set. Pure Vanilla opened on a busy Oak Bay thoroughfare with no time for fanfare. The staff has been too busy selling out of organic artisan bread by eleven o'clock in the morning and producing delectable lunch specials like the mushroom, arugula and asiago panini with lentil soup that I recently enjoyed.

What's not to love here? The interior is bright and welcoming ("the colour of golden pastry," my husband says); the staff, under the direction of front-end manager Shoshannah Buck, are young and blond and charming; the vast picture windows provide a continuous spectacle of people to watch, and the food is pure ReBar, owner Audrey Alsterberg's long-time successful modern-food restaurant in Victoria's Bastion Square.

You can drop by for Torrefazione coffee and a sticky bun, have a full lunch or just stock up on six kinds of bread (from whole wheat-walnut to fig-anise), buns and beautiful cookies (chocolate cherry crackles, shortbread and white-iced fleurs-de-lys), fresh fruit galettes, the café's signature chocolate swoop cakes, tiramisu cakes and luscious lemon tarts that will take you back to the 1950s. I love that the cakes and tarts come in three sizes to fit every celebration.

Being the nosy foodie that I am, I went snooping behind the scenes where the gleaming new bakery was in full production: half a dozen female bakers were mixing, rolling, and lifting trays into ovens, and Audrey was making a huge vat of pesto. Audrey has quietly fashioned a large segment of Victoria's modern, good-food culture: ReBar has had a loyal following for its wholesome, predominantly meat-free home cooking since 1988 and Cascadia, her flagship downtown bakery, has an equally appreciative audience for its hearty baking and café fare.

Share Organics

Susan Tychie dropped by my house herself with a hamper brimming with fruit and veg. The produce is normally delivered by one of her five helpers on Tuesday or Wednesday by bicycle or car share (Susan books a vehicle through the fuel-efficient Victoria Car Share).

Share Organics' brown-box delivery service includes produce from Sooke's exemplary ALM Organic Farm.

She has just returned from a "once-in-a-lifetime holiday" with her children in Spain, yet her jet lag is not noticeable, particularly when she starts to tell me about the produce she's brought. The winter months are, not surprisingly, her busiest. The farmers' markets have closed up and gardens are less productive, so she gets a lot of calls on grey days from folks like me seeking some inspiration in the kitchen.

Susan supports farmers who use organic growing methods and maintains a "local first" policy. She imports from the British Columbia mainland or California when she has to. Today she's brought me white Kennebec potatoes, Macintosh apples, oranges, lemons, kiwis, Bosc pears and a big bunch of bananas, hearty Lacinato kale, beets, onions, romaine lettuce and a bag of oyster mushrooms.

I follow her suggestions of sautéing the onions until caramelized, then laying the kale over top to wilt and finally drizzling with a little balsamic vinegar; sautéing the oyster mushrooms and mashing the potatoes with a whole head of roasted garlic. Finally, I grill some sole, cut up the fruit for an easy dessert, and presto — a healthy dinner is on the table.

It's always fun to create meals from the brown-box delivery programs. I'm a big fan of Susan's Share Organics because the produce is fresh and mainly local, she offers a good range of add-on products (from Cowichan Bay Farm chicken and Wild Fire breads to Silk Road teas and Nature's Path cereals) and her heart is in the right place.

A former employee of Victoria's Nature's Fare health-food store, she began her own business as a food co-operative among a handful of families. It evolved from there into a weekly box program for 140 singles and families throughout Victoria. Susan says she caters mainly to young families and university students.

Her produce comes from well-regarded local organic growers such as Mary Alice Johnson of Sooke's ALM Farm, Heather and Lemont of Saanichton's Northbrook Farm, Brian Hughes of Deep Cove's Kildarra Farm and Violet Leclair of Metchosin's Bentback Farms. Susan says she enjoys "connecting with the farmers." She loves it when the veggies arrive at her own door to be sorted into the boxes. She tells me: "Often I'll get lettuce bouquets so beautiful you could walk down the aisle with them!" The romaine she's brought me is just such a bouquet.

With her commitment to "be as green as possible and sell as reasonably as possible," Susan is making a big impact on the health of many local families. Check out her website's new virtual farm tours which instantly connect customers with the farmers who grow their food.

Spinnakers Brewpub

I slipped into Spinnakers Brewpub early one Monday morning for a tour and chat with beermaker Lon Ladell. The pub's recently launched organic brews, Honey Pale Ale and Nut Brown Ale, were receiving rave reviews and I wanted to know more about them.

It seems that, in addition to being organic, these are Victoria's only aquifer ales. The brewpub has dug its own well, from which water is pumped through a light filtration system. Lon says that "incredibly good water" is one of four essential ingredients in the Spinnakers beers. The other essentials are malted barley, hops and yeast. Says Lon: "Knowing what you want to make and how you want it to taste can only be accomplished by starting with good ingredients."

Spinnakers gets its malted barley from an organic barley farm in Saskatchewan. Lon takes me upstairs to see part of his annual order of six to eight tons. We nibble on some nutty crystal malt kernels and he tells me how he got into the business. After working at Royal Oak Dairy in Victoria, where he made cottage cheese and other dairy products, he began at Spinnakers as an apprentice. After a couple of years, he was offered the opportunity to set up a brewery in Bourges in France's Loire Valley. Spinnakers' owner, Paul Hadfield, encouraged him to go, and later welcomed him back.

a fine stop for an organic cool one on a hot day ...

The Loire brewery gave Lon great experience in his own craft but also gave him an insight into slow food. "There was a fromagerie down the road owned by an old woman. I'd stop for cheese, and a little farther on, pick up a baguette." When the French brewery was up and running, he came back to Spinnakers as planned.

He loves what he does and delights in the creative aspect of his work: "I can taste a beer in Belgium, as I have done, and know how to make it." Lon and his fellow beermakers at Spinnakers produce 132,000 litres of beer each year, and the demand is increasing.

Lon first creates a mash of malted barley and hot water and lets it steep for an hour or so at 64.5° to 65°F. The starch in the barley is converted to sugar water, called "wort," which is then transferred into a large kettle and boiled for one to three hours, depending on the type of beer being made.

Whole-leaf hops (specifically, the female flower of the hop vine) are added, and then the mixture is cooled down to provide a perfect environment for the yeast. The beer is then transferred either to an English-style open fermenting vat or to a closed, German-style vat — again, depending on the beer. Because the beer mixture is not filtered or pasteurized, there is always some risk of spoilage, so the beermakers have to keep a close eye on this stage of the process. In the fermenting process, Lon says the yeast basically "eats the sugar [the wort] and creates alcohol and carbon dioxide." I ask about the nutritional value of beer, and he points out that a glass of beer gives more than the daily requirement of vitamin B.

Following fermentation, the beer is stored in large cooling vats. Light ales are kept at 3°C in one cooling room. The traditional English beers, which tend to be less bubbly and are served warmer, are stored in another room at 8° to 13°C.

Lon and his friends are big proponents of local, organic slow food. He says he would like to see organic barley grown on the island. This year, the yields were not good on the prairies, and he "can't support the fossil fuel it would take to bring supplies from farther afield."

Spinnakers, with its prime location on Victoria's Inner Harbour, charming adjacent bed-and-breakfast accommodation and restaurant now in the very capable hands of former Oak Bay Marina chef Mel O'Brien, makes a fine stop for an organic cool one on a hot day. The beers are also available at local liquor stores and on tap at top bars like the one at Brasserie L'École.

As we tuck in, one of the eagles steals our attention by sweeping seaward for its own breakfast. A man sets up his tripod on the rocks. The elderly couple next to us finish their breakfast. He walks around to pull out her chair, and they head out for a leisurely stroll along the beach. We are in no hurry, either. We finish our own breakfast in the lounge, sunk deep into armchairs with coffees and newspapers at hand, yet still glued to the view.

Travel with Taste Tours

One day, when Kathy McAree was in her teens, she asked her grandmother: "How do I know how to make all these things?" Said her grandmother: "When you were younger, you watched your mother in the kitchen like a hawk." Kathy's grandparents owned a restaurant in her native Winnipeg, giving her early exposure to the foodie life.

Kathy was working as an account representative for Kelloggs Canada when she decided to take a break and do some travelling. Her wanderings took her to Ecuador, Australia, New Zealand, Las Vegas and Vail, but it was a hands-on cooking vacation on the Amalfi Coast that ended up changing her career. She knew then and there that she wanted to offer her own culinary tours.

A keen gastronome, Kathy is now sharing her love of good food and wine with locals and tourists through her Travel with Taste Tours of the island. The tours range from a seven-hour wine tasting in the Cowichan Valley to behind-the-scenes culinary tours on Saltspring Island to week-long itineraries that

Brie and Pear Ginger Chutney on Baguette

KATHY MCAREE, TRAVEL WITH TASTE TOURS

Serves 20 to 30 people as an appetizer. When she isn't conducting culinary tours of Vancouver Island and the Gulf Islands, Kathy can usually be found in faraway places researching new food ideas. This recipe comes from her recent tour of wineries down under in New Zealand and Australia.

Chutney:

2 lbs	Anjou pears, seeded and diced	910 g
1 c	sugar	113 g
1 c	apple cider vinegar	240 ml
1 c	water	240 ml
1 tbsp	mustard seed	15 ml
1 tbsp	fennel seeds	15 ml
2 tsp	chili flakes	10 ml
2 tbsp	grated fresh ginger	30 ml
1 c	golden raisins	113 g

Combine all ingredients in a thick-bottomed pot. Bring to a boil, turn down and simmer for 1½ hours, stirring occasionally. This chutney can be made days ahead of time and kept in the refrigerator until needed.

Cheese:

1 kilo	Brie, cut into chunks	2.2 lb

Place the Brie chunks in a baking dish and spoon the desired amount of chutney over the top. Bake in a hot oven for 5 to 7 minutes or until the cheese softens but is not completely melted. Serve with warm slices of baguette.

include private meetings with chefs, cooking classes, mushroom foraging, six-course meals in Relais & Châteaux dining rooms, hands-on cooking classes and visits to interesting farms, cheesemaking operations and bakeries. (Relais & Châteaux is an association of luxurious, privately owned hotels and restaurants in 51 countries around the world.) Says Kathy: "I want my clients to leave thinking Vancouver Island is an amazing place for culinary delights."

It's not difficult to be impressed on one of Kathy's intimate tours. Taking groups of four to 44 participants at a time, she does all the driving and organizing. Her clients can literally sit back and enjoy themselves, without having to worry about how many glasses of wine they sample or where the next meal is coming from. Working closely with many of Vancouver Island's fine food producers and purveyors such as Fairburn Farm, Hilary's Cheese Company, Spinnakers, Brasserie L'École, Marley Farm Winery, Salt Spring Vineyards, Hastings House, The Bread Lady and Sooke Harbour House — to name only a few — Kathy has created the kinds of itineraries that foodies from across the planet are lining up to indulge in.

Wild Fire Bakery

One might expect the owner of Victoria's hip, happening, wildly successful, only fully organic bakery to be a more imposing figure. The fact is that Cliff Leir is a genuinely unassuming guy who rides his bike over to the bakery to meet me, breaks bread with me and answers my questions thoughtfully. One of his bakers had been off the day before, so Cliff pulled two shifts back to back. A strong cup of coffee revives him as we sit chatting in a window seat. He tells me that the three years since he and business partner Erica Heyerman started Wild Fire have been "overwhelming and wonderful."

I find Cliff to be both modest and happy. He is pleased with the bread he produces and the crew he has working for him, whose praises he sings several times during our meeting. The bakery is now at a stage where Cliff and his bakers "are all learning from each other," and what they're producing reflects that collaboration.

The ingredients are all organic, from the flour and butter to the olive oil and sea salt. Says Cliff: "The highest-quality ingredients emphasize the best flavours." Most of the flour comes from Anita's Flour in Chilliwack. Anita's white whole-wheat flour is the basis of all Wild Fire's whole-grain breads. It's golden in colour, sweeter and nuttier in taste than regular whole-wheat

> "All organic, all the time."
>
> — on the chalkboard at Wild Fire Bakery

Cliff Leir and Erica Heyerman, organic bakers extrordinaire, at their Wild Fire Bakery.

flours. The spelt comes from an organic spelt pool on the prairies. Cliff started his magic wild yeast four years ago with wheat flour and artesian water from Cobble Hill. As is the practice in developing levain, he made a stiff ball, added more flour and water, then waited for the fermentation. He feeds his yeast four times a day with more flour and water. For him, the process worked perfectly from the start. Even the great Jeffrey Steingarten (*The Man Who Ate Everything*, Vintage Books, 1997) had to make many attempts over many months to cultivate an active culture. Obviously, you either have it or you don't.

Cliff travelled to Italy to participate in the Slow Food Conference and was thrilled to meet "people so passionate about food." He connected with a number of bakers, "people on the other side of the world who are doing what I'm doing." They talked bread — grains used, shapes made — and sampled each other's products.

Cliff is hooked on the history of bread, "this basic, nourishing food that can bring people together." He is concerned that organic foods are often seen as economically exclusive, and so he supports eating locally and seasonally to stimulate the local economy and help people connect to their food and community.

As we chat, an old friend of Cliff's drops by to say hello and buy his daily bread. Cliff cuts thick slices of a newly launched onion and rosemary ciabatta and we all get lost in its crispy, flavourful crust and moist, soft interior. He talks about bread pairings: like wine, different loaves can be served at different stages of the meal. A crusty fougasse, for example, pairs perfectly with salad or soup; plain baguette is the best foil for the cheese course.

 Cliff is moving toward pairing breads to sandwich fillings in the bakery's funky café. Today, there's a cold frittata with mayonnaise on focaccia; nourishing tomato-lentil soup is bubbling in the crockpot and there are several personal-sized thin-crust pizzas on offer. Stopping in every week for my whole spelt loaves, I find it impossible to leave without trying something from the pâtisserie selection: fudge cookies, meringues shaped like mushrooms, vegan carrot muffins, lemon soufflé tarts, for heaven's sake. And the greatest indulgence: florentines. Okay, so now I'm not just running in for bread; I've settled in to the café where that great Caffé Fantastico coffee, chai and apple cider are always on tap and there's lots of New Age reading material.

Future plans for Wild Fire Bakery include a roof garden with herbs, fruits and edible flowers that will be used in the breads and pastries. While Cliff and Erica believe in staying small, they want to make a visible statement with the garden: using compost from the bakery, they will show that even the tiniest urban bakery can produce some of its own ingredients. That garden will perhaps inspire other downtown dwellers and businesses to develop edible green areas.

Zambri's

It's four o'clock and Zambri's restaurant is between sets. Lunch has concluded and dinner is on the horizon. The owners, siblings Peter and Jo Zambri, and their staff have a short intermission, but nobody's sipping champagne. In that time, the restaurant is fully cleaned, dinner is prepped, candles are set out on the tables, flowers and fruits are arranged. Before the curtain goes up, Peter Zambri pours two glasses of Venezia Guilia, hands me one, and invites me into the kitchen.

It is always an honour to be taken behind the scenes. As I follow Peter, his phone rings. Without missing a step, he banters a little with Chef Edward Tuson of Sooke Harbour House while he leads me to a section devoted to the evening's antipasti. In immaculate stainless steel containers are roasted red peppers; mushrooms marinated in olive oil, balsamic vinegar, carrots and basil; marinated kalamata olives; red Italian onions roasted cut-side down in balsamic vinegar, olive oil, salt and pepper; celery sticks with Gorgonzola and mascarpone. These

Jo and Peter Zambri on the line at Zambri's, voted best casual restaurant in 2005 by Vancouver magazine.

will be added to house-made meats and wonderful cheeses from Ottavio's Gastronomia to comprise the antipasti platters for which Zambri's is known.

The previous Sunday, Peter took delivery of a 200-pound pig from Andrei Fedorov of Mon Plaisir Farm in Sooke. He'd spent the day preparing pancetta from the belly, coppa from the neck, even fromage de tête. A highly regarded chef who is also a talented butcher, Peter takes pride in using every part of the animal. He bemoans the absence of traditional salami making here, and is determined to keep making his own and challenging himself to "always learn."

Peter's been cooking all his life. He effectively started his professional career as a teenager when, with his buddy Rob, he operated a catering business out of his mother's basement in Toronto. It's a career that has taken him from stints of cooking in Italy, to Toronto's Windsor Arms Hotel, Vancouver's Wedgewood Hotel, Château Whistler and Sooke Harbour House (it was Peter who hired Edward Tuson and the two are good friends). At Sooke Harbour House, Peter was the chef, but he also gardened and developed the inn's highly efficient organic composting system. When the concept for Zambri's restaurant came together in 2000, it was the culmination of Peter's, and his partner and sister, Jo's, life-long commitment to serving good food, simply prepared.

Peter is a great supporter of local organic vegetable producers including Mary Alice Johnson of ALM Farm, Dave Wiebe of Cowichan Valley Organic Farm, Michael Ableman of Madrona Valley Farm and Candace Thompson of

Eagle Paws Organics. He tells me he particularly loves the summertime, when he can buy everything locally. This summer, he will also cook with the herbs grown by his girlfriend, Suzanne Reimer, in their backyard garden. Several island vineyards are represented on the select wine list: Blue Grouse, Alderlea and Venturi Schulze. I'm impressed that Peter sees the restaurant as a place not only to feed people, but also to educate them in the benefits of local, seasonal and, as much as possible, organic cooking. This is a man whose food ethic I have always admired. Though many will not know this, he cooks a free lunch on Saturdays for the Moss Street Market vendors from their leftover produce.

The night before I visited Peter in his kitchen, I attended a general meeting and special dinner for Vancouver Island's Slow Food convivium held at Zambri's. The dinner began with lasagne made with local organic winter broccoli, then Cowichan Bay Farm chicken involtini with Saltspring Island Cheese Company's truffled goat's cheese fonduta, and finished with Poplar Grove blue cheese semifreddo with an Alderlea Hearth (port) glaze and an Italian anise cookie.

The organic onion-sourdough bread had been baked by Cliff Leir from Wild Fire Bakery. The convivium's membership includes some of the most gifted island chefs, and it is a mark of Peter's own ability and his complete lack of pretension that he not only pleases the palates of so auspicious a group, but also has fun with it. Says Peter: "I love to cook, especially for people who are happy and enjoying themselves." With his cooking, what's not to enjoy?

SAANICH / BRENTWOOD BAY

Arbutus Grille & Wine Bar at Brentwood Bay Lodge

Entering the foyer, one is instantly captivated by the soaring West Coast architecture that demands nature be let indoors. Large windows draw one's glance across the room to the charming bay with its fishing and pleasure boats. Even in the guest rooms, that sense of being surrounded by the lushness of the outdoors is ever-present. Though the rooms are luxurious, I found myself regularly looking out, as one does on the waterfront, so as not to miss any bird flying past, any shimmer of light on the bay.

The background of superb luxury in the rooms, world-class spa and kayaks at the ready for relaxation and recreation, is really just a foil for the dining experience. While one can dine pretty well in the Marine Pub (with its fun summertime deck), it is the Arbutus Grille & Wine Bar that truly deserves one's time. I wandered in for a 7:00 P.M. reservation one evening, after first indulging in a vino stomp in the spa.

(If that treatment sounds like exertion, it is only on the practitioner's part. My legs and feet were soaked, then exfoliated with crushed local pinot noir grapes, sea salt and ylang ylang oil. I was told the grapes contain an antioxidant that prevents free radicals from entering the system. With a glass of the nearby Chalet Estate's Cabernet Merlot close to hand, it all sounded good [and felt even better!] to me.)

I was greeted at the wine bar by the lodge's affable general manager, Matthew Opferkuch, who proffered the evening's first pleasant surprise, a glass of 2003 Ortega from Salt Spring Vineyards, which I enjoyed in the company of Carol Wallace, who had grown the grapes on her Saanich farm. She was excited that the wine had been made entirely from her grapes. Carol's daughters help out on her property and often drop around to the lodge's kitchen door with baskets of black currants, walnuts or other produce for the chef. For me, making that direct connection from the grower to the glass was the beginning of a wonderful evening.

Dinner was a tasting menu paired with mostly local wines. We started with wild sockeye tartare with pea shoots and watercress atop a petite brioche, a favourite *amuse bouche* of Matthew's. Matched with the dry, white Sole 2002 from Venturi Schulze Vineyards, it set the tone for several clean, simple courses.

I commented on the interesting china, which had apparently been selected by the restaurant's founding chef, Brock Windsor. The soup bowl was not only the size of a pudding basin, it was cleverly designed to slant toward the diner and gave its contents — basil-wrapped sablefish with duck essence, roasted pearl onions, enoki and shiitake mushroom and baby bok choy — great presence. Other courses were presented on equally intriguingly shaped china.

Executive Chef Alain Léger had chatted to me in the dining room before service and alerted me to his love of braising, so I was pleased to sample his grilled lamb chops and braised lamb cheeks with parsnip purée and roasted fall root vegetables. Paired with an Okanagan wine, organic Hainle Vineyard's Zwiglet Z 2002, this entrée was deeply satisfying.

Léger is a Quebec transplant, who was interested in cooking from an early age. "My mother would leave notes before she went to work: 'Can you find such-and-such in the fridge?' Eventually I took an interest in actually preparing the meals." He went on to attend the Institut de tourisme et d'hôtelier du Quebec and worked at Diva at the Met in Vancouver under the tutelage of famed chef Michael Noble and pastry chef Thomas Haas before taking the job of executive chef at Vancouver's Pastis Restaurant.

He was the product development chef for Earl's chain of 52 restaurants in Vancouver when Opferkuch called with the big question: "How would you like to move to the island?" Léger brought his commitment to organics and using local produce in season to his position at Brentwood Bay Lodge. Drawing on the produce supplied by Saanich Organics, JC Herbs and FAS seafood, he is putting great taste on the plates, both in the Marine Pub and Arbutus Grille.

For me, a highlight of the tasting dinner was dessert, where pastry chef Bruno Feldeisen's talent shone brightly. King Arthur's apple cake with pear vanilla compote and cinnamon ice cream preceded a chocolate tart with burnt

Cinnamon Smoked Breast of Cowichan Bay Duck with Huckleberry Verjus Brown Butter

CHEF ALAIN LÉGER, ARBUTUS GRILLE & WINE BAR AT BRENTWOOD BAY LODGE

Serves 4 as an appetizer.

For the duck:

12–14 oz	duck breast (two)	170–198 g
2 tsp	grapeseed oil	10 ml
2 tsp	fresh thyme, leaves only	10 ml
1/2 tsp	cinnamon, ground	2.5 ml
10	juniper berries, crushed	10
	ground black pepper and coarse sea salt	

Trim all excess fat from the duck breast and score the skin. Marinate the duck overnight with the grapeseed oil, thyme, cinnamon, juniper and pepper. The next day, smoke the duck over alder chips for approximately 30 minutes. Season the breasts with the sea salt and then sauté skin side down in a moderately heated sauté pan, pouring off excess fat until the skin is crispy. Turn the breast and continue cooking flesh side down for a few minutes until the breast is medium-cooked. Set the duck aside in a warm location to let rest for 10 minutes before serving.

For the sauce:

1/2 c	verjus, red	120 ml
2 c	brown duck stock	480 ml
1/4 lb	unsalted butter	113 g
2 tsp	raspberry vinegar	10 ml
1/4 c	huckleberries (fresh or frozen)	60 ml
	sea salt	
	ground black pepper	
2 tbsp	leek, cut in brunoise	30 ml
1/4 tsp	tarragon, chopped fine	1.25 ml

In a saucepan simmer the verjus until it is reduced by two-thirds and set the reduction aside. In the same pan place the duck stock and reduce it until it becomes concentrated and fairly thick. Set aside. When you are ready to serve the dish, preheat a wide saucepan and place the butter in it. Cook the butter until it melts and the milk solids begin to brown. When the butter is brown pour it immediately into another warm saucepan. Add the verjus reduction and the duck glacé along with the huckleberries and raspberry vinegar. Add the sautéed leek and chopped tarragon. Season to taste and serve. The finished sauce should look separated. To serve, slice the duck in thin slices. Arrange with some salad greens such as arugula or mizuna on a warm salad plate. Spoon some sauce beside the duck and serve immediately. NOTE: Leftover sauce can be refrigerated and reheated.

orange sauce and espresso ice cream. His ability is reflected in his résumé. An apprentice chocolatier at Les Palets Dior in Moulins, France, Feldeisen worked with Alain Ducasse at the Michelin three-star Grand Hotel in St. Jean de Luz and was chocolatier at the Hotel de Paris in Monaco (another three-star eatery in which I have had the pleasure of dining). Before coming to the Brentwood Bay Lodge, he had supervised the kitchen of Prince Al-Whalid bin Salal in Saudi Arabia. Needless to say, it was an honour to eat anything created by this paragon of the pastry kitchen.

The other leading man in Arbutus Grille's dinner productions is Brian Storen, the resident sommelier, whose descriptions of the wines and their vintners are remarkably detailed and highly entertaining. Even before the inn had opened, Storen garnered two prestigious awards for the inn's wine list at the Vancouver Playhouse International Wine Festival. He brings 40 years of experience at Sooke Harbour House, The Wickaninnish Inn and Whistler's Bearfoot Bistro to his role in the dining room. Storen is also responsible for the wine picks in the inn's Wine & Spirits Shop, which include an impressive range of island pours: Salt Spring Vineyards, Alderlea, Marley Farm Winery, Chalet Estate, Vigneti Zanatta, Thetis Island Winery and Venturi Schulze are proudly represented. There is an equally drinkable selection of island beers and ciders, including Phillips, Spinnakers and Gulf Island breweries and Merridale Ciderworks.

I am increasingly impressed by wait staff whose expertise about the food they're serving knows no bounds. A stellar example is Mark Wachtin — formerly of The Marina Restaurant in Victoria and Glow World Cuisine in Nanaimo — who spoke so knowledgeably to each of the eight courses I ate for dinner that I thought he had prepared them himself. Always the gentleman, he greeted me at breakfast the next morning with a coffee pot in his hand and the welcome suggestion before he poured: "Elizabeth, let me instead make you a French press."

Marley Farm Winery

For me, there is always something magical about driving out the Saanich Peninsula, and I have many fond memories of accompanying painter Cynthia Eyton on her early-morning forays to photograph sleepy country scenes "when the light is filtering." This morning, I'm alone and enjoying the "mists and mellow fruitfulness" of late autumn. I have an appointment with Michael and Beverly

Marley Farm Winery's Veggie Patties

BEVERLY MARLEY, MARLEY FARM WINERY

Beverly says: "Patties are the traditional fast food in Jamaica and everyone has their own 'original recipe.' Here is one of my favourite fillings (favoured by Rasta-farians, who are vegetarian), but don't feel limited by this — beef, chicken, lobster, ackee and calalloo (spinach) are very popular. Have fun!"

Patty pastry for 15 6" circles. A 397 g package of puff pastry will make 10.

2 c	flour	480 ml
1 tsp	curry powder	5 ml
1/2 tsp	turmeric	2.5 ml
1/2 tsp	salt	2.5 ml
1 tsp	baking powder	5 ml
1 1/2 c	cool water	360 ml
1/2 c	shortening	120 ml
2 tsp	shortening	10 ml
2 tbsp	butter	30 ml

Mix the dry ingredients in a bowl. Add the 1/2 cup shortening and butter. Cut in with a knife or lift through with your fingers until it is like coarse breadcrumbs. DO NOT OVERDO! Make a well in the centre, and add half of the cool water. Pull and lift the flour through the water, gradually adding more liquid as needed. You want a soft dough, so do not knead. As soon as the dough holds together and is not sticky, STOP! Roll the dough into a 10" x 14" rectangle, brush with 1 tsp shortening and fold over in thirds. Roll again into a rectangle in the opposite direction. Repeat the procedure, then roll out again, but this time do not brush with shortening. Just roll it into a tube, and cover with plastic in cool place. When your filling is ready, cut the dough into 15 pieces. Roll each piece into a 6" circle (Beverly works on parchment paper so she doesn't have to use much flour). Put 1 large tablespoon of filling in the centre. Brush edges with milk or cream (you can add a little turmeric for colour). Fold in half and press the edge well to seal. Make two tiny slits in the top and press gently to spread the filling to the edges. Place on parchment paper on a cookie sheet. Brush with the milk/turmeric mixture. Bake at 350ºF for about 30 minutes. OR you can use frozen puff pastry. Beverly says: "The trick is to split the pastry in half, so you have fewer layers. The flavour will be milder, so I add a bit of curry and hot pepper sauce to the milk mixture."

Marley, lord and lady of the hugely fun and colourful boutique winery that they run from their 47-acre homestead in the Mount Newton Valley.

As I pull in, a worker is quietly pruning the vines, preparing them for their long winter slumber. Beverly's pet pigeons flutter about. A bevy of ducks waddles past. It's a bucolic scene and a well-deserved one. In 1975, Mike and Beverly travelled a great distance from political unrest in Jamaica to start their new life in Canada, a country they chose for its freedom and safety. Mike was an engineer in his home country but taught himself property development here. One day he attended a meeting of the Vancouver Island Grape Growers Association about family wineries and right then and there ("because I'm not spontaneous at all," he laughs), he decided to plant grapes.

It helped that Beverly had always loved to make fruit wines and dandelion wine and that Mike is "a big pinot grigio fan." They planted five acres of Ortega, pinot grigio and pinot noir in 2000 and by 2003, with help from consulting winemaker Eric von Krosigk, were bottling their own grapes. Michael finds there is more mineral content in the soil here than in the Okanagan — a distinctive element of the region's *terroir*.

The Marleys use no chemicals, but spray rigorously with organic kelp and they make their own compost to continually improve the soil. Their sheep mow and fertilize the fields. As Beverly puts it, they aren't trying to be "holier than thou"; they just want to do things the way they believe is right. "We farm with a conscience. When our grandchildren take over, this land is going to be even better than when we found it."

She leads me into the tasting room and gift shop, which are run by her daughter-in-law, Danielle. As reggae music sets the tone, the promise of "a kaleidoscope of flavours and bouquets" is gloriously fulfilled. On pour today is Michael's pride and joy, the clean and fresh Pinot Grigio; as well as Novine White, the estate-grown blend of pinot grigio and Ortega; Kiwi, with its sweet aromas of apricot, lemon zest, apple and kiwi and smooth, full finish; and Blackberry Gold, the harvest-style wine that I serve as port after dinner. Beverly makes wine from local kiwi, rhubarb, quince, pear, gooseberries and many others. She smiles and tells me: "Every time you come here, you'll get a taste sensation you've never had in your life."

Yet there are more sensations than just great wines here. Beverly has always been fascinated by vinegars. Thanks to an early experiment with grapes that produced "awful wine but fabulous vinegar," she is now making lively blueberry, bumbleberry, kiwi and peach vinegars. She tells me they're actually harder to make than wine.

Depending on the day you visit, you may also get to participate in one of the Marleys' much-anticipated community events: the Kiwi Squeeze gets everyone in on the fruit-squeezing process; at Ewe Hoo, sheep-shearing to wool-spinning and felt-making are demonstrated; and Summer Frolic features an exciting horse-driving competition, a sport that is a great passion of Beverly's. Beverly says she gets a lot of pleasure from "people who have tasted the great wines of the world, then try something like my kiwi wine and love it," but she also loves sharing the farm life with children through these community events.

In the early fall, I attended Grape Notes at Marley Farm, an exuberant annual event featuring good eats and dancing that raises funds for the local hospital. On another evening in summertime, on long communal tables in their courtyard, the Marleys presented a sumptuous Jamaican feast to their friends and suppliers. The estate wines flowed and the steel drums played reggae long into the night. It was a great celebration of local, seasonal foods and wines and an impressive benchmark of generosity.

When the Marleys started the winery, they named it Carriage Hill Estate Winery, but were later persuaded by *National Post* wine writer Michael Vaughn to change it to reflect their roots and honour Michael's second cousin, the legendary reggae *mon* Bob Marley. And nothing rings truer here at Marley Farm Winery than the words of his song: "Let's get together and feel all right."

Shady Creek Ice Cream Company

I'm with my young writer friend, Leyland Cecco, when we are greeted at the door to the Shady Creek Ice Cream Company by office manager Deeny Patel and asked to don hairnets. Having spent a great deal of time researching this book clad in some form of protective clothing, I give full marks to the island's small food producers for the care they take with regard to sanitation, often beyond the governmental Food Safe requirements. And, of course, I'm impressed by any 14-year-old guy who doesn't blink at wearing a net.

Inside, the rap music and inviting aroma of vanilla beans draws us to the cooking area where ice-cream maker Ben Lyon is busy slicing vanilla beans and dropping them into a large vat of simmering cream. He is preparing both the company's best-selling vanilla bean ice cream and the seasonal cinnamon ice cream.

Shady Creek Ice Cream began in 1997 when former police department employee (she looked after women prisoners) Christie Eng started experimenting in her kitchen. She missed the excellent ice cream she and her family had been able to buy in Calgary and was looking to change careers. The company

Martin and Christie Eng proffer tuiles with roasted banana ice cream at the Harvest Bounty Festival.

has evolved slowly, gradually taking over the first floor of the Engs' home in Saanich. Today, Christie produces over $100,000-worth of ice cream annually.

She is associated with the Social Ventures Network, an international organization of socially responsible entrepreneurs. I first heard of this group at Hollyhock, on Cortes Island, which hosts a meeting of its members every September. Members include people like Judy Wicks of Philadelphia's White Dog Café Foundation, known for its success in linking local farmers and chefs; Ben Cohen of Ben & Jerry's Homemade Ice Cream whose business embraces both a social and a financial mission; and Happy Planet Foods, which makes those great smoothies and donates 10 percent of profits to environmental and humanitarian organizations. Says Christie: "It enhances the quality of the food we

Blackberry Lavender Trifle

CHRISTIE ENG, SHADY CREEK ICE CREAM COMPANY

Makes 8 generous portions. I was honoured when Christie created this recipe especially for this book. It's the ultimate modern take on the English classic, and I love that it incorporates local wild blackberries and Cherry Point Vineyard's excellent blackberry port.

	sponge cake torn up into roughly 2" pieces	
2 c	Shady Creek Lavender Ice Cream	480 ml
1/3 c	Cherry Point Vineyard's Cowichan blackberry port (may substitute rum or sherry)	80 ml
1 c	whipping cream, whipped	240 ml
1 c	fresh seasonal berries soaked in 1/6 c (40 ml) blackberry port	240 ml

Remove the ice cream from the freezer. In a glass bowl or four individual goblets spread a thin layer of the whipped cream — about one-fifth of it. Randomly set pieces of sponge cake into the cream. Sprinkle with the blackberry port. Dab in another one-fifth of the whipped cream to support the next layer. Drop dollops of slightly softened lavender ice cream somewhat evenly over the whipped cream. Add a few of the berries. Cover with the remaining whipped cream. Top with the remaining berries soaked in port.

produce that we care about the quality of our environment and the world we live in."

The ingredients are all high quality, many organic: Callebaut chocolate, Dutch cocoa, Australian ginger, maple sugar from Quebec, local blackberries and raspberries, lavender from Happy Valley Lavender and Herb Farm, Santa Cruz lemons, coffee from the Saltspring Roasting Company and many gallons of Avalon Dairy's pure whipping cream. Cardamom, cloves and cinnamon are ground for the chai tea-flavoured ice cream (Christie credits Victoria chef John Hall with educating her palate in the development of this flavour). The blackberries are cooked, then strained through a chinois to remove seeds before being made into sorbet. Star anise is roasted, ground, then steeped in cream to make the popular licorice ice cream.

Ben refers to "the science of ice cream," and shows me the amazing computer-generated recipes he works from. It is Christie's husband, Marvin, who inputs the number of tubs of each ice cream flavour required for a particular day's order. The computer program then determines the quantities that will be needed for each recipe to meet the order. Generally, Christie and Ben make ice cream Monday through Wednesday, and freeze it on Thursday and Friday. Often they produce 200 tubs a day. It gets so cold in the freezing area that Ben wears a scarf.

 Christie and her son, University of Victoria student Erin Eng, personally deliver the ice cream up and down Vancouver Island. They load up to 1,600 tubs into her refrigerated truck and drive to Parksville and points north. Chefs call Christie all the time for special orders (killer bee honey and lime sorbet being one of the more interesting). Christie served a startling seaweed ice cream at the 2004 Harvest Bounty Festival that blew me and everyone else there away. Shady Creek is often on the menus at The Fairmont Empress Hotel, Butchart Gardens, Government House (ginger ice cream was available to Queen Elizabeth II and Prince Philip during the 2002 Golden Jubilee visit), The Med Grill, Truffles Catering Group, The Canoe Brewpub and Restaurant, the Wesley Street Cafe, Glow World Cuisine and the Atlas Cafe. New flavours include lemon-thyme and maple nugget ice creams and passion fruit and strawberry-thyme sorbets. Buy it from the island's best grocers and you can eat it straight from the tub the way Leyland and I did on our way home.

Southern Vancouver Island Foraging Trail

This joint package between The Aerie Resort in the Cowichan Valley and Brentwood Bay Lodge and Spa gives people the opportunity to "discover the culinary richness of Southern Vancouver Island" without having to plan anything but the date they want to arrive. Coordinator and culinary public relations consultant Deirdre Campbell tells me: "People like the fact that mostly everything is organized for them."

Guests start at either resort and hop the charming Mill Bay ferry two nights later to cross Saanich Inlet to reach the other. Each two-night package includes suite accommodation, full breakfast, five-course dinner for two on either night, lunch and menu discussion with Chef Christophe Letard at The Aerie, self-guided gourmet farm tour in the Cowichan Valley and an eco-foraging tour at Brentwood Bay Lodge.

lemonade and lavender shortbread, lavender soaps and lavender plants and seeds for sale. Lynda composes a new lavender recipe every year to encourage her customers to cook with the ancient plant.

How did she choose lavender in the first place? "I didn't," she tells me. "It chose me." Lynda had regularly visited an elderly lady to pick lavender until one January, the lady arrived on Lynda's doorstep with a huge plant. She had decided to move to a smaller home and wanted Lynda to have her lavender. From that plant, Lynda took 500 cuttings and started her first garden.

Metchosin Farmers' Market

The Metchosin market is a favourite of mine because it is so naturally presented. It's held on Sundays, outdoors, just behind the fire hall, and never fails to impart that lovely sense of being in the country. The pace is slow, the vendors are friendly and the produce always looks and tastes like it has been picked only minutes before you arrive.

You'll find organic farmer extraordinaire Dieter Eisenhawer with his tiny, perfect fingerling potatoes, arugula, beans and tomatoes; Yoshiko Unno and Tsutomu Suganami of Umi Nami Farm with their exquisite Oriental vegetables; Gini and Peter Walsh of Swallow Hill Farm with apples, Asian pears, blueberries and rhubarb; and Bernie and Marti Martin-Wood of Two Wings Farm with the most amazing salad mix, heirloom tomatoes and organic seeds.

There are 15 to 20 stalls at every market. Call ahead for the date of the Harvest Festival in the fall, when local musicians, clowns and a rooster-crowing contest add to the fun.

SOOKE

Cooper's Cove Guesthouse and Angelo's Cooking School

I'd driven by an immaculate little blue house perched above Sooke Basin many times before a knowledgeable voice on the other end of my phone said: "You really should check out the cooking classes at Cooper's Cove." I was delighted to find former Culinary Team Canada chef Angelo Prosperi-Porta offering afternoon cooking classes followed by kitchen suppers and lovely sea-view rooms for the night. Prosperi-Porta, "a Canadian born with a Roman heart," and

Whole Seed-Crusted Salmon Fillet with Chervil Lemon Butter

ANGELO PROSPERI-PORTA, COOPER'S COVE GUESTHOUSE AND ANGELO'S COOKING SCHOOL

Serves 8. Sometimes you get what you wish for. Thank you, Angelo, for permission to reprint this recipe from your cookbook before it hit the press!

For the fillets:

8	5 oz	skinless salmon fillets (Angelo prefers coho or spring salmon)	8 142 g
		salt and pepper	
	1/3 c	finely ground flax seeds	80 ml
	1	egg white, lightly beaten	1
	2 tbsp	each of whole flax, sunflower, poppy, pumpkin and sesame seeds. The variety of seeds can vary depending on what is available. You will need about 3/4 c (180 ml) in total.	30 ml each
	3–4 tbsp	extra virgin olive oil	45–60 ml

For the sauce:

3/4 c	dry white wine	180 ml
1 c	fish stock	240 ml
	juice and zest of 1 large lemon	
1–2 tbsp	honey	15–30 ml
3 oz	cold unsalted butter, cut into small pieces	85 g
1 1/2 c	fresh chervil, stems removed, coarsely chopped (amount approximate)	340 g

Season the fillets on both sides with salt and pepper. Dredge both sides lightly with the ground flax seed, dip the flesh side only into the egg white and press the egg white-coated side into the mixed seeds to coat. Set aside. Heat a large skillet big enough to hold all the fillets or use a smaller skillet and cook the fish in two batches. When the pan is hot, add 3-4 tbsp olive oil and add the fillets seed side down. Sear about one minute to get a well-toasted crust, adding more oil if necessary. Turn over and cook about two minutes more. Remove from the skillet and place in a warm oven (225°F to 250°F) while you make the sauce. Drain the excess oil from the pan. Return the pan to the heat, add the white wine and reduce by approximately half. Add the fish stock and reduce by two-thirds. Add the lemon juice, zest and honey to taste. Reduce the sauce slightly, then add the butter and quickly whisk or swirl to incorporate. Add the chopped chervil and cook for a few seconds more. Season if necessary and portion onto serving plates, placing the fillets on top of the sauce.

Ina Haegemann, his German-born partner, have created a unique culinary experience that has been featured on Oprah but is still something of a secret locally.

In the comfortable and well-equipped kitchen, I joined other guests for a cooking class that featured many local, seasonal and organic ingredients. Prosperi-Porta proffered a large bowl of seaweeds harvested that morning by Diane Bernard, owner of Sooke's Outer Coast Seaweeds. We sampled sea lettuce, sugar kelp, alaria, dulse and, my favourite, feather boa — "all very healthy and full of minerals," said our host. From the seaweeds, corn meal and wheat flour, we made bread molded into fanciful seaweed shapes.

Prosperi-Porta simmered white wine and diced cucumber for a sorbet and told us what excites him about cooking: "It's not just the act of eating. When I cook the dishes I grew up with, it keeps my heritage and family memories alive." He grows most of his own produce and is proud that his fruit trees are descendants of his father's trees, that he brought the *minucia* in his garden from Italy.

We all got involved making seaweed pesto to be served with seared albacore tuna, then learned how to concoct a surprisingly simple fresh fruit terrine. Prosperi-Porta left the kitchen at one point to "go fishing," and returned with a stunning sockeye salmon. He gave us tips on buying fresh fish: the eyes should be clear, the gills bright red, and the whole fish firm to the touch. He demonstrated scaling and filleting, then made a tasty crust for the fillets of flax, sunflower, poppy, pumpkin and sesame seeds. We later enjoyed the salmon with a chervil lemon butter sauce, accompanied by sautéed spaghetti squash, radishes and green beans with garlic and mint.

After the lesson, we soaked in the hot tub before returning to the kitchen to feast on our earlier efforts. Haegemann had laid the centre island with white china and flowers from her garden, Prosperi-Porta poured a dry riesling, and the Buena Vista Social Club set the tone on the stereo. We ate and drank, laughed a lot and had some fantastic new recipes to take home the next day.

Prosperi-Porta's classes may be booked as part of a two- or three-night getaway at Cooper's Cove Guesthouse. For those inclined more to eat than cook, his sublime meals are available for breakfast and dinner. This is a spot to unwind, to learn about food from someone who really has reverence for his ingredients and a true mastery of his craft, and to eat remarkably well.

Angelo shares some of his culinary secrets in his recently released, much-anticipated first cookbook: *Flavours of Cooper's Cove.*

Little Vienna Bakery

Andreas and Michelle Ruttkiewicz's Little Vienna Bakery has slipped into Sooke like a well-fitting glove, which is ironic, really, as one doesn't think of this as a town craving strudel or Sachertorte. In fact, they hadn't planned on settling in this small community, but Michelle tells me: "There are some 40 bakeries in Victoria. We saw interesting changes in Sooke and decided to take the plunge." And I am always standing in a long line of jovial locals when I drive out to satisfy my cravings for pastries as fine as I found years ago in Vienna's Café Demel. Michelle tells me they are "amazed at the number of people who thank us every day for being here."

I love to take my time perusing the pastry display case, where mille feuilles, raspberry linzers and slices of nusstorte, Mozart torte and poppy seed torte compete for my attention. I inevitably pick a slice of apple strudel because it takes me back to my European heritage — and because I know of no better rendition of this sweet pastry. Even my father, whose roots into the pastry shops of Germany and Austria go deeper than my own, is smitten with Michelle's strudel. And of course there is more to Little Vienna Bakery than pastries.

Its cheery premises are located just past Sooke's only traffic light. The decor is an eclectic mix of big gilt mirrors, local artwork (major shows are often hung here by the Sooke Arts Council) and cosy tables. A piano against one wall often inspires impromptu concerts by local pianists, and book readings by local authors are on the menu in winter. In summer, it's a pleasure to kick back on the outside deck with a local beer like Phillips India Pale Ale and a hearty sausage served with Bavarian mustard.

I sit down to chat with Michelle against the bustle and merriment of Christmas shoppers and diners. She tells me she is thrilled with the reception her bakery has received and is particularly pleased that they are now employing 11 locals. Staff range from students to retirees and "they feel like an extension of our family." Miles Nickerson, who makes me a good, strong *caffè macchiato* at the front counter, is also a noted guitarist and often plays during special events. Two sisters who help in the kitchen are students at the local high school. Michelle is teaching her staff what she knows, from her pastry training at Frau Freidle's conditorei in Vienna to the memories of the café society that she and Andreas grew up with on St. Denis Street in Montreal.

Michelle tells me she sees Little Vienna as "a gathering place where I hope people can be very much at home." That sense of hominess is the Ruttkiewiczs' aim. They are recreating both pastry shop and *Heuriger*, the

Michelle's Sachertorte

MICHELLE RUTTKIEWICZ, LITTLE VIENNA BAKERY

Serves. 14. Michelle's Sachertorte takes me back to the great Café Demel in Vienna where the cake is said to have been invented, and where I first tasted it. I like that her version is accessible to the home cook. While she uses the German Schokinag chocolate at the bakery, she promises success with everyday chocolate chips.

1 c	butter	240 gr
1 c	dark chocolate chips	240 gr
1/2 c	icing sugar	120 gr
1/2 c	granulated sugar	120 gr
3/4 c	fine breadcrumbs	180 gr
12	egg yolks	12
12	egg whites	12
2 c	ganache (recipe follows)	480 ml
3/4 c	apricot glaze	200 gr

Melt chocolate in microwave (melt one minute; stir; melt one minute) and let cool to room temperature. Separate the eggs. In a mixing bowl, combine the granulated sugar and the egg whites and whip into a meringue (stiff peaks). In a large mixing bowl, cream the butter and add the icing sugar. Add the yolks to the butter mixture, a few at a time, and cream until smooth. Add the melted chocolate to the butter mixture. Fold a small amount of the meringue into the butter mixture to lighten. Then add all the butter mixture to the meringue, folding gently. Finally, fold in the breadcrumbs. Spread the batter in a 9" buttered and floured cake pan and bake at 325°F for one hour. When still slightly warm, remove cake from pan and cut into two layers. Fill with a 1/4" layer of apricot glaze and brush top and sides with warmed glaze. Let cool. Pour the warm ganache over the top and sides of cake. Enjoy with freshly whipped cream.

Ganache

1 c	whipping cream	240 ml
1 1/4 c	dark chocolate chips	260 gr

Heat the whipping cream in saucepan over medium heat until warm. Add the chocolate chips, reducing the heat to low. Stir occasionally until completely melted and a smooth consistency is obtained.

Austrian family restaurants where patrons go to sample the new wine, especially the young rieslings, and to enjoy live music and simple food like roasted chicken, rosti, potato salads, dumplings and savoury strudels. Michelle says she will soon introduce the famous Emperor's Pancake with plum compote to delight her customers in winter.

Michelle and Andreas — who tell me their bible is *Women are from Venus, Men are from Mars* — seem to have found the right recipe for working together to create something that Sooke never knew it needed but now can't live without.

Markus' Wharfside Restaurant

At the end of Maple Avenue, just before you hit the water, stop at the small blue cottage on the left. Markus and Tatum Wieland have opened one of those friendly little restaurants with great food that one reads about in *Saveur* and then always hopes to stumble across. I'd heard that Sooke Harbour House and many of the area's bed-and-breakfast establishments were sending guests there, so I felt the restaurant came well recommended.

I arrived solo without a reservation and found myself warmly greeted and shown to a window seat with a spectacular view of Whiffen Spit and the Olympic Mountains. The decor is simple but elegant, with white tablecloths and colourful art on the walls. My server was knowledgeable about the menu, and I'd soon selected a vegetable risotto to start, followed by sautéed prawns with a garlic, white wine and herb butter sauce. A glass of gewürztraminer came to mind, and a generous glass was set before me to enjoy with some Siciliano bread from the neighbouring Little Vienna Bakery and that lovely view.

Markus' Wharfside Restaurant was the vision of Markus and his father when they visited Sooke and came upon the cottage a year ago. A crowd of workmen moved in to transform something that had been neglected into something charming. Says Tatum: "It was such a beehive of activity in here for months that I didn't actually see the vision until the tables were set!" Today, she works front-of-house, keeps the books and is taking a wine course through the International Sommelier Guild, while her husband runs the kitchen. It's a successful division of labour that has garnered them a loyal local following.

Markus was born in Mexico to German parents and raised with an appreciation of "cooking from the region." He prefers to use local ingredients as much as possible and is "not too much into fusion." His food is what it is, and that's a good thing. A supporter of the Slow Food philosophy of eating regionally, he draws on Sooke's ALM Organic Farm and Demamiel Creek Organics for

Braised Smoked Black Cod with a Tomato, Green Spanish Olives, Spicy Peppers and Onion Broth

MARKUS WIELAND, MARKUS' WHARFSIDE RESTAURANT

Serves 4. Markus' simple preparation brings the taste of the Mediterranean to Sooke — and now to your table.

4 200-g	fillets of non-dyed smoked black cod, boned and skinless	
8	new potatoes, cooked and peeled	8

For the Tomato Broth:

1 1/2	medium yellow onion, sliced in very fine julienne	1 1/2
4	large, ripe, beefsteak tomatoes	4
8 tsp	grapeseed oil	40 ml
3 oz	Spanish green olives, some slivered and some whole	85 g
2 oz	pickled yellow peppers (mild or hot depending on desired heat level)	60 g
4	bay leaves	4
	sea salt	

Core the tomatoes and score an "x" on the bottom of each one. Blanch the tomatoes by immersing them in boiling water for a few seconds until the skin starts to peel away. From the hot water, immediately transfer the tomatoes into a prepared ice bath. This step loosens the skin from the tomato for peeling. When the tomatoes are peeled, cut them in half, remove the seeds and put them into a strainer set over a bowl. Keep the juice that separates from the seeds for later. Sauté half the sliced onion with half the grapeseed oil until the onion appears glossy. Then add the tomatoes and tomato juices to the onion, simmer until completely cooked and season the mixture with sea salt. Let it cool in preparation for blending. When it is cool, blend mixture into a smooth liquid. On medium heat, in a large shallow pot, sauté the remaining sliced onion in the remaining grapeseed oil. When the onion appears glossy add the olives and the whole pickled yellow peppers, making sure not to brown the onions. Combine with the blended tomato broth and simmer for five minutes. When this step is finished, season the mixture with sea salt, keeping in mind that the cod fillets are already salted before they are smoked and will add a fair amount of salt to the dish. Place the black-cod fillets in the pot, making sure that the fillets are just covered by the tomato broth. As well, the peeled potatoes and the bay leaves can be added to the pot. Bring the broth to a light simmer on the stovetop. When the broth has simmered, cover the pot with a lid and transfer to a preheated oven at 400°F for 7 minutes. This dish is best served in large shallow bowls accompanied by a spoon, the potatoes and a generous scoop of the tomato-onion-pepper-olive broth. A butter lettuce salad with a simple olive oil, lime and garlic vinaigrette is a great complement to this dish.

fresh produce and farmer and food photographer Andrei Federov for ducks and turkeys, Cowichan Bay's Hilary's Cheese Company and local fishers with commercial licences.

Markus has a world of experience, having apprenticed at Seehotel Silber in Konstanz, Germany, and cheffed in Switzerland, Italy and France before opening his own place, the Alabaster Restaurant, in Vancouver's Yaletown. He then catered in Vancouver and did some private cheffing in Mexico before a short stint at Sooke Harbour House drew his attention to Sooke and the idea of opening a small restaurant there.

Tatum says she is enjoying being a restaurateur and working with her husband. The two met in the Okanagan where they were both show-jumping horses. Now that they are settled in Sooke, they have bought a horse and are getting back into the ring in their spare time. Also in their future is a plan to sell takeaway lunches and homemade foods from the restaurant. Markus and Tatum say they are working on an idea to ensure visitors can enjoy a casual lunch and still leave room for their first-class dining experience in the evenings.

I end my meal with the *grande dame* of all desserts (permanent note to self: we only live once!), a trio that includes tiramisu, Belgian chocolate mousse and, my favourite, pannecotta with caramel sauce, and a good coffee. Tatum says she likes that "every night we make people happy." As one of those happy people, I take the slow road back to Victoria and plan my next visit.

Ragley Farm

Josephine Hill left her job as a systems manager with a wholesale food company in Victoria to become a working farmer on 30 acres in East Sooke. Her husband, Rob, was a key grip in the Vancouver film industry and now works on the farm and on his cars. They've never looked back.

Saturdays (and Sundays in season), Josephine opens up part of her barn to sell the fruits of her labour. Customers can take a wicker basket, then fill it with tomatoes, collard greens, chard, baby radish, spring onions, squash, arugula, mesclun, jalapeños and many more veggies. The large baking rack holds still-warm loaves of whole wheat, sourdough, fruit and olive breads, and blueberry and cranberry apple muffins. Josephine grinds all her own flour. One morning when I visited, she was a little low on bread because the power had been out for five hours the night before.

Near Christmas, Josephine takes orders for her boxes of exquisite holiday cookies. She often has samples of her baking, not that the palate needs to be tempted first. I am particularly fond of her spekulatius cookies, which she kindly delivered just before the big day. She makes a wonderful range of organic jams, such as black currant, cascadeberry and apple-ginger. Farm-fresh eggs are always available.

The atmosphere in the barn is warm and friendly, with a steady stream of regular, mainly local, customers dropping by. They buy and they catch up on the week. Even their dogs catch up with each other. I was amused by one car that drove up with its owner's dog hanging out the window to announce his arrival to the Hills' dogs.

Josephine says it was Rob who first spotted the farm and knew she would love it; when it finally came on the market in 1995, they made the move. They had a lot of work to clear the place up, but now thrive in their rural lifestyle. The farm has an interesting past, having been settled by Reverend and Lady Walker. Lady Walker, daughter of Lord Seymour, Marquess of Hertford, was also related to Lady Jane Seymour. She was a noted agricultural pioneer, setting up the East Sooke Farmers' Institute around 1927 and hosting many of its meetings at Ragley Farm.

The Seaweed Lady

In some ways, Diane Bernard has naturally progressed to her nickname: The Seaweed Lady. She was born to Acadians and lived half her life in the Maritimes. She has a strong background in coastal communities and a passion for the ocean, so, as she says: "I came by my new profession honestly."

That new profession — gatherer and purveyor of west coast seaweed under the Outer Coast Seaweeds banner — has local chefs and gastronomes buzzing. At the 2002 Feast of Fields, Diane teamed up with Chef Edward Tuson of Sooke Harbour House to serve a raw seaweed salad to the 600 participants. It was a huge hit. In the lineup was Lisa Ahier, then chef at Long Beach Lodge in Tofino, who encouraged Diane to "walk into restaurant kitchens with your bucket and show chefs what they can do with seaweed."

Diane credits Lisa, and her friends, Sinclair and Frédérique Philip of Sooke

The Seaweed Lady, Diane Bernard, gathers seaweed near Port Renfrew.

Seaweed Salad with Tahini Soy Dressing

LISA BARBER-AHIER FOR OUTER COAST SEAWEEDS

Serves 6 to 10, depending on size of portions. A great Asian creation using seaweed — a healthful and delicious natural Vancouver Island ingredient.

Seaweed Salad

2 c	Egregia seaweed	480 ml
2 c	Alaria seaweed	480 ml

Rinse, then blanch the seaweeds in boiling salted water for 2 to 3 minutes. Rinse again and de-rib. Use the Egregia in its natural shape after the ribs are removed. Cut Alaria into thin strips. Add the seaweeds to the following thinly sliced or julienned vegetables:

1 1/2 c	leeks	360 ml
1 1/2 c	carrots	360 ml
1 1/2 c	cucumbers	360 ml
1 1/2 c	red peppers	360 ml

Toss with the Tahini Soy Dressing to taste; sprinkle with toasted black sesame seeds and serve.

Tahini Soy Dressing

6 oz	tamari soy sauce	180 ml
4	limes, juiced	4
4 oz	sherry vinegar	120 ml
6	minced shallots	6
4 tbsp	molasses	60 ml
1 1/2 tsp	light brown sugar	7.5 ml
3	chipotle peppers (in adobo)	3
1 1/2 c	olive oil	360 ml
8 tbsp	sesame oil	120 ml
1 1/2 tbsp	minced ginger	22.5 ml
1 c	tahini paste	240 ml

Combine all ingredients and purée very well in a blender. Store chilled for up to one week.

Harbour House, for mentoring her in her new venture. Sinclair encouraged her to begin working with the chefs, so she spent a season taking them out to see the seaweed and introducing them to their "good, healthy, distinctive yet subtle" properties. At first, she found it was the "progressive, more avant garde" chefs who took an interest, but now she is inundated with enquiries. Once people see and taste the possibilities, they're hooked.

The nutritional value of seaweed is extremely high. As Diane points out, seaweed has no root system. It attaches itself by its stipe to a rock, a log or to other seaweed, and so "the nutrients taken in directly from the ocean" are all available to the eater. Seaweeds are "nutritionally dynamic. They're high fibre, low fat and have no cholesterol."

Diane collects her seaweeds west of Sooke, often hiking out great distances along the Juan de Fuca Strait where "no industry or big ships" interfere with the environment. She harvests eight to ten different types. Her personal favourite is Alaria or winged kelp, a versatile variety with a very rich, sweet-pea taste and rhubarb smell. Her family goes through about a pound of seaweed a week and, as she says: "I've got teenagers!" I'm reminded of the tofu-eating teens on Saltspring Island (see: Soya Nova Tofu), and start to have hope for the next generation.

In addition to her online wholesale business, Diane is now supplying the retail market through Lifestyles and Planet Organic markets in Victoria and will soon be selling through a couple of local brown-box programs.

Sooke Harbour House

It's fair to say that Vancouver Island gastronomy started with Sinclair and Frédérique Philip. From their "romantic little white inn by the sea," they have heightened our awareness and raised our expectations of food in general and reawakened our taste buds specifically to the pleasure and purpose of eating fresh, local, seasonal ingredients.

There is a reason why Sooke Harbour House has been a veritable training ground for the best local chefs, including Bill Jones, David Feys, Gordon Cowan, Brock Windsor and Peter Zambri, and a Mecca for gardeners such as Tina Fraser wanting to learn and apply organic methods to the cultivation of over 400 edible flowers and herbs. It has played a huge role in the revival of market gardening. Many Vancouver Island farmers regard Sinclair as a mentor because of the interest he takes in their operations and the knowledge he so generously shares. Tugwell Creek Honey Farm is one beneficiary of his

Chef Edward Tuson adds love and humour to the pot at Sooke Harbour House.

tutelage: Sinclair encouraged Bob Liptrot and Dana Le Comte to produce honey and mead at their nearby apiary, and they now have a thriving business that includes the production of linden honey, so prized by the European guests at Sooke Harbour House. The Philips persuaded Diane Bernard to start up Outer Coast Seaweeds, now another successful local food business. Mary Alice Johnson of ALM Organic Farm, Karen Barr of Ladybird Farm and Josephine Hill of Ragley Farm are part of the inn's family of suppliers. Mara Jernigan of Fairburn Farm says: "What Sinclair and Frédérique have achieved at Sooke Harbour House is really a remarkable piece of Canadian culinary history."

The reason for their far-reaching impact is not only that they care; they have a long-held conscience about sustainable farming and land preservation which extends beyond their own business. They want to ensure that agricultural land is used for farming, not development, and they want to see other people — growers, grocers and chefs — succeed in the food business.

In some ways, the couple's position in the local food chain was inevitable. They have plowed a lifetime of knowledge and enthusiasm into making their inn the "Sixth Best Small Hotel in the World" (*Travel and Leisure*, 2002). Its authentic local cuisine was voted first in the world by *Gourmet* magazine in 1997, and it won a Pinnacle Award for best independent restaurant in Canada in 2002. For five consecutive years, the inn has been awarded the *Wine Spectator*'s rare Grand Award for having one of the world's 88 best wine lists, and in 2002, Frédérique was named Woman of Distinction for business and entrepreneurship in Victoria. Most recently, the inn received the highest Audobon Green Hotel Rating in BC, with four green leaves in recognition of its green hotel policies, water reclamation and recycling system and "grass-paved" parking lot.

Frédérique tells me their story really began in France, when Sinclair was taking a Ph.D. in political science and international economics and Frédérique was studying economics at Grenoble. Ten years later, they went to Toronto to be with Sinclair's mother, who had fallen ill. When his mother passed away, they headed west because "Sinclair had always wanted to be by the ocean." They drove around and ended up at Whiffen Spit in Sooke, a far less populated area 25 years ago.

There, at the water's edge, was the 1929 clapboard house that would be improved incrementally, as the Philips could afford it, to become what it is today. They moved into the basement with their three children (the fourth, Rissa, was born in Sooke) and began to convert the house into an inn. They had no experience as innkeepers, but Frédérique remembers thinking: "It shouldn't be that complicated." The Philips' children grew as the inn grew, and all have worked in various capacities. Nishka tends the gardens, Benjamin is a sommelier and waiter in the dining room, and Jasmine is the ever-gracious hostess. Rissa, who is currently in Europe, has bussed in the dining room.

What impresses me, as I have coffee by the fire with Sinclair one crisp autumn day, is how uncomplicated it all appears and how immensely relaxed both he and the inn make me feel. Intellectual, food activist, gastronome and oenophile, he is, most importantly, a very decent guy who treats his own success as a gift to give back — to his guests and to others in the local food and farming industry.

I ask about organics and Sinclair says it's the only ethical choice. He is proud to have influenced many local growers and producers to transition to organic. And he is pleased to have popularized formerly unpopular ingredients and created great interest in growing and foraging for indigenous ingredients. Those include many First Nations foods, from uncommon fish to berries, prolific local mushrooms (when we later meet up with Chef Edward Tuson, Sinclair excitedly tells him about the Slippery Jack boletes he found on his morning forage), and bitter winter greens, which people used to regard as inedible. Sinclair had

Co-owner Frédérique Philip lights the candles before dinner at Sooke Harbour House.

65

Simple Sea Lettuce Emulsion to Accompany Fish or Vegetable Dishes

EDWARD TUSON AND SINCLAIR PHILIP, SOOKE HARBOUR HOUSE

Serves 4 to 6. Says Sinclair Philip: "Sea lettuce can be found at the highest intertidal levels and it is the easiest to recognize because it is light green, quite thin and unlike any other seaweed on our Pacific Coast. It is best fresh, and this delicious recipe requires fresh sea lettuce."

1/8 c	fresh sea lettuce, rinsed and chopped coarsely (*ulva lactuca* or *ulva fenestrata*)	28 g
1/2 c	fish or shellfish stock	120 ml
1/8 c	unsalted butter, cut into ½" cubes	30 ml
2 tbsp	dry white wine	30 ml

Pour the fish stock into a small, stainless steel saucepan and bring to a boil. Then add the white wine and remove from stove. Pour all the ingredients into a blender, put the lid on and blend at high speed for three minutes. Pour the blended ingredients back into the saucepan and bring to a boil over high heat. Serve once the sauce reaches the boil.

a pretty good idea what would grow in Sooke because it has a climate similar to where he lived in France.

I ask about Slow Food — Sinclair is the Canadian representative to the International Slow Food Council — and he tells me that he and Frédérique have "always lived by Slow Food values, as we understand them." He says it's all about using and promoting "foods in their regional, seasonal and historic context," and preserving traditional foods such as First Nations dishes.

I'm anxious to see how philosophy translates into cuisine, so Frédérique offers to take me into the kitchen. En route, she shows me some images for the first of three books she is producing, *The Art of Sooke Harbour House*. These are photographs of some of the inn's food-themed art collection. Each image has inspired Chef Tuson to create a special recipe that will be included in the book. Proceeds will go toward developing the art department at the local high school.

A great inn being the sum of its parts, it would be remiss of me to not mention the menu of spa treatments designed by Frédérique. At Sooke Harbour House, the treatments actually come to the guests, in their rooms (or, if preferred, they are given in the exotic Potlatch Room where one can have a massage behind the curtains of a marquee straight out of the Arabian Nights). Frédérique recognized something that we spa aficionados have long decried: after a relaxing treatment, one is forced to get dressed and leave the sanctuary. The answer is in-room everything, from sea salt scrub to Swedish massage.

Before leaving me and my thousand hungry questions with Chef Tuson, Frédérique tells me: "Following the seasons is everything to good cooking." She finds it strange that chefs are making a big story about going to the markets. "We've always done that," she says, "and we didn't do it to be trendy."

Edward Tuson has a 10-year history at Sooke Harbour House where he loves that "every day is different." I love the fact that he is different from what one might expect of a chef with so stellar a reputation. I'm not referring to the nose ring or the tattoo; I'm impressed that he's like the boy next door, a genuinely humble guy who takes a lot of time showing and explaining things.

He says he's "a farmer at heart," and he lived a few other lives before coming to cooking. He delivered furniture for Sears Roebuck in Los Angeles and

The white clapboard house on the water's edge in Sooke has become an internationally acclaimed inn and restaurant — Sooke Harbour House.

worked on an oil rig in the Beaufort Sea before enrolling in the chef-training program at Vancouver Community College. That was the year he'd hurt his back and figured construction jobs were out of the question. Besides, cooking had always been part of his repertoire from an early age. His mother was a hairdresser who worked at home, and he would often "try to cook her dinner."

While cheffing at places like Vancouver's Pan Pacific Hotel, Edward used to come to Sooke to snorkel for abalone. That's how he met fellow diver Sinclair. He signed on at Sooke Harbour House for five years, then took off in 1995 on an adventure across Asia (the Bangkok portion of that journey was spent with Peter Zambri of Victoria's Zambri's restaurant). Gathering culinary knowledge wherever he went, Edward finally returned to Vancouver Island in 1999, working briefly at The Aerie, Micheline's and the Malahat Mountain Inn, before settling back into the kitchen at Sooke Harbour House.

"It should be required that every young chef studying in Canada eat here at least once!"

— Mara Jernigan

As we chat, his staff works around us: Jenny is wrapping Sooke Harbour Dungeness crab and chervil with pickled rutabaga to accompany her sea cucumber and wild porphyra seaweed fritter; Geoff is braising sculpin in a sweet cicely root, Alexander seed and wild pine mushroom broth; and Josh is preparing black currant grand fir sorbet to include with his pear-calendula petal terrine.

There is a great deal of creativity in the kitchen and a lot of room for individuality. Edward lets his staff know what's come in fresh that day, then leaves each person to write his or her own portion of the evening's menu. The results are electrifying: spicy albacore tuna served rare on a buckwheat-noodle, root-vegetable and cilantro salad with fennel-seed duck sausage, a clam parsnip fritter and a tamari, red wine vinegar and ox-eye daisy vinaigrette. As we contemplate the dish, Edward cuts me a thick slice of that albacore tuna and I'm lost for several minutes. Or: caramelized apple and dried cranberry terrine in a calendula-petal-and-apple glaze with lavender marshmallows, frozen sour cream jellies, pumpkin seed wafers and nasturtium leaf juice.

Edward is "Entrée Dude" to his staff; he handles the creation of the main offerings and fine-tunes the rest. He also visits the local farms and markets, takes early-morning calls from fishers on their boats, manages the supplies, writes recipes and gives interviews to the likes of *The New York Times*, *Bon Appétit* and *Canadian Living* (not to mention demanding book authors!). And yet, this is an executive chef who is always on the line during service. He tells me it's all made worthwhile "when someone tells me I've cooked them the best meal they've ever eaten in their life."

I move from back of house to the oceanside dining room to eat the best meal of my life with Toronto chef and sommelier, Daniel Beiles. It is a graciously served and elegantly presented six-course dinner. The kitchen's attention to detail and relentless pursuit of excellence is evident, from the scrumptious warm albacore tuna, apple, red onion, sourdough tartlet with chickweed–ox-eye daisy salad, Korean mint, cilantro yogurt and pickled ruby beet to the roasted Peking duck breast with a buttermilk and grand fir glaze, lapin cherry-fennel sauce and split-pea tortilla torte. Daniel appreciates the opportunity to sample a flight of British Columbia wines with his meal and is overwhelmed by his tour of the cellars.

Tugwell Creek Honey Farm

Dana Le Comte trained as a fashion designer at Ryerson College and worked as a merchandiser in Vancouver, so I'm not surprised that she manages to look fabulous in protective clothing. We're talking full beekeeper regalia: head-to-toe canvas suit, gloves and large straw hat with netting. She and her husband, Bob Liptrot, have invited me to visit them and the 3 million bees that reside at Tugwell Creek Honey Farm in Sooke. No worries, I say, and pull on my own space suit.

Bob has been fascinated with bees since he was seven. He used to help an elderly neighbour with his hives and always received a chunk of sweet honeycomb in return. He went on to earn a Master's degree in entomology, then took apiculture (beekeeping) at Simon Fraser University. He has more knowledge about his charges than most people, but I can instantly see an intuitive asset: he is completely in tune with the bees and is able to work with them without protective clothing (don't try this at home).

It's one thing to see bees in a museum setting; it's something else to stand with beekeepers as they dismantle a hive and introduce you to the clan. Each of

Honey Spice Cake with Mascarpone and Honey Icing

DANA LE COMTE, TUGWELL CREEK HONEY FARM

Dana originally created this recipe for my column in *Focus* magazine. It's light and not overly sweet, and the icing is gorgeous. When my baking partner, Phyll Remple, and I made it, it attracted a swarm of happy tasters.

Honey Spice Cake

1/2 c	40% bran cereal flakes or bran buds	120 ml
1/2 c	water	120 ml
1/2 c	butter	120 ml
1/2 c	sugar	120 ml
1/2 c	honey	120 ml
1	egg	1
1 tsp	vanilla	5 ml
1 3/4 c	sifted all-purpose flour	420 ml
1 tsp	baking powder	5 ml
1/4 tsp	each soda, salt, cinnamon, cloves and ginger	1.2 ml
1/2 c	finely chopped walnuts (optional)	120 ml

Heat oven to 350°F. Combine bran flakes or buds and water. Set aside until most of water is absorbed. Cream butter and sugar until light and fluffy. Continue creaming while adding honey in a fine stream. Add egg and vanilla. Beat well. Sift together the dry ingredients. Add alternately to creamed mixture with the bran mixture. Fold in the walnuts. Spread batter in a greased, lightly floured baking pan that is 9" in diameter and 2" deep. Bake about 30 minutes or until cake tests done in centre. Cool on wire rack five minutes. Remove cake from pan. Finish cooling on rack.

Mascarpone and Honey Icing

1 lb	mascarpone	454 g
2 1/2 tbsp	honey (or more to taste)	37.5 ml

To make icing, mix room-temperature mascarpone and honey together and beat for three minutes until smooth. Ice cake, then drizzle an additional tablespoon of honey on top.

the couple's 90 hives contains some 40,000 to 60,000 Carniolan bees. The proletariat includes 13,000 to 20,000 foraging workers and at least 26,000 workers that stay in the hive to contend with brood-rearing, comb constructing, housecleaning, defense and temperature regulation. The brood consists of thousands of eggs, pupae in sealed cells and larvae being fed. Significant family members are the drones, of which there are 100 to 300, and the queen.

As I hover over the new observation beehive, Dana points out the queen (she is larger than the others and marked with a little dot of blue nail polish), and I'm fascinated by her obvious coterie of attendants. These bees are assigned to stay with her at all times to groom, feed and protect her. She's the J-Lo of the insect world, and I learn that these queens are in big demand. A good breeder can fetch as much as $150, and it is not unusual for queens to be delivered from one beekeeper to another via the postal service.

The queens breed after completing their mating flight with five drones, whom Shakespeare aptly described as "the idle bachelors." Yet there are no winners here: the drones die in the process (suffice to say, the penis snaps off), and the queens go on to lay some 2,000 eggs per day for the rest of their lives.

The workers have finely honed phonetic and kinetic forms of communication. The "dance of the honeybee" is a much-studied ritual, whereby the foragers return to the hive and, through sound, taste and smell, "provide information regarding the location of a particular source of forage." The recipients of that information can then head out on their own to collect pollen.

The ultimate winners, of course, are you and I, and a visit to Tugwell Creek Honey Farm can only heighten our appreciation of one of nature's perfect foods. Dana and Bob chose their ten-acre farm for its proximity to Survey Mountain. Located 25 kilometres inland, it provides an ideal warm, dry climate and a proliferation of hawksbeard, fireweed and salal for foraging. The couple transports their hives to the mountain, as well as to nearby Muir Creek, where the bees collect nectar from linden tree blooms, and the Sooke River Potholes, where they feast on blackberry flowers.

A whole lot of buzzing going on at Tugwell Creek Honey Farm.

I first sampled Tugwell Creek Honey at Feast of Fields and it has become a firm favourite. New this spring is Dana and Bob's meadery, a first for the island, where you will be able to buy Vintage, Melomel and Sack meads. Mead was traditionally drunk in the "honey month." The father of the bride would supply his son-in-law with all the mead he could drink during what is now known as the honeymoon.

Dana says they are delighted to have control of the whole process, from hive to honey and honey wine. She is happy that their business has become a family affair: her sister and mother come from Vancouver to help during the harvest and daughter Teagan enjoys the excitement. Bob and Dana expect another assistant any day now as Dana is pregnant with their second child.

In the meantime, if you're tired of trawling superstore aisles in the city, get thee to the meadery. Dana and Bob offer a delicious and educational respite down on the honey farm.

Saltspring Island

Happily, Saltspring Island has not come a long way since I used to go over with my middle-class hippie friends in the 1970s. The counter-culture is alive and well, and the various nouveaux who have built expensive summer homes have come for the peace, not to create any new scene. Sure, it can get pretty busy in the summer. You wait longer for the ferries. You probably have to queue for your latte at the Saltspring Roasting Company or Morningside Organic Bakery and Café. The Bread Lady may be sold out of your favourite loaf if you don't get to the Saturday market early enough, but switching over to island time tends to keep all of this in perspective.

Saltspring really is the organic capital of British Columbia, and the many growers are refreshingly vocal about food supply and sustainable agriculture.

The Bread Lady

Heather Campbell's mother always said: "It doesn't matter about your china; it's sharing the food you have with other people that counts." She would divide whatever she had for supper by the number of people at her table, and Heather does the same today. On Friday nights, before she bakes 400 to 500 loaves of bread, she cooks and leaves her porch door open. Neighbours and friends know they can just drop by. Some eat, some drink; all contribute to the lovely sense of joie de vivre that Heather exudes.

When I arrive on a Saturday afternoon, the week's work is done. Heather has just returned from the Market-in-the-Park, where she regularly sells every loaf she bakes. She and her architect husband, Phillip van Horn, are looking forward to a sunset picnic with friends that evening. There's a beautiful salmon lying on the butcher block, about to be cooked. Phillip has gone off for a swim. Heather and I sink into a couch and talk baking.

Unlike many people I've met who have changed careers to become food producers, Heather always sought an alternative lifestyle and always baked bread. It was a natural evolution for her to turn a passion into a business. She says she likes doing hands-on things, loves "making something that I really like and passing it on to others. It's a way to pass your energy around."

For 15 years, she and Phillip lived "in the bush" on 25 acres in the Ottawa Valley. There was no power or running water and no phone. When they came to Saltspring in 1991, the locals warned them that the lifestyle was quite rustic. To them, it was practically luxurious.

A friend of Heather's had heard Alan Scott, author of *The Bread Builders*, speak at a conference and Heather liked the sound of his wood-fired bread ovens. She bought plans from Scott (which Phillip revised somewhat to make the oven stronger) and had a local mason build her a four- by six-foot oven. The oven holds 35 loaves at a time, and she bakes up to 700 loaves of bread a week. She mixes and hand-shapes every loaf, but has help loading the oven — from Phillip, and from Mark Stevens, who grows seeds for Dan Jason of Saltspring Seeds at his own farm down the road. People are very much connected on the island. Heather says it's one of the most caring places she's ever lived.

Heather's bread is sold at the seasonal Saturday market and year-round at Admiral's Sushi Bar and NatureWorks in Ganges. One morning a week, she and Charlie Eagle of Bright Farm sell at a small organic market in Ganges (Tuesdays, 10:00 A.M. to 2:00 P.M., 112 Hereford Avenue). People who know her phone ahead to place their orders.

The bread is made with certified organic flour and mainly organic ingredients. I find it impossible to choose from 95 percent rye, 100 percent spelt, whole wheat levain — plain, or with walnuts, raisins, apricot/hazelnuts, dates/ginger or rosemary. Heather is always experimenting, and one week, produced cranberry with white and dark chocolate. Her customers couldn't get enough.

When I finally get up to leave, Heather invites me to come back for dinner "any Friday evening." I'm truly touched and reminded of something Mara Jernigan once said: "You can go to Italy and eat in all the best places, but if an Italian family invites you into their home, you'll remember it forever."

Bright Farm

I'm sitting on the back porch of Charlie Eagle and Judy Horvath's farmhouse, sampling juicy Italian plums straight off their trees and then chewing on the dried version — prunes that Judy proffers from one of her collection of big kitchen jars. Hastings House chef Thomas Render and I are spending a Sunday touring farms and food producers on the island, and this is our first stop.

Charlie and Judy came up from the Bay Area in the early 1990s and bought their 10-acre farm in about two hours, en route to the ferry. It was a fortuitous move. They had been homesteading on a remote property in California since 1980, but, with their daughter, Bree, ready to begin school, they felt they wanted somewhere more community oriented. Saltspring was the answer, and Judy found the house and property so idyllic that she cried the first time she walked through the door.

I find it idyllic as well, and Charlie tells me most visitors feel a sense of wonder here. The property was originally 153 acres, bought for $153 by Thomas and Jane Mouat in 1890. It has a creek running through it that drains St. Mary's Lake and runs through to the Vesuvius estuary. It is something of a bird sanctuary. As we wander about the farm, we stop to watch a turkey vulture, a hawk and then a great blue heron soar above us.

Charlie's main crop is garlic: Chinese, Spanish, Early Red Portuguese and Korean, some of which I'd bought at the Saltspring Garlic Festival in August. He sells it in big fat braids. This was a good year — 560 braids! Other crops include potatoes, beans, corn, carrots, leeks, lettuce, chard, zucchini, broccoli, winter squash and celery. There is a vast greenhouse of tomatoes, tomatillos, hot peppers and cucumbers. There are watermelons and cantaloupes and gorgeous Concord grapes (Charlie and Judy make Concord jelly together).

And then there's the orchard, an amazing planting of 200 varieties. The trees were moved to Bright Farm as a complete collection in 1993. They were just "little two-foot whips when I planted them," says Charlie. They'd been amassed by a woman from Sloan River who collected heritage apple varieties. Charlie and Judy press some 40 to 50 varieties into juice and also make cider. People buy caseloads of the farm's 20 varieties of crabapples to make jelly. Because the nights have been cold this summer, Charlie is anticipating a good, sweet apple harvest this year.

As we wander through the orchard, Thomas spots a hawthorn bush. He's just found a recipe for hawthorn jelly and a discussion ensues, mainly around how long

Braids of Bright Farm's Korean garlic for sale at the Saltspring Island Garlic Festival.

it would take to pick enough of those tiny berries to make a batch of jelly. We pass the chicken coop, a field of sheep (Charlie counts on the neighbour's ram busting through the fence every year to propagate his herd) and a couple of hives (the bees are mainly kept to pollinate his crops, but he also harvests as much as 40 pounds of honey annually).

The orchard is watered directly from a large pond on the property. Gravity draws the water from Jane's Spring (named for original owner Jane Mouat) into a storage tank for the drip-irrigation system that waters the rest of the farm's plantings. Charlie has help in the form of a dozen WWOOFers (Willing Workers on Organic Farms) throughout each year. Some of them stay on the property in a sweet little cabin behind the house. They all sit down to Judy's hearty dinners after their working day.

Charlie is clearly proud of his daughter, who loves the farming life (yes, these young people do exist!). Bree is taking a degree in environmental studies in Santa Cruz, but can't wait to move back to Bright Farm when she graduates. She worked in the gardens of Hastings House as a teenager and, like her mother, she enjoys selling at the local markets.

Back on the porch, Charlie and Judy are singing the praises of their dinner in the kitchen at Hastings House four days earlier. It seems the experience of dining stove-side was "incredible," and Charlie rushes off to get some of his homemade cider to send back with Thomas for the kitchen brigade. I make a mental note to book a seat at that particular kitchen table as soon as possible.

Hastings House

The winding drive to Relais & Châteaux's Hastings House takes us past fields of sheep before arriving at a charming cluster of buildings, all facing Ganges Harbour. There's a converted barn, an authentic Hudson's Bay Company post (now The Post House, a honeymooners' delight) and a stately replica of a sixteenth-century Sussex manor house built with locally quarried stone.

Received as if we've come home, my little group of foodies is invited to join the manager, Shirley McLaughlin, in the front parlour of The Manor House for morning coffee, or "elevenses" as the English affectionately call the respite. Meandering along the garden path, we are inspected by one of two resident cats, the indomitable Mr. Hastings. Some years back, word got out that Chef Marcel Kauer was leaving bowls of fresh cream and tidbits of fish at the kitchen door. Mr. Hastings and Squeaky were first in line and soon took up permanent, luxurious residence here.

Inside, the perfect welcome awaits. A fire roars in the open hearth, and organic coffee from the Saltspring Roasting Company is set out in Minton china cups. There are freshly baked strawberry muffins and a selection of jams made from the inn's own heritage fruit trees. The *Gulf Islands Driftwood*, Saltspring's leading (and only) newspaper, is at hand. We sink into chintz and happily give ourselves over to our edible journey's most relaxing stop.

Hastings House is located on the site of an old working farm of 25 acres. The Manor House was built in 1940 for Warren Hastings to replicate a home he had owned in Sussex. Features like the large inglenook fireplace in the lounge are typical of those found in Tudor homes in Sussex. When Donald Cross bought the property from Hastings in 1980, he brought in a local architect, Jonathan Yardley, to develop it into a country resort.

It faces south across Ganges Harbour, which provides a continuous show of boating activity, particularly in summer. The lush, rolling lawn, with its immaculate flower beds, is dotted with Adirondack chairs just calling guests to curl up with a book, or sit, as I did, with a glass of port after dinner and watch the sun set.

The Manor House at Hastings House.

On one visit, I enjoyed a room upstairs in The Manor House, which reminded me of a cosy hotel I'd stayed in near Salisbury Cathedral many years before. The suite's living room faces the harbour, and you can read before a wood-burning fire (remember those?). It's private and cosy with thoughtful appointments throughout. Your name is on the door, and a stuffed toy cat can be hung out to alert the housekeeper that the room can be cleaned (its other side is a dog that appears to have bitten off part of the housekeeper's uniform, a sign that privacy is desired).

Of course the highlight for any gourmet trailblazer is dinner, and Hastings House doesn't disappoint. Many celebrities have dined here, although the inn is discreet enough to divulge only the names of those whose presence was already known, including Johnny Carson, Martin Short, Goldie Hawn and Kurt Russell.

There are several choices for dinner: the Verandah dining room where no jackets are required, which is often booked for weddings and special parties; the

Poppyseed Crusted Pacific Halibut, Beetroot Risotto and Lemon Thyme Beurre Blanc

THOMAS RENDER, HASTINGS HOUSE

 Serves 4. A creative contrast of colour, texture and flavour: firm, black-crusted fish married with creamy, maroon risotto. Plated on white china, it's a work of art!

Beetroot Risotto:

1 c	arborio rice	240 ml
2	shallots finely diced	2
1	fresh bay leaf	1
1 1/2 c	beet juice	360ml
1/2 c	white wine	120ml
1 1/2 c	chicken stock	360 ml
4 tbsp	butter	60 ml
2 tbsp	grated Parmesan cheese	30 ml

Sweat the minced shallot in 1 tbsp (30 ml) of butter until translucent. Add arborio rice and stir to coat evenly with butter. Add bay leaf. Add 1 c (240 ml) of liquid and stir gently until most of the liquid has evaporated. Continue this process until all the liquid is used and the rice is creamy but still firm. Fold in remaining butter and Parmesan. Season with salt to taste.

Halibut:

4	5-oz (150g) portions halibut	4
	Dijon mustard	
	poppy seeds	

In a hot fry pan, brown the halibut on the outside and remove to a baking tray. Brush lightly with mustard and sprinkle on some poppy seeds, pressing gently so they adhere.

Beurre Blanc:

3	sprigs lemon thyme	3
1/2 c	white wine	120 ml
1	lemon, juiced	1
1	shallot, minced	1
1/2 lb	cold unsalted butter, cut into cubes	227 g

In a saucepan reduce the wine, lemon thyme, lemon juice and minced shallot until 2 tbsp (30 ml) remain. Strain out the solids. Return liquid to saucepan and warm. Add cold butter to the sauce a few cubes at a time, whisking vigorously. Continue adding all the butter, taking care not to heat the sauce too much as it will split.

NOTE: Adding 1 tbsp (15 ml) of whipping cream will stabilize the emulsion. Season with salt to taste. Just before serving, place halibut in a preheated oven at 425°F and cook until firm to the touch. (Be careful not to overcook it!) Place risotto in the centre of the plate. Place the halibut on top. Spoon the sauce around. Garnish with fresh lemon thyme sprigs.

Snug dining room next to the cellar, for private parties; the main dining room; and, in summer, the porch, where a lucky party of four can dine privately. Foodie fanatics can have it all by dining at a special table right in the kitchen (this experience books up fast, so do call well in advance). It all adds up to a true English country-house feeling, where someone like me imagines intrigue in every corner.

Executive Chef Marcel Kauer is Swiss-born and -trained. At the age of 16, he did his apprenticeship in his uncle's restaurant in Germany, then went into the army. When his parents were travelling in Vancouver, they ate at La Raclette, and his father asked if the restaurant would employ Marcel. They agreed, and Chef Kauer came to Canada. He worked both at La Raclette and at the Galiano Lodge, spending half of the week in each kitchen. He said it was a busy time for him and challenging because he "had no English." He loved it when the lodge was quiet and he could go fishing.

Kauer came to Hastings House 13 years ago and is now both chef and co-manager. He believes in cooking with the seasons, from what's available. "Wait until the food comes to you," says Kauer. What doesn't come from the Hastings House gardens, he buys from local growers, going off the island only for things like bulk potatoes and flour.

Chef de Cuisine Thomas Render joins us at the kitchen door, and we all inspect the day's produce delivery. There are slender eggplants, several varieties of tomatoes and peppers, green beans, portobellini mushrooms, pattypan squashes, greenflash cantaloupes, leeks, yams and a large tray of fragrant basil. As various members of the kitchen brigade pass by, they touch and comment, all impressed and excited by the quality. Most of it comes from Charlie Eagle's Bright Farm on the island. Sweet little strawberries arrive from Rosalie Beach's Wave Hill Farm, and saddles of venison from Broken Briar Fallow Deer Farm near Chemainus. Michael Ableman's Madrona Valley Farm supplies the golden and red plums, as well as green, and prized white, asparagus. Blueberries come from Cathy Bull's Bluebeary

79

Pastry chef Carley Makela with bread just baked for the evening meal.

Hill Farm in Victoria. Kauer says they also buy 300 to 400 pounds of blackberries from local pickers who come to the kitchen door every summer. Many of those berries find their way into Hastings House jams and jellies, which guests can buy to take home.

Earlier in the day, sockeye salmon and snapper came in for the evening's menu. Typically, they get calls from the boats of local fishers like Don Bemi with the day's catch. They meet the boats at the dock in Ganges, and it's seriously fresh fish for supper. Lamb, which is featured on the Hastings House menu every night by popular demand, comes from Mike Byron's neighbouring farm.

Tofu comes from Soya Nova Tofu on the island. Chef Render loves the smoked tofu and includes it in delicate strudel as well as vegetable sautés. Tempeh, the cultured soy curd that is mixed with barley and allowed to ferment, is now being made on the island and used by Hastings House.

Chef Render apprenticed in the Okanagan, then worked in restaurants in Vernon and Kelowna. He's worked four seasons at Hastings House, alternating with stints at The Raintree in Whistler and other restaurants in the off-season.

Pastry chef Carley Makela is pulling loaves of whole-wheat bread out of the oven. A graduate of the Pacific Institute of Culinary Arts in Vancouver, she originally learned how to bake from her grandmother. Following stints at Cin Cin and other Vancouver restaurants, she is now responsible for the tea trolley, breakfast and all pastries at Hastings House. Her desserts — like the Dark Belgian Chocolate Brownie Torte with Blackberry Ice Cream which I enjoyed — are fresh and creative without being overly fussy or loaded with unnecessary ingredients. Carley recently won a top award with her Simply Grand Chèvre Cheesecake at the Grand Marnier Dessert Challenge in Victoria.

The Garden at Hastings House

I venture into the herb garden, where Shelley Kobylka and her friendly dog, Tessa, are tending to plants in one of the greenhouses. Shelley had been working as a landscape gardener in Duncan when an interesting ad appeared in the local paper. The rest is happy history. From March to November, she grows all the flowers for the dining rooms and the 18 guest suites. She works closely with the housekeeping staff, ensuring that flower colours complement the furnishings and that fragrances are never overpowering.

As well as the ornamental flowers, there are many grown for the kitchen, including nasturtiums, calendula, roses, day lilies and scented geraniums. Shelley regularly picks a selection of flowers and takes them to the chefs, so they can see what's available for cooking. She is gradually converting the flower garden over to perennials, but it's a big job as there have been as many as 5,000 annuals planted each year.

The flower beds around The Manor House and guest suites are changed regularly and instantly. Shelley has developed a system of growing plantings in pots that can be moved quickly to a bed with a wheelbarrow, unpotted and, presto — winter pansies where summer's petunias once bloomed.

Herbs and veggies are prolific in the 70-square-foot kitchen garden, which has been designed in the European wheel shape. There's a bay leaf tree in the centre, and each section of the wheel holds something different: herbs, salad greens, Oriental mix, snow and snap peas, cabbage, rhubarb, artichokes, arugula, sorrel (we nibble the lemony leaves as we talk), green beans, cantaloupe, beets, peas and Swiss chard. Before new plantings go in, Shelley, Chef Render, Michael Ableman and Charlie Eagle sit down to plan what will be grown for the Hastings House menu.

It's a popular garden where guests are often seen strolling around. Shelley says people come out to the gardens because "they like to see where their food comes from." She enjoys conversations with guests and is flattered when they photograph or sketch the garden with a view to recreating aspects of it. "One couple from Minnesota actually paced it out and planned to copy it in detail back home," she tells me.

Like all gardens on the Gulf Islands, these are surrounded by tall fences to keep out the bold local deer who also appreciate fresh veggies. Shelley tells me that the fawns, who "don't know what they like yet, eat everything." She sprays rotten eggs around the fences to further deter the deer. Shelley maintains organic-growing methods in the gardens, even treating the slugs to repellants such as piles of eggshells and inorganic strips surrounding plants, but she says it's an ongoing battle.

The heritage orchard has crabapple, apple, plum and pear trees from which come the delectable jams and jellies served for breakfast and tea.

The sheep grazing on the property are delightful, and you could, as I did, spend hours just watching them. Spring is of course the most fun, with the newborn lambs frolicking about. There's an admirable orphan project in operation, managed by the local 4-H club that cares for lambs which have become separated from their mothers.

House Piccolo

Saltspring Island never fails to amaze me. You can literally cross the street from farmers' market to fine dining without changing your blue jeans. Even though the attire is casual everywhere, the attention to food is generally high-class all the way. Such was my first experience at House Piccolo. I arrived for dinner in jeans and was treated as if I were in head-to-toe couture.

The 30-seat restaurant (which expands to 48 seats with outside seating in summer) is in a cute little blue house right in the village of Ganges. Inside, it has a homey feel, with paintings by the owner's aunt and various European knick-knacks on the walls. There is a whole display of Russian dolls that were originally owned by a Finnish prime minister interspersed with copper pots and awards, including awards of excellence from *Wine Spectator* for every year since 2000. There is also a proud certificate of membership (by invitation only) in the prestigious international gastronomic society, La Chaîne des Rôtisseurs.

The meal was one of the best I'd ever eaten, from the complementary salad and warmed house-made bread to start, to the meltingly rich, yet surprisingly light gorgonzola tart with port wine, toasted cumin seed and Bosc pear chutney and the Saltspring Island lamb chops with a hearty aïoli, designer vegetables and scalloped potatoes. Sticking to one glass of wine, as is my custom, I enjoyed the fruity Bacchus from Cowichan Valley's Alderlea Vineyards (Piccolo's wine list is an extensive, much-lauded collection of over 250 selections). I'm often asked where I put all the food I eat, but I had no trouble finishing my meal with the unique lingonberry crêpes with vanilla ice cream and a bottomless cup of Saltspring Island Roasting Company coffee. Everything was excellent and the service was friendly, but not intrusive.

Besides the local coffee, the restaurant uses Saltspring Island ingredients as much as possible. The lamb is always local; Moonstruck and Saltspring Island

Chef Piccolo and Kirsi Lyytikainen in the kitchen of House Piccolo.

cheese companies supply the cheese; vegetables come from Bon Acres, and lettuce comes year-round from Living Lettuce, an organic hydroponic farm nearby. Saltspring Island Sea Products smokes the salmon. Even the beer is island-made, from the Gulf Island Brewery in the Fulford Valley.

In 1989, Piccolo Lyytikainen and his girlfriend, Kirsi, were ready to move away from the big city — in their case, Helsinki. They had no preconceived ideas but, as an avid boater, Piccolo knew that he wanted to live by the sea. They came to Saltspring Island at the invitation of his uncle who lived here. It was Christmastime, and they liked the place very much. They returned in the summer to really check it out and ended up deciding to get married and make a permanent move in January 1991. Whatever happened, Piccolo tells me, there would be boating 12 months of the year! Piccolo brought a wealth of cooking experience and Kirsi, bookkeeping and self-taught pastry-making, from their Finnish homeland.

He credits his mother with his life-long interest in good food. "She actually had more than salt and pepper in her spice cabinet, so our food had different flavours," he tells me. Her good cooking gave him "a little kick," and he began his career driving for a catering company, then working in restaurants in Helsinki "from the very bottom to becoming a schnitzel cook."

Warm Gorgonzola Tart

Serves 6 to 8. Rich and deeply satisfying; a little slice goes a long way. It took some cajoling on my part to get the recipe from Chef Lyytikainen and understandably so, as it's one of his most popular appetizers at House Piccolo.

7 oz	Gorgonzola cheese	200 g
4	egg yolks	4
1 3/4 c	heavy cream	420 ml
1 tbsp	flour	15 ml
	9" pre-baked, unsweetened tart shell	

In a mixer or blender, mix the cheese, egg yolks and flour well. Once consistency is smooth, blend in all the cream at once. Do not whip the cream. Pour the mixture into the tart shell and bake at 350°F for about 40 minutes. Let the tart rest for 20 minutes before cutting it into slices. Delicious served with a fresh green salad and vinaigrette.

Somewhere in between, he worked in the boat electronics industry. His boss owned a small island, and Piccolo ended up becoming a cook on the island for guests of the company. He loved that "summer gig," because he could take his own boat to work and was able to cook with great local ingredients. Back in Helsinki, he decided to get some proper training under a Swiss chef at the restaurant Bellman. And then came the trip to Canada, and Piccolo and Kirsi's love affair with Saltspring Island.

They found the little house on Hereford Avenue right away. It had been a Mexican café, then a restaurant called Carol Feeds the Planet (only on Saltspring!), and the decor needed a lot of work. They weren't sure they could afford it, but decided to do it anyway. The couple worked together and with friends to reno- vate the place, and opened in October 1992. They originally served breakfast, lunch and dinner on blue-and-white checked tablecloths, but gradually honed their style to dinners-only on white linen.

When I ask Piccolo where he wants to be in five years, he tells me, "Right here. We have the one thing that everyone wants — to live on Saltspring."

Jana's Bake Shop

It's always fun to discover a culinary gem, and Jana's Bake Shop, Saltspring Island's tiny perfect bakery and coffee bar, is such a place. I try to drop in for quiche whenever I'm on the island because Jana Roerick makes the best quiche of any baker anywhere. Whether blue cheese, kale and jalapeño pepper or carmelized onion and Gruyère, the combinations are fantastic, the pastry is light and flaky, and each personal-sized quiche is made in a deep dish so you really get a nice portion. With a cup of Saltspring Roasting Company's coffee, this is one of the best lunches I know.

The little shop is inviting with a fun collection of coloured cookie cutters hanging on the walls, and a welcoming open kitchen from which Jana greets you as she puts another tray of baking into the oven. With only a few stools at her coffee bar, there is always the opportunity to meet someone and have an interesting conversation while you munch away.

Jana and her husband, Marcus Dowrich, are true islanders — he's from Trinidad; she hails from Toronto's Ward Island — so they "couldn't have asked for a better move" when they chose Saltspring. Marcus had been raising South African Boer goats and Jana was supplying restaurants with her wonderful cakes in Tobago when the urge came to move back to Canada. "Of course, we wanted to find the warmest place in the country," Jana tells me. Marcus started studying the Gulf Islands and they decided on Saltspring. They love it, says Jana, "but Marcus does miss his goats!"

Jana graduated as a baker from George Brown College in Toronto and puts her skills into making things people most love. Her chicken, beef and vegetarian pot pies, soups and roasted vegetable and beef lasagne portions are always on hand in the freezer for take-home dinners. The individual quiches, calzones and a great selection of sweet treats like date squares, chocolate loaf, deep-dish butter tarts and the "disappearing" chocolate-pecan junkies are consistently in demand. Jana also supplies cakes, pies and fruit crumbles to Moby's Pub.

It's good to hear that Jana and Marcus have no plans to "grow" the business (as we urbanites would say). They are delighted that Saltspring Islanders have embraced them. Customers regularly tell Jana that they love being able to watch her rolling pastry and making tasty fillings when they come in. Jana's Bake Shop is the closest thing I know to walking into my mother's kitchen and being made to feel she's baking something special just for me.

Cranberry Orange Muffins with Crumble Topping

JANA ROERICK, JANA'S BAKE SHOP

 Makes 12 muffins. When I have a serious writing dead-line, I escape to the privacy of my father's study. The best moment of many days spent there recently was when Mother appeared at the door with a cup of tea and one of these tasty muffins.

Preheat oven to 375°F to 400°F (as Jana says: "You know your own oven!"), and butter a 12-cup muffin tin.

Crumble topping:

1 c	flour	227 g
1 c	brown sugar	227 g
1 c	rolled oats	227 g
1 tbsp	cinnamon	15 ml
1 tsp	baking powder	5 ml
4 oz	softened butter	113 g

Mix the first five ingredients together well. Mix in the butter with your fingers until the mixture is crumbly. Set aside.

Cranberry mix:

1	large orange, ends and seeds removed	1
2 c	cranberries	454 g

Purée the orange in a food processor or blender. Add the cranberries and pulse to break them up. Set aside.

Muffins:

4 1/2 c	all purpose flour	1021 g
2 c	brown sugar	454 g
1/2 tsp	salt	2.5 ml
2 tsp	baking soda	10 ml

Mix all the dry ingredients together. Set aside.

2	eggs	2
2 c	buttermilk	480 ml
3/4 c	vegetable oil	180 ml

Beat the wet ingredients together until blended. Add the cranberry/orange mixture to the dry mixture to coat the berries. Then stir the wet mixture into the dry mixture. Divide the muffin mixture among the 12 muffin cups, topping each with one-twelfth of the crumble mixture. Bake until firm to the touch — approximately 30 minutes.

Madrona Valley Farm

Jeanne-Marie Ableman and I are sitting on a chaise longue under a heritage apple tree, one of the farm's cats stretched in the sunshine at our feet. Before us are fields of strawberries, basil, chard, many lettuces and herbs. Jeanne-Marie is peacefully feeding her son, five-month-old Benjamin, and telling me about her journey from California's Goleta Valley to Saltspring's Madrona Valley.

She is originally from San Francisco. Her husband, organic-farming pioneer and activist Michael Ableman, is also American, but spent time herding sheep and working on farms near Nelson, BC. They came together at Fairview Gardens in Goleta, the farm that Michael is credited with saving in the early 1980s.

It's a compelling story, and one I've enjoyed reading about in one of Michael's books, *On Good Land*. When he arrived at Fairview Gardens in 1981, the area was still largely agricultural, but over the years, development encroached until it became the only surviving farm property. In 1995, Michael and a group of local activists formed a non-profit society and raised money to buy the land, ensuring that it would remain a working organic farm in perpetuity.

That same year, Michael, Jeanne-Marie and Michael's son, Aaron, took a biking holiday on Vancouver Island and the Gulf Islands, staying in bed-and-breakfasts

> *"How was this grown? What materials were used in its production? How far did it travel?"*
>
> — Michael Abelman, speaking to the 2002 International Federation of Organic Agriculture Movements (IFOAM) conference, Victoria

and, as Jeanne-Marie tells me, "meeting great people with connections to farming," including Dan Jason and Mara Jernigan. The decision to look for a place of their own on Saltspring evolved naturally and, after looking for a couple of years, they bought a unique Victorian farmhouse on five acres.

Corn Pancakes with Maple Blackberries and Lavender Yogurt

REBECCA TESKEY, MADRONA VALLEY FARM

Makes 4 servings. Every time I make these pancakes, I mentally connect to Madrona Valley Farm, where Michael and Jeanne-Marie Ableman's hard work and commitment to sustainable, organic agriculture gives me a whole new appreciation for the ingredients.

1 1/2 c	ripe blackberries	360 ml
3/4 c	pure maple syrup	180 ml
	(Canadian dark is preferable to light or amber)	

In a small saucepan, bring the maple syrup and 1/2 c (120 ml) of the berries to a bare simmer. Gently mash these berries. Put the remaining fruit in a bowl and pour the maple/berry mixture over. Let stand while you make the pancakes.

Lavender Yogurt:

1 c	natural 3% or whole milk yogurt*	240 ml
1 tsp	chopped fresh lavender leaves	5 ml
	the purple flowers from one sprig of lavender	

*Organic yogurt will drain much faster than regular yogurt because it almost never contains stabilizers like gelatin or guar gum. Place a layer of cheesecloth or a clean dishcloth in a fine mesh sieve. Put this over a bowl to catch drips and empty the yogurt into the sieve. Stir in the lavender leaves and flowers. Let drain 1 to 1 1/2 hours.

Corn Pancakes:

1 1/3 c + 2 tbsp	cornmeal or a coarsely ground cornflour	320 ml + 30 ml
	(not masa harina)	
1 3/4 tsp	baking powder	8.75 mL
pinch	salt	pinch
2	eggs, separated	2
1/4 c	unsalted butter	60 ml
1 tbsp	brown sugar	15 ml
1 c	buttermilk or milk, or 1/2 c (120 ml) of each	240 ml
1 c	corn kernels, freshly cut**	240 ml

**Michael Ableman grows a bi-colour, hybrid variety of corn that is so sweet and juicy you can eat it raw. It is important to choose a local organic corn because the sugar in corn starts to turn into starch as soon as it is picked. Chances are that your local corn will have spent less time off the stalk.

In a large bowl, whisk together the first three ingredients. In a small saucepan, melt the butter with the sugar. Place the buttermilk in a glass measuring cup and whisk in the egg yolks and the butter/sugar mixture. Make a well in the centre of the dry ingredients, add the milk mixture and blend until just combined. Fold in the corn kernels. Beat the egg whites in a clean, dry bowl with a small pinch of salt until soft peaks are formed. Fold the egg whites into the batter. Drop batter to form 2" to 3" rounds on a lightly oiled griddle or non-stick pan, and cook the corn cakes until they are well browned on both sides. To serve, make a semi-circle of three or four cakes on one side of a plate. Using a slotted spoon, place a mound of the blackberries in the center of this. Top with a dollop of the lavender yogurt. Serve the remaining berry syrup on the side, warmed if you like. Garnish with a sprig of lavender.

"Even though it's bottomland that floods in winter," says Jeanne-Marie, "we're fortunate to have Cowichan soil and one of the most fertile areas on Saltspring." The previous owner was a hobby organic farmer, so the foundation was there for their vegetable beds. Michael did some intensive planting and established an irrigation system off the property's two ponds. He follows organic-gardening practices, including the use of cover crops so the soil is held intact in winter; drip tape on the vegetable and herb beds to ensure low water use; companion planting (for example, seed garlic shades the lettuce); and protective tenting to keep veggies warmer and hold the moisture that naturally evaporates off the plants.

Jeanne-Marie redecorated the house to provide bed-and-breakfast accommodation, which *Gourmet* magazine described as, "traditional but unfussy, as relaxed as the hosts themselves." There is a self-contained cottage next to the raspberry patch that's perfect for families. Guests can buy eggs and produce from the farm and make their own meals. I think of all the city families I know whose children would benefit from this simple experience.

I'm delighted that the food is organic, that I can see most of it growing before it appears on my plate, that the sheets and towels are air-dried and smell divine and that all the cleaning products are natural. Guests are treated to superb organic breakfasts. I devour tiny strawberries and custard enhanced by the stimulating conversation in the dining room. It's all about the food and the issues surrounding the food, and it's presented in such a natural, easy way that

one learns willingly. For me, the essence of the Madrona Valley Farm experience is the hosts themselves and their interest in sustainable agriculture.

It's hard to believe that, on top of the farm and bed-and-breakfast operations, Michael still works part-time at Fairview Gardens, and Jeanne-Marie takes their abundant produce to the island's Market-in-the-Park every Saturday morning. They do it all with minimal help. Horticultural students come to learn about organic gardening, and guests are welcome to pick up a hoe. Michael says: "If people leave here without gaining some new understanding of food and how it comes to them, we haven't done what we set out to do."

Rebecca Teskey is a self-taught chef who came to Saltspring from Winnipeg with her mother to "look around" and ended up staying when she was offered work at Madrona Valley Farm. She respects the "integrity of the food" that she works with at the farm. "There's a big difference when you are cooking French beans that you've spent three back-breaking hours picking. You want to do the best job of cooking and presenting them that you can."

Market-in-the-Park

Nothing takes me back to the 1970s more than the Saltspring Island market, held on Saturdays from May to October. Market-in-the-Park, as it is now known, is a testament to community pride and unwavering commitment to sell only items made, grown or baked on the island. With over 120 vendors at the height of the summer, the market has become a top-billed event. It makes a wonderful day-trip for non-residents. In addition to produce from familiar growers and food producers including Michael and Jeanne-Marie Ableman of Madrona Valley Farm, David Wood of the Saltspring Island Cheese Company, Heather Campbell, "The Bread Lady," Rosalie Beach of Wave Hill Farm and Chintan and Satva Hall of Monsoon Coast Exotic World Spices, there is a plethora of handcrafted items from charming gumboots "planted" with flowers to natural soaps and hemp clothing. Many non-profit groups — from The Land Conservancy to the Raging Grannies — raise awareness at the market.

Wave Hill Farm's Rosalie Beach at her flower stall at Market-in-the-Park.

Monsoon Coast Exotic World Spices

Nobody is more hospitable than Satva Hall, a warm and dynamic man whose career has taken him from the clothing and jewellery businesses to his real passion: creating exotic spice blends. He spent his early 20s travelling through Pakistan, and when the war ended in 1973, he walked into India. At a train station, there was the "Vegetarian Eating Room" and the "Non-Vegetarian Eating Room." As a lifelong vegetarian, he decided he had found his country. Then he found his future wife, Swiss-born Chintan, whom he met at an ashram in northern India. He says "the whole India thing touched him deeply" when he was young, and it has stayed with him.

In true Indian fashion, he first invites me for a cup of chai — in this case, his Railway Chai, "spicy and warm with ginger and pepper, fragrant with cinnamon, cardamom and cloves." We sit on the couple's sun-drenched porch, drinking the tea and nibbling papaya, avocado and pear slices that have been sprinkled with chat masala, which is based on garam masala, but goes best with fruits, and his divine Monsoon Balti Spread on crackers. Hall's spices are incredibly flavourful, complex and fresh tasting, but not over-the-top hot. He says he is mainly catering to North American taste buds, many of which are just

Couscous with Roasted Veggies and Feta

Serves 4. Satva Hall has recently been "roaming afield from my original Indian mandate and created two new masalas: Tobago Habanero Curry, a hotter Caribbean-style mixture, and Ras el Hanout, the star of the Cairo souks." He says the following Ras el Hanout recipe "is a big hit at potlucks. Experiment with quinoa or bulghur wheat in place of the couscous!" I enjoy making it all three ways — to rave reviews.

5	garlic cloves, crushed	5
3 tbsp	extra virgin olive oil	45 ml
3 tsp	balsamic vinegar (optional)	15 ml
	salt and black pepper, to taste	
5	red, yellow or orange bell peppers (a mix), seeded and sliced	5
4	ripe tomatoes, quartered	4
1	large red onion, sliced in 1" pieces	1
1 1/4 c	sheep milk feta, cut into 1/2" cubes	300 g
3/4 c	Kalamata olives, pitted	200 g
	vegetable stock (or water) approx 1 1/2 times the volume of the couscous	
1 1/4 c	couscous	300 g
4 tsp	Ras el Hanout	20 ml
2 rounded tbsp butter		30 ml
1/4 c	fresh pine nuts	60 ml
1/4 c	Italian parsley, coarsely chopped	60 ml

Preheat oven to 400°F. Crush the garlic and mix with the olive oil, balsamic vinegar, salt and pepper. Toss with the peppers, tomatoes and onion until everything is well coated. Remove the veggies from the marinade, place in a roasting pan and roast in the preheated oven for 30 to 40 minutes (until the vegetables turn brown at the edges). Add the feta and olives to the marinade after the veggies are removed. Turn the vegetables once halfway through cooking, adding olives and feta when you do. While the veggies are roasting, make the couscous as per package instructions using vegetable stock or water and adding the Ras el Hanout and butter. Lightly toast the pine nuts in a dry pan. Mix the vegetables and couscous together and serve hot, topped with the pine nuts and parsley.

waking up, but can also satisfy his "macho customers," who want seriously hot flavour.

Satva imports spices from India and develops his own spice combinations. Traditionally added at the end of cooking, his concoctions give it those unmistakable exotic flavours. The room he does his mixing in has a deeply intoxicating aroma of cardamom, coriander, chilies and star anise, to name but a few of the dozens of individual spices he employs.

It's both a simple and a complex process. Satva says there's a lot of experimentation, but he is gifted with a taste for layering flavours, so he doesn't make too many mistakes. He says: "It's great when the wow factor happens, when it all comes together like one of Chintan's mixed-media artworks." At the moment, he is on a mission to create totally organic mixtures. He has been sent some organic spices from Orissa that he's experimenting with and is also working with Saltspring Island seed guru Dan Jason to see what spices might be grown on the island.

Monsoon Coast is receiving a lot of attention — B.C.'s *EAT* magazine recently rated it "one of the best 100 food experiences in the province" — but for now, it is strictly a small, family-operated concern. Satva develops the spice blends; Chintan leaves her artwork to help with packaging. When they're in full production, Chintan's mother comes over to help. Chintan says it's nice to have her mother involved; they can work and have a good chat at the same time.

Moonstruck Organic Cheese

I often order a glass of red wine and a simple cheese plate for dinner, a habit I got into when travelling in Australia one year. It enabled me to sample a great variety of local cheeses and still have room for sticky toffee pudding for dessert! At the Marriott Hotel's Fire and Water restaurant in Victoria, Chef Jeff Keenliside recently presented thick pieces of Moonstruck Organic Cheese Company's Blossom's Blue (a blue-veined Stilton-style cheese) along with thinly sliced baguette and fig compote. I enjoyed the cheese so much I resolved to visit its makers as soon as possible.

Julia and Susan Grace have been making "fine quality, highly ripened, good-dining kinds of cheese" on Saltspring Island since 1998. Their reputation is huge among connoisseurs of good cheese and deservedly so.

When I dropped in with Cynthia Eyton on one particulary wet and muddy day in December, we were offered hot coffee and seats by the fire in the Graces' living room. It was a warm welcome and typical of those I experience in rural homes. Farm work never actually stops, but generosity always seems to prevail. I wanted to know how the business of creating what *Macleans* magazine called "sin on a cracker" came about.

Julia and Susan weren't always in the cheese business. They began with a market garden and brown-box program for island residents. Then Susan, who Julia says "was always drawn to the animals," bought one and then another Jersey cow. By 1996 Julia had a lot of milk on her hands and "started to fool around with butter, yogurt and a nice cheddary kind of cheese." She would tuck the new products into her customers' brown boxes and their response was fabulous.

Eventually the women decided that "farming protein was a lot easier than growing leaves," and they considered making cheese in earnest. At that time, they had a couple of things in their favour. No one else was producing 100 percent organic cheese commercially so they were able to obtain a provincial government licence for a dairy and cheesemaking operation, and Julia's mother had left her some money which enabled them to get the business going.

"We don't produce supermarket cheese," says Susan. "Our cheese sits on your tongue and makes you go 'oohhh.' We want the flavour to be there, the taste to last in your mouth in a pleasant way." Those great tastes, such as the nutty creaminess of White Moon, the peppery, woodsy flavour of Savoury Moon or the sweet, buttery blue bite of Baby Blue, are, says Susan, "all about the milk." And that milk is from the famed Jersey cows. As someone who was Jersey-born, and raised on its cows' milk, I can heartily attest to the milk's superior quality.

Twenty-five of the Graces' 28 Jersey cows are dry when we visit, leaving three producing milk "to keep the soft cheese accounts going over the winter." By March the calving will begin. Lisa Lloyd of Saltspring's Stowell Lake Farm raises the "youngsters" for Susan, returning them to the herd when they are ready to milk. Susan credits Lisa with teaching her how to milk in the first place, and she also mentions fellow cheesemaker David Wood of the Saltspring Island Cheese Company as having been "a great help to us over the years." David, who has a delivery van, regularly delivers Moonstruck cheeses for the Graces, while the women, who own the requisite lab equipment, do cheese testing for David. They all benefit by "shouldering one another along."

By May, Saltspring's Market-in-the-Park gears up for the season, and the Graces go into full cheese production as they have a booth at the market every Saturday in addition to wholesale and retail orders. They were able to take a short break in the fall to attend the first Slow Food Terra Madre conference in

Blue Cheese Dressing

BILL JONES, FOR MOONSTRUCK ORGANIC CHEESE

When I asked Julia Grace for a recipe, she said: "My favourite is good crackers and red wine, so I think I'll call a chef and beg for help!" Her plea resulted in this fantastic recipe from Bill Jones of Deerholme Farm and Cottage. I love this dressing made with Moonstruck's Beddis Blue cheese, drizzled over iceberg lettuce. What can I say about the lettuce? I'm a child of the 1950s! (reprinted with permission from *Chef's Salad*, Whitecap Books, 2003)

1 tsp	chopped garlic	5 ml
2 tbsp	mayonnaise	30 ml
1	lemon, juice only	1
2 tbsp	water	30 ml
1/4 c	Moonstruck blue cheese	57 g
1 tsp	chopped fresh parsley	5 ml
	salt and pepper to taste	

Place the garlic, mayonnaise, lemon juice, water, cheese and parsley in a blender and process until well blended. Thin with a little water if necessary to make a pouring consistency. Season well with salt and pepper and chill until needed.

Turin. Later, they "rattled around Italy" visiting other cheesemakers, an experience they found "uplifting and humbling at the same time." Julia says that they came back to Saltspring "feeling really good about our cheese."

Ultimately, they credit the animals with creating such a good product. Says Susan: "The integrity of the cheese comes from the good milk." Even though it's an expensive process to be both producing the milk and making the cheese, they say the Jerseys give such high-quality milk that they want to keep it all going. Julia also wants to experiment more, to get "wilder and funkier" in her cheesemaking. She ripens the cheeses on open shelves, "letting those huge molds grow, washing them down and developing the flavour." That is real cheese to her, and she makes us laugh when she tells us: "When I see a cheese without a good rind, it looks naked to me."

You'll find Moonstruck organic cheeses on the menus of Cafe Brio, Fire and Water in the Marriott Hotel, Spinnakers, Hotel Grand Pacific's Mark dining room, Butchart Gardens and the Temple in Victoria, and at Sooke Harbour House, where an entire cheese course is created from these truly world-class cheeses.

Morningside Organic Bakery and Café

Alan Golding and Manon Darrette have created a café that not only serves "everything organic, all the time," but provides a comfortable venue for good conversation, an outlet to talk things over. Says Alan: "There are a lot of scary things happening in the world. We've been disconnected. We need to be bold, to reconnect with each other." Those reconnections are regularly made over cups of excellent coffee, house-made muffins and pizza.

Alan is a gentle man, with a lifetime of mindful thinking and responsible action, who has created a modern-day salon in a little adobe building at Fulford Harbour. The café came about at the right time, after he had looked for the ideal situation on some of the other Gulf Islands.

Alan and Manon had been living in Victoria, and came to Saltspring in 2002 to take in the Market-in-the-Park. Getting off the ferry at Fulford Harbour, Alan had an instant, wonderful feeling about the place and said to Manon, "We're not going to the market. We're staying here." They looked around, discovered that the little café on Morningside Road was vacant, and signed the lease that day.

The café menu is focused on nutritious, organic fare made from mostly local ingredients. The Caffé Fantastico coffees and Wild Fire breads and pastries, delivered daily from Victoria, are exclusive on Saltspring to Morningside Café. There is a wide range of organic fine foods available for purchase, including olive oils, balsamic vinegars and teas. In spring and summer, local organic produce is sold in the café's courtyard. Alan has also been working with island farmers to grow some special vegetables for the café menu. Eventually, they hope to grow herbs on the roof of the building, an urban-gardening concept that would be well suited to this little place.

Alan's aim to provide "food for the stomach and food for the mind" has already been more than fulfilled here. I find myself returning not only for the good eats, but also for the inspiring conversation.

Salt Spring Flour Mill

What must be the world's smallest flour mill is located on north Saltspring Island. As I approach the architecturally designed home of Pat Reichert, I find myself looking in vain for a water wheel. The actual mill is in a tiny yellow room in the back of the house. Its main feature is a wood-framed stone mill that's beautiful enough to be a piece of furniture.

Pat greets me at the door of the mill and asks if I'd like a demonstration. Once the mill starts grinding the grain, which she brings in from her partner's family-owned, certified organic farm in Saskatchewan, I can see her passion for milling. This is a second career for Pat and one she hadn't exactly planned, but which seemed like the right thing to do at the time.

She's always baked. When she was working as a social researcher, she travelled a lot and found herself coming home and baking bread "to ground myself." A few years ago, she saw a photograph of a stone mill and felt herself connecting to it. It wasn't long before she started looking for her own mill, which turned out to be more difficult than she had imagined.

Her research finally led her to the only person who still makes mills in Canada, and he agreed to make hers. It's constructed of untreated solid pine whose natural resin prevents bugs from developing in the flour. Pat tells me that grain and flour should never be milled against metal as it destroys nutrients. Inside the mill are two specially tumbled granite stones from the Tyrol that work together to grind the grain.

Pat produces only about 15 to 20 pounds of flour at a time, using a cool-milling process in which the stones turn very slowly; fast action creates heat and heat reduces nutrition. She estimates she has personally ground 12,000 to 15,000 pounds of flour in the last three years.

Most of her flour and cereal products are distributed through the local Market-in-the-Park, at NatureWorks health-foods store and through the Growing Circle Co-op, on whose board she sits. Local restaurants such as Hastings House use her flours.

Pat says she is pleased to be doing something useful for the community. In the old days, people would take their grains to the local mill to have them turned into flour. She says she would love to "bring that quality back to Saltspring." She is proud to be offering fully certified products that are distinguished in the marketplace.

Not only does Pat produce flours, she has some delicious cereal combinations, as well as quick bread, muffin and pancake mixes. When I visited her at her home, she was working on an expanded line

Fresh Apple Cake

Pat Reicheart, Salt Spring Flour Mill

My European heritage has made me a big fan of cakes that aren't too sweet. Pat's Fresh Apple Cake can be whipped up in no time, and it is the perfect accompaniment to afternoon tea.

In a small bowl, stir together:

1 1/2 c	Salt Spring Flour Mill All Purpose Multi Grain Flour	340 g
1 tsp	baking soda	5 ml
1/2 tsp	nutmeg	2.5 ml
1 tsp	cinnamon	5 ml
1/2 tsp	allspice	2.5 ml
pinch	salt	pinch

In another small bowl, stir together:

1	egg, lightly beaten with a fork	1
1/2 c	light vegetable oil	120 ml
1/3 c	liquid honey or sugar	80 ml

Preheat oven to 300°F. Lightly butter and flour a 9" square or round cake pan. Peel three small apples, then cut each into quarters and take out the cores. Coarsely chop the apples. Measure 1 3/4 cups of chopped apples and place in a medium-sized mixing bowl. Pour 1/4 cup of sugar over the chopped apples and stir to coat all the apple pieces with the sugar. Let stand for 10 minutes.

After the apples have been sitting in the sugar for 10 minutes, add the egg mixture to the apples and stir. Then add the flour mixture and stir *only* until the whole mixture is combined. Do not overstir. Pour the mixture into the prepared cake pan. Place the pan in the centre of the preheated oven and bake until the cake springs back when lightly pressed. This will take about 30 to 35 minutes. Remove the pan from the oven, and let the cake cool in the pan for about five minutes. Then evenly sprinkle about 2 teaspoons of icing sugar over the top of the cake using a sifter.

NOTE: Pat says: "This cake is delicious when it's warm, with or without a scoop of ice cream. If there are leftovers they make a perfect treat in your lunch bag the next day."

of heritage-grain products as well as cake mixes, which include a tempting double chocolate cake. Later in the year, I ran into Pat at Saltspring's Seedy Saturday event, where she was launching Hearty Seed, Lemongrass and Cilantro and Mediterranean bread mixes. For those wanting organic baked goods without having to start from scratch, these products are a godsend.

Salt Spring Vineyards

Happy, who trained to be a seeing-eye dog but ended up failing the course, appears to be greeting us with great enthusiasm when Cynthia Eyton and I open the gate to the Salt Spring Vineyards. We're not surprised that it's really Cynthia's adorable Lhasa Apso, Jasper, who has caught Happy's eye and the two of them become fast friends. We are warmly greeted by the vineyard's co-owner, Janice Hartley, and steered straight to the tasting room for a welcome glass of 2004 Christmas Release Blackberry Port, which Janice describes as "alcoholic blackberry pie." It makes for a delightful mid-morning refreshment.

Janice and her husband, Bill, are new to the winery business, but then so is Salt Spring Island. In 2002, they were granted the island's first-ever licence to operate a winery. Pragmatic folk, Janice said they felt they had "done everything they wanted to do" in their previous business, the River Run bed-and-breakfast in Ladner, and decided to make their next project a winery. They chose the Fulford Valley on Salt Spring because it was on the same parallel of latitude as Vancouver Island's Cowichan Valley wineries, and Salt Spring has a long history of successful orchards so they knew the climate would be conducive to grape growing. Their vineyards sit high on Lee Road, which ensures that late spring frosts are unlikely to harm the grapes. The location also gives them great visibility for attracting customers.

They began to clear and groom the property in 1998 and planted two acres of pinot gris, pinot noir and chardonnay in 2000. The following year, they added another acre of pinot noir and the early-ripening red, Leon Millot. When they were granted their winery licence in 2002, their neighbours, Elaine Kozak and Marcel Mercier, were also granted a licence half an hour later for their Garry Oaks Winery. The Fulford Valley is emerging as an interesting wine area on the island. The Hartleys' winemaker, Paul Troop, will soon be launching his own vineyards of experimental varieties across the road.

Janice tells me the pinots are very well suited to the area because they like a longer, cooler ripening period. She feels "they have a better flavour than the Okanagan, maybe because of the higher mineral content in the soil here." I'd wager their dedication to organic growing practices also contributes to the

Saltspring Island Lamb Moroccan Style

Colleen Bowen of Colleen's Kitchen Catering for Salt Spring Vineyards

 Colleen Bowen is in charge of producing harvest lunches for the workers. "It's such a fun and festive time with friends, family, locals and children all pitching in. We use all the wonderful Salt Spring produce available and pride ourselves on feeding everyone in style! "

Debone a leg of lamb, trimming away excess fat. Cut into thick slices and marinate for six hours or overnight.

Marinade:

	juice and zest of one large lemon	
10	garlic cloves, crushed	10
1 c	sundried tomatoes, chopped and drained	227 g
1/4 tsp	dried chile peppers	1.25 ml
1/4 tsp	saffron	1.25 ml
1/2 tsp	cinnamon	2.5 ml
1/4 tsp	cloves	1.25 ml
1/4 tsp	nutmeg	1.25 ml
1/2 tsp	salt	2.5 ml

Layer ingredients below in a cast iron pot, tagine or casserole dish, in the order listed.

4	medium potatoes, cubed	4
2	yams, cut into chunks	2
2	onions, sliced and lightly browned	2
	a layer of sliced lamb	
1/2 lb	whole green beans	.23 k
1 c	chopped dried apricots or figs or both	227 g
	another layer of sliced lamb	
1/2 c	green and black olives, pitted	113 g

Add two lemons cut into quarters and two whole heads of garlic with their tops cut off. Pour the remaining marinade plus one glass of Salt Spring Vineyards' Merlot over everything and place in a 325°F oven. Slowly cook for three hours.

NOTE: "Wonderful aromas will fill your kitchen, but resist opening the lid and do not stir until the dish is done. If needed, this dish can be thickened at the end with a bit of corn starch. Serve over couscous, rice or chunks of Heather Campbell's [see: The Bread Lady] bread! This is totally yummy paired with a glass of Salt Spring Vineyards' Merlot."

improved taste. Says Janice: "We believe that grapes free from herbi-cides produce healthier and tastier wines." On offer the day we visit are their 2004 Ortega, Blanc de Noir and Christmas Release Black-berry Port as well as the 2003 Pinot Noir and Merlot Bin 537 (this one is made with fruit from Oliver, BC, and won a silver medal at the All Canadians). Janice is par-ticularly excited about their 2004 wines because "we had fabulous weather."

When I ask what she is most proud of at the winery, there is a curious pause. Janice says she associates pride with its "seven deadly sins" meaning, so we laugh and I reword the question. What fulfills her here on her five-acre vineyard? She tells me she "always feels happy when I walk out into the vineyards." Believing that "we are here to be stewards of the land," she is pleased that they have been able to utilize what they've got. She enjoys the sense of community on Lee's Hill and appreciates it all the more when she comes back from a visit to the city. "It's always nice to come home to our Slow Islands in the gulf," a term that has recently been adopted by some Gulf Island residents to express their idyllic lifestyle (and, inherently, express their desire to keep it that way!).

Bill Hartley is a pilot who also teaches flying in Vancouver. Janice is a certified accountant who also teaches a course in entrepreneurship in Royal Roads University's School of Business. When they decided to go into the wine-making business, they both took courses in oenology at the University of Cali-fornia at Davis. She says that she and Bill "work really well together. The winery is fun and people are happy to be here." She teaches her students the process of planning for success that makes such a venture possible and often brings them to the vineyard to see for themselves the fruit of her business model.

Cynthia and I buy blackberry port (we love the fanciful, award-winning labels designed by Vancouver wine rep Bernie Hadley-Beauregard) and jars of Chow Chow, a relish made by one of Janice's friends on the island, before col-lecting Jasper and heading back to Fulford Harbour to catch the ferry. As we leave, Cynthia turns to me with a smile: "It's always impressive to see what education, foresight and planning produce."

Saltspring Island Cheese Company

I was introduced to David Wood's famous goat and sheep cheeses in Victo-ria at Ottavio's, and found them not only delicious, but beautiful. Each perfect mound of cheese is decorated and flavoured with different edible flowers (from

Rosalie Beach at Wave Hill Farm), peppercorns (David recommends the peppercorn cheese with a nice scotch: "There's something so right about that combination"), white truffles and roasted garlic. They make a notable addition to the cheese tray. There's a marcella (dried-out soft goat cheese) and a croutin chevignon, which holds its shape when baked. There are creamy camemberts including a delicious blue camembert, some aged sheep's-milk cheeses, and a hearty feta. The thing about sheep, though, is they take the winter off, so the goat cheese is really the Woods' bread and butter.

Before visiting the fromagerie and meeting the cheese-maker himself, I have been invited to picnic atop the island's 1975-foot Mount Maxwell. At its lookout, we open the lovely, wicker picnic hamper to reveal a cornucopia of delights packed this morning by Chef Render at Hastings House. There are a tasty chicken salad, fresh fruits, bread, a root-vegetable terrine with onion confit and an assortment of David Wood's cheeses, some freshly baked gingersnaps, chocolate cookies and almond shortbread. The wine is the popular Millefiori 2000 produced by Venturi Schulze Vineyards of Vancouver Island. I couldn't wait to see how this diverse range of cheeses was produced.

> "You get to do things with your kids like milking the sheep."
>
> — David Wood,
> Saltspring Island Cheese
> Company

David's story is not untypical of the kinds of people who settle on Saltspring. He paid his dues in Toronto with the highly successful David Wood's Fine Foods in trendy Yorkville, wrote a couple of cookbooks, then, 14 years ago, picked up the family and bought a peaceful sheep farm on Saltspring. He says the change in lifestyle has been good for family life: "You get to do things with your kids like milking the sheep." It's hard work, but they are making a living and loving their new life.

David considers himself a "gumbooter," one of the hardy and hearty south Saltspring Island residents whose outdoor lifestyle requires them to keep gumboots at the ready. (There is also an implication that these are the real Saltspringers who collect oysters, clams and seaweed.) As I tour the fromagerie with him, I sense a quiet pride of accomplishment. The goat cheeses are made from milk brought in from "goat people" in Abbotsford on the mainland, and from Mill Bay on Vancouver Island. They're mostly fresh cheeses; because of the smaller fat globules in the milk, they have a great silky texture — not gritty or grainy in the mouth. I happily learned from David that the higher the moisture content, the lower the fat. His soft goat cheeses have only 19% fat content — what a pleasure!

The milk is pasteurized (heated to 145°F for half an hour, then cooled), then a culture is added and it's left to ripen. This, says David, is the curds and whey or "Miss Muffet" stage. The whey or water is drained off, leaving the curds — the fat and protein. "Differences in time, temperature and acidity make a huge difference to the finished product," says David, so these aspects are closely monitored. His soft goat cheeses age for four days; the camemberts take 25 days. He makes 280 soft cheeses per day and 120 camemberts.

We gathered around the Sweet Heart stove in David's kitchen and sampled his beautiful cheese. It's a food memory I recall each time I buy Saltspring Island Cheese in Victoria — another rewarding link from field to feast.

Saltspring Island Garlic Festival

Garlic ice cream, anyone?

From early August until the end of September, that distinctive waft is in the air at the many garlic festivals across North America. West-coasters can celebrate on Saltspring Island, where the island's garlic growers come together for a real love-in on the first August weekend. There's the odd off-island grower like the exuberant Ken Stefanson of Gabriola Island, who brings his Russian Hard Neck, Porcelain and Purplestripe varieties — fresh, pickled or made into chutney and potent chocolate bars.

Saltspring Island grower John Wilcox displays his abundance of garlic at the Saltspring Island Garlic Festival.

Dozens of vendors set up tents at the Farmers' Institute Grounds on Rainbow Road in Ganges, and people come from as far away as the mainland to stock up on the season's first juicy harvest.

Yes, there is lots of garlic ice cream on offer, but it's a bit too early in the day for that, so I buy a braid of Korean garlic from Charlie Eagle's Bright Farm, and wander from stall to stall absorbing the festivities. Garlic has come a long way, baby, since its odour offended those unaccustomed to Mediterranean flavours, and it's now firmly embedded in the North American culinary lexicon.

Soya Nova Tofu

I consider a visit to Soya Nova Tofu a quintessentially Saltspring Island experience. There's something wonderfully communal about the operation, which is also home to owner Deborah Lauzon. Located in one of the island's old orchard areas, Soya Nova Tofu has been in production for 20 years.

Deborah invites Thomas Render and me to join her in her "office." She sets out real sofas and tables on her patio in summer and receives her visitors in the sunshine. All around her, her employees are coming and going. They're just finishing off a long day of production and the place is really buzzing. All her employees are young; many sport interesting dyed hair and tattoos. All seem wildly passionate; Deborah calls it "energized enthusiasm."

When there's work to do, she has a policy of "hiring whoever walks through the door," and she is proud that all three of her children — Zoltan, Nova and John — are tofu makers.

What, I ask, is her secret? I mean, how is it that these young people are so obviously turned on to tofu? She laughs. When her own kids had parties, she always cooked something for them. Being a vegetarian for 30 years, she often

made tofu burgers and they loved them. She says the kids of Saltspring eat tofu: burgers, soy-sausage rolls and her famous Zed Spread. Now, her grandchildren are enjoying the benefits of tofu. When they are "strung out on candy from a birthday party," she feeds them tofu with nutritional yeast and tamari, and watches them "mellow right out."

Deborah gives the okara (the pulp by-product of tofu production) to local farmers to feed their animals. She would like to see more farmers using this high-protein organic feed.

Wave Hill Farm

Those are Rosalie Beach's rosemary sprigs and edible flowers atop the artisan chèvre made by the Saltspring Island Cheese Company, and her jewel-like strawberries and figs are on the menu at Hastings House, yet this enterprising woman is actually best known for her flowers.

Today, I have a bouquet of Rosalie's dahlias on my desk, globes of deep fuchsia, purple and pink that take me back to the tranquillity of her flower garden every time I look at them. The garden itself is overwhelming, both in colour and in variety: dahlias, tiger lilies, casa blanca lilies (Rosalie's favourite) and daisies. Giant purple and golden cardoons have also found their way into the flower bed. The day I visit, Rosalie is about to make up a special order for the IFOAM conference in Victoria: 200 handmade bouquets that she will deliver herself.

She takes me on a rambling tour of her orchard, greenhouses and market garden. I soon see that not only did she and husband, Mark Whitear, save this property, but she is deeply passionate about growing and wholly committed to their new life in Canada. The couple spent 25 years in England where they raised three children and Rosalie lectured on holistic health care.

Forty years ago, Rosalie's parents bought a 575-acre property on Saltspring Island. Twelve years ago, when they were forced to sell off a few acres to pay the enormous taxes, Rosalie and Mark decided to try to keep the place. The couple moved to Saltspring, converted some of the land to organic farming, started a natural-selection timber business, and felt they were finally home.

The flower garden meets up with the vegetable and fruit gardens, where Brussels sprouts and broccoli are underplanted with mizuna, and companion planting is used extensively. There are strawberries, cascadeberries (a cross between a wild trailing blackberry and a loganberry), figs, asparagus, grapes, watermelons, Ogen melons, St. Nick melons (they keep until Christmas), plums, potatoes and herbs. There are greenhouses for tomatoes, cucumbers, peppers and aubergines.

Theirs is the oldest orchard on the island, planted in 1855 by pioneers Trage and Spikerman. It originally had 1,600 trees. Rosalie loves the Braeburn apples for their taste. Her Wolf River variety is well-known for its flavour and for the size of its fruit ("One apple, one pie," says Rosalie). She also grows the King of Tompkins County, Baldwin, Wadhurst Pippins, Gravenstein, Mann and Fallow Water varieties. As we wander through the orchard, "the slug patrol" marches by: a family of Rouen ducks. The sheep regard us from a distance. Rosalie and Mark press and sell apple and grape juices in the fall.

As many as 20 WWOOFers (Willing Workers on Organic Farms) work on Wave Hill Farm every year. Once, one of them asked Rosalie why they never eat citrus fruits. She replied that, with so many fruits and vegetables in season on the farm, they had no reason to buy oranges from some place else. One night, she and Mark counted 23 vegetables, herbs and fruits on their dinner plates. To me, theirs is an enviable, self-sustained existence.

Rosalie and I walk back to her barn (actually, it's underneath her house), past the fence lined with grapevines, lavender and rosemary. She tells me how those plantings remind her of holidays in Provence. She loves gardening and loves Saltspring Island, and, gazing at the dahlia bouquet on my desk in Victoria, I reflect on her enviable state of contentment.

PENDER ISLANDS

Iona Farm

As I attempt to stroll casually by Ellen Willingham's vegetable stall at the Pender Island Farmers' Market, apparently I'm not casual enough. "Taking notes this morning?" is her friendly enquiry. The old notepad has blown my cover, and we have a great chat over samples of her divine goat cheese with fresh herbs and garlic.

Ellen and Rob Willingham are both Anglican priests and crisis counsellors who came to Pender Island seeking a healthier lifestyle. They had been practising in separate parishes in Winnipeg, their youngest daughter had been diagnosed with leukemia and they felt they had a lot of stress to deal with. On a visit to the west coast, the family visited a cousin on Pender Island. Amazingly, after having coffee with his cousin, Rob bought her house and the Willinghams went back to Winnipeg to sell their home there.

Ellen says they have never regretted the move. Eventually, they were told about the Iona property by Tekla Deverell, and they decided to farm in earnest. The 20-acre farm is mainly forested, but they have five large vegetable gardens and pens for their goats, sheep and chickens. They began farming to feed themselves and later started selling at the Saturday Market. They've been certified organic since 1995.

Ellen tells me they are essentially "boat people," who used to enjoy sailing on Lake of the Woods in western Ontario. The Gulf Islands reminded them of that.

The organic beans went fast at this farmgate on Pender Island.

"We feel like seals, torn between wanting to be on land or water," she jokes. She and Rob are always on the water on Sundays, heading out on their diesel-powered boat, although they spend the day apart. One of them gets off on Mayne Island, to conduct the Sunday service there; the other carries on to Galiano Island to lead that congregation. When they're not leading services, farming or at the market, the Willinghams provide crisis-counselling services on the island.

I buy a big tub of chèvre and some of Ellen's green peppers, and then move on to speak to her tablemate. Tekla Deverell, formerly a psychologist living in Vancouver, is the island's undisputed doyenne of organic gardening and wife of the famous crime writer Bill Deverell.

From Tekla, I buy the freshest walnuts and I ask her what brought her to Pender. She smiles and tells me: "I followed Bill." Now, Tekla owns one of the island's most beautiful and prolific organic gardens, and she loves bringing her produce to market.

Jane's Herb Garden

It's absolutely correct that my cell phone packs in halfway through my conversation with Jane Gregory as I drive off the ferry. After all, Pender Island is a relatively small place and everyone knows everyone else. I shouldn't have to evoke big-city technology to get directions to her garden. A helpful walker at the side of the road points me right, and minutes later, I find Jane waiting at her front gate to greet me.

I'd remembered her sweet little rosemary plants on the tables of Aurora restaurant at Poets Cove Resort, and wanted to meet the lady who also grows all the restaurant's herbs and sprouts. Born in Buckinghamshire in England, Jane was working in a legal process-serving company in White Rock before moving across to Pender Island. As we survey her raised beds of herbs (all grown without sprays or fertilizers), she tells me she has always loved gardening. "Herbs are wonderful to brighten up a meal or transform vinegar or a bar of soap into something special."

With her two daughters, Samantha and Melanie, "now in school mode," Jane has expanded her business of fresh herb plants and cut herbs to include a full herbal product line of preserves, soaps and sweets. She rises at 3:00 A.M. on market days (the Pender Farmers' Market is held Saturdays from May to October) to make her famous glazed orange buns. When she has fruit available — apples, plums, strawberries or rhubarb — she makes pies that have garnered just as loyal a following as the buns.

Jane makes wonderful soaps using organic goats milk from Ellen Willingham of Iona Farm. I tried rosemary and orange from a range made with such enticing ingredients as raspberry, lavender, oatmeal and almond. The soaps are made from scratch and take six weeks to cure. Her preserves include hot pepper jelly, kiwi jam with pine nuts and cranberries, and an amazingly complex and addictive fig, walnut and brandy conserve. Jane recommends the fig conserve with pork or turkey, but mine didn't last beyond the cheese course that night and a midnight nip to the fridge to eat the rest directly out of the jar!

On the sweet side, Jane makes toffee that is a good match for my favourite commercial brand, MacIntosh's Creamy Toffee, and vanilla fudge that she tells me is "really creamy and not terribly sweet." Its popularity meant there was none left for me to try, but it certainly has given me a good reason to return.

Morning Bay Farms

They say that on the Gulf Islands, the proverbial "six degrees of separation" is only two degrees. My husband and I ventured down a very long and winding dirt road to find a picture-perfect cabin with smoke coming out of the chimney and a stunning view across to Saturna Island at its back door. We knocked and the door was answered by a couple I had met before. Keith Watt and Barbara Reid had been at the Marley Farm Winery one hot summer's evening two years ago, and I remembered that they were going to start a winery on one of the islands. Here they were now, with that winery about to open its doors to the public.

Keith invited us to join him on an invigorating walk around the vineyards, which he calls "the most difficult thing I've ever done." It's not hard to see the work that went into clearing the land, installing a drip irrigation system and planting the vines. Says Keith: "We were able to make good use of what we cut down," with wood from the land going into the house and new winery building.

Keith is a former CBC Radio journalist; Barbara worked in wholesale clothing for the April Cornell Trading Company in the United States. When they bought the 25 acres, they thought it would suit apple orchards, because Pender Island has a history of apple growing. They decided to start with a market garden and sold their bounty of lettuces, purple cabbage, Oriental greens, Brussels sprouts, eggplant, watermelon, herbs and saffron to the Pender Farmers' Market. Last year, they grew 3,000 pounds of veggies for the market, making them "the largest organic farm on Pender Island."

One day, Keith was looking across to Saturna Island and thought he spotted grape vines. He soon discovered that he lived directly across the pond from Saturna Island Vineyards. Calling on Eric von Krosigk, consulting winemaker to many local wineries, to appraise Morning Bay Farms, he got the green light for grape growing.

"In 2001, we planted Schoenberger and Marechal Foch here on the east side, and pinot noir, pinot gris, riesling and gerwurztraminer on the south-facing upper bench." It seems the upper bench can get as hot as 40 degrees in the summer, which perfectly suits the white varietals. While the grapes grow, he has been taking courses at the University of California at Davis, and experimenting with wine-making, using grapes sourced elsewhere.

Keith hasn't been able to find out too much about the property, because it's never really been farmed. There is an old barn and cabin where a woman lived and kept goats in the 1950s. Keith and Barbara have restored the buildings and moved them to the upper bench. One-quarter of their property is in the Agricultural Land Reserve, and that's the section on which they have been given permission to build the winery. "We're fortunate that winemaking is being encouraged as a sustainable agricultural industry," Keith tells us.

With the winery opening this spring, folks will be able to drop in for a tasting, then head down to the market garden with the gorgeous view to U-pick raspberries and strawberries. Morning Bay Farms will also host special events with music and food throughout the summer, so you may want to call ahead in order to include one in your visit there.

Pacific Shoreline

One of the ironies of living on a Gulf Island, surrounded by water and fish, is that it is not easy to buy fish. It has to do with the whole licensing and regulatory system of the fishery and the fact that shellfish must go to Nanaimo to be inspected and then to Vancouver to be cleaned before being sold just metres from where they were first gathered.

Between them, Bonnie and Cal have been involved in the area's fishery for over 60 years. Bonnie grew up in a fishing family on Long Beach on Vancouver Island's wild west coast. She and Cal, a fellow fisher, met in Victoria one night after she and her mother dropped into a pub after bingo.

Several years back, the couple recognized a need for fresh fish among all the Gulf Islanders and began mooring their boat for a few hours each week at docks on Mayne, Galiano and Pender islands. Naturally, they have a loyal following on each island, with many people appreciating their fresh-from-the-boat deliveries. When they're not delivering, they run a fish-export business from their home on Pender Island.

My sister and I met this industrious couple at 2:00 P.M. precisely on a Thursday afternoon at the Hope Bay dock on North Pender. A sign had been hung there earlier in the day: "Salmon today 2:00 P.M." I saw a similar sign when I was on Saturna Island the following week. Cal was happy to remove head, tail and fins from the fine spring salmon we selected for dinner. We took it back to the cottage, stuffed it with sliced onions and lemons and rosemary, and threw it on the barbie. With some fine fresh

Cal and Bonnie of Pacific Shoreline selling the day's catch from their boat on Pender Island.

corn from the island's mainly organic Southridge Farms Country Store, carrots bought on Mayne Island the previous afternoon and a blackberry crumble made from the berries I'd picked at the side of the road, we feasted like queens. We had foraged for the freshest local ingredients, supported local producers and were now revelling in our bounty. What better island foodie experience?

Pender Island Bakery Café

Dorothy Murdoch is a long way from hotel management in Vancouver, and she's a lot happier. "I'd had my eye on this bakery for a couple of years," she tells me, "and when it came up for sale, I was ready to buy."

She is delighted to finally be working for herself and providing employment for eight islanders. She operates as a bakery by day and pizzeria by night, when creations like The Gulf Islander (smoked oysters, anchovy, tomato sauce, spinach and three cheeses) and The Spicy Thai (breast of chicken with sweet Thai chili sauce, peanut sauce, lime juice, cilantro, mozzarella and peanuts) get rave reviews.

Dorothy is not a baker, and many people thought she was crazy to operate in the same plaza as the island's main grocery store with its in-house bakeshop. It seems she saw something they didn't: a craving for back-to-basics, made-from-scratch baking. She hired the shop's original master baker, Dorian Wilde, and took on a pastry baker and several assistants. From the day she opened, Dorothy has put the Pender Island Bakery Café on the map. Her impressive range of breads and buns — many organic — walk out the door. We took Cornish pasties (a nod to Dorothy's English roots), spanakopita and the biggest cinnamon buns ever back to the cottage for lunch, and it was thumbs up all around the table.

Dorothy is very attuned to the baby boomers' desire for organics and interest in knowing what's in their food. She serves only organic coffees from Reingold, a German roaster in Vancouver, and uses organic ingredients in baking whenever possible. Sitting at the window on a sunny Sunday morning, my niece and I enjoyed our Americanos and, yes, just one more of those sinful cinnamon buns.

Poets Cove Resort and Spa

When Executive Chef Martin De Board was seven years old, he remembers peeling carrots to the beat of "Black Magic Woman." He laughs at that one, but tells me that music and cooking go really well together. While he and his team prep, he likes to have the tunes going. ("Listening to the Gypsy Kings, you get spice! You get colour! When we hear reggae, we're more organic," he winks.)

I've dropped in to meet De Board in Aurora, the fine-dining restaurant at Poets Cove Resort. As the restaurant is being set up for lunch service, he reflects on the past four months in his new job at an all-new resort and shares his vision for farming on Pender Island. De Board was asked to head the kitchen just weeks before the resort's grand opening in March 2004. He arrived with his sous-chef, Brett Huber, a formidable team from the Westin Hotel in Whistler. It was a busy and challenging time. He remembers lights needed to be refitted in the dining room only hours before service. "When the workers had finished, we realized the table settings were covered in dust, so everything had to be removed, cleaned and re-laid." Saying he "couldn't have done the opening without Huber," De Board is now clearly on a steady course.

The resort, which was built on the site of the former Bedwell Harbour Resort, often has 300 boaters in port and 100 other guests housed in the lodge and cabins. That translates into a couple of large dinner sittings in the dining room and ongoing

Quick Seared Sablefish on Pak Choy and Orange Glaze

MARTIN DE BOARD, CHEF, POETS COVE RESORT AND SPA

Serves 4. Chef's note: "Even though this recipe is very light, it is a great dish in winter because of the freshness of the oranges. I recommend using Valencia oranges and serving the fish with roasted fingerling potatoes."

Fish:

2 lb	sablefish medallions	890 g
1 tbsp	canola oil	15 ml

Orange glaze:

2 c	freshly squeezed orange juice	480 ml
3 tbsp	unsalted butter	45 ml
1 tsp	soy sauce	5 ml

Pak choy salad:

4 bunches	pak choy or baby bok choy	4
3 tbsp	hoisin sauce	45ml
	knob of butter	

For the orange glaze: Reduce the orange juice to about a cup (250 ml). Pass through a fine mesh *chinois*. At service heat and add soy and whisk in butter a little at a time.

For the pak choy: Clean all the cabbage and dry. Toss in a hot skillet with a little butter and hoisin sauce and season to taste.

For the sablefish: Season the fish generously and rub with oil. In a very hot pan sear the fish for 45 seconds each side.

To plate, place the sautéed pak choy in the middle of the plate. Place two fish medallions on top, pour the orange glaze around. Garnish.

patronage in Syrens lounge every night. De Board says one of the most challenging things for him is finding a large enough supply of local ingredients. As someone who remembers "eating tomatoes that tasted like tomatoes" from his grandmother's garden in his hometown of Vaudreuil, Quebec, he loves the seasonal offerings. In summer, he serves a fresh tomato salad "just with salt and pepper," and people ask how he makes it taste so good.

He would like to patronize Pender Island farms more, but finds they "just can't get enough" to supply the restaurant. He's pleased to see local producers "going back to doing things properly," but says that with the restaurant's volumes, they "could use the entire herd of sheep on Pender." Maybe more telling was the offer of kale made by one grower, "but he could only supply 12 portions a week and I need 200," laments De Board. Jane's Herb Garden on Pender Island is able to supply the herbs and sprouts, and Moonbeams Coffee Roaster, the coffee.

I mention how delighted I was with dinner the previous evening, which had been cooked by Huber, and was pleased as always to see mention on a menu of the ingredients' origins. The Warm Local Goat Cheese Cake with Red Beet Purée and Honey Syrup featured chèvre from Saltspring Island Cheese Company. It is a signature dish De Board developed for a wine-tasting seminar in Whistler. The local Sautéed Mixed Mushrooms with a Herb Citrus Phyllo Arc held Jane Gregory's pea shoots. The Duo of Cowichan Bay Duck — duck breast topped with cassis jelly on a potato croquette and duck confit wrapped in a crepe — and Duo of Gulf Island Lamb — lamb sirloin stuffed with roasted garlic and White Grace cheese served over a caramelized shallot tart and sour cherry jus, and lamb tenderloin marinated in balsamic vinegar served over a local goat cheese polenta cake, tomato coulis and sautéed spinach — were both impressive examples of respect for ingredients and a refined understanding of how to prepare them.

When I had the chance to chat with Huber after service, he told me about another compelling ingredient in the dining room: the "purple and orange sunsets" in summer that customers and staff alike make a point of stopping to enjoy. Huber is a Saskatchewan-born, self-described "mama's boy" who grew up on her good homecooking and worked in pubs before graduating from Dubrulle's in Vancouver in 2000 and joining De Board at the Westin. He tells me he loves to cook "fine dining" but particularly enjoys "the heart and soul" of bistro fare — cassoulet, braised lamb shanks. Says Huber: "Anything that takes eight hours to cook has to be worth trying."

De Board tells me he became interested in food by watching his grandmother cook and then cooking with his mother. He later trained at the Institut de tourisme et d'hôtellerie du Quebec (as did Brentwood Bay's Alain Léger), then worked for Club Med in Turks and Caicos before heading to the Westin Hotel. At Poets Cove Resort, he has found his *metier*. He's still developing the bistro menu in Syrens bar one floor down and is working at "adding more Vancouver Island vintages to the wine list," but generally things are on key, attributable in part to playing the right tunes in the kitchen.

I next pay a visit to the resort's Susurrus Spa, an experience that turns out to be as culinarily oriented as the restaurant, though not nearly as caloric.

In the calm of the spa lounge, curled up in a comfy chair before the fire, I take a quiet moment to enjoy a cup of lavender, nettle and peppermint tea. I've booked a salt glow with nourishing lotion, but Spa Manager Trish MacKinnon instead suggests their latest Nutty Chocolate Body Buffer made with avocado oil, walnut shells, wheat germ oil, chocolate and vitamins. One whiff of the product sends my endomorphines a-buzzing, but I'm assured there is no caloric consequence to the treatment. I'm guided to a private room to succumb to *le massage au chocolat*, which is followed by an application of Chocolate Whip Creme with echinacea and burdock.

Trish tells me that "people are increasingly looking for results-oriented treatments using natural products." Without synthetics in the body products, she tells me, "you get real results." As in the food and beverage realm, people now want to know where ingredients come from. Susurrus Spa offers many face and body treatments with the Éminence organic skin-care products from Hungary as well as locally made natural-product lines. Trish opens a few jars to let me feast on the aromas of face masques made from pumpkin and orange, sour cherry and eight greens and sends me off with a sample of Seven Herb Treatment, a "hyperactive nourishing herbal extract masque" that I've now incorporated into my weekly routine.

Before leaving Poets Cove, I paid a visit to the deli where boaters stock up on staples and shoot the breeze with hot cups of Moonbeams coffee. Someone looked across the cove and remarked that "it is calm as a millpond out there." Sadly, that signalled the right sort of weather for a ferry ride back to Victoria, and I took my leave.

SATURNA ISLAND

The southernmost Gulf Island has only 320 permanent residents, a population that Michael Vautour of Saturna Island Vineyards describes as one big family. Certainly, after taking a walk on the island's foodie side, I felt I'd made new friends.

Haggis Farm Bakery

I follow Priscilla Ewbank by car to Haggis Farm Bakery, which she co-owns with her husband, Jon Guy. Partway there, an oncoming car stops in the middle of the road, and Dottie, Priscilla's dog, is transferred to her car. Seems Dottie has been out for a walk with another dog, and her play date is now over.

The bakery is a clapboard building a kilometre or so from the Saturna General Store, which is also owned by Priscilla and Jon in partnership with Hubertus Surm. As we walk in, we enjoy the residual aroma of the 600 loaves that were baked the day before. Priscilla shows me the walk-in cooler ("refrigeration is very important here"), the stacks of grains that are milled on-site, the big mixer, oven and cooling racks. Behind the bakery is a greenhouse where tomatoes, basil and peppers are grown for the store's café.

Besides the bread, cookies and cereal baked twice a week for customers all over the Gulf Islands, Victoria and Vancouver, the bakery produces pasta and some special-order cakes. Priscilla attributes the success of the bakery to Jon: "He's an excellent baker — he's a Virgo. It's really his heart and head in the whole operation."

My conclusion is that both Priscilla and Jon, together with their dynamic, extended family, are all responsible for the success of Haggis Farm Bakery and the Saturna General Store and Café. And their success is a reflection of their commitment to the land and to each other.

Saturna General Store and Café

The hub of the island's food and social scene has to be the big ol' general store, which offers everything from a post office to groceries and video rentals. There's also an excellent selection of B.C. wines and a café where I could happily eat every meal.

Co-owner Priscilla Ewbank takes me to an outside table, telling me she needs some air after packaging a bread order for Vancouver and Victoria until four o'clock that morning. Her husband, Jon Guy, is now making the off-island deliveries in their new refrigerated truck. Bread deliveries have come a long way since Jon started baking a decade ago and their two eldest daughters took the loaves door-to-door by horseback.

Today, they appear to have it all — a thriving store, bakery and café that together employ 23 islanders — but, understandably, it's been a long journey. They met as students at Berkeley during the

Co-owner Priscilla Ewbank takes a break for breakfast at the Saturna General Store.

heady 1970s, and came to Canada when Priscilla decided she "didn't want Jon to be cannon fodder in Vietnam." She tells me that the suburban values she was raised with, but never embraced, collided with the activist scene at Berkeley. She and Jon then attended Simon Fraser University, but Priscilla thought it restricting, and found herself looking across the pond to Saturna Island.

When they first arrived on the island, they lived and worked at Jim Campbell's farm. They milked cows and helped with the haying, and Priscilla spun and wove wool from the sheep. Today she says she is "so grateful to have experienced that way of life, and realize how it informs my own."

As we chat, a young woman comes out with Priscilla's breakfast — a beautiful, fat omelette with ricotta and spinach, and a side of bacon. The plate is decorated with nasturtium flowers. Priscilla introduces her youngest daughter, 20-year-old Jessie.

That Jessie is the café's head chef this summer is no surprise: she began cooking her famous pizzas at the age of 12, and worked for Hubertus Surm at the Saturna Lodge & Restaurant as a teenager. She now cooks at the café in the summers and lives in Mexico and other warm climes every winter. She says: "Cooking makes sense to me," and it's obvious that she has a gift for bringing out the best in her ingredients and a refreshingly un-fussy sense of presentation.

The evening's dinner menu reads like a gastronome's dream: Organic Mayne Island Greens with Buttermilk Feta Dressing and Summer Vegetables; 40-clove Roasted Chicken Breast with Roasted Vegetables; Haggis Farm Pasta with Basil Pesto and Parmesan; Tagliatelle with Roasted Eggplant; and, for dessert, the blueberry tart, cheesecake or their specialty: big, luscious fruit pies.

One by one, the café staff drop by our table, each one hugging Priscilla, and introducing themselves to me. I find myself in the centre of a warm and loving extended family. Katie often stays with Priscilla when she works evenings, as her family lives on the other side of the island. Amy divides her time between the café and Saturna Lodge & Restaurant. Kolton is working in the kitchen before heading off to university on the mainland in September. Priscilla says she believes in "teaching the kids well" and giving them something meaningful to do. I think of how a lot of city teenagers I know would turn around in this hugely nurturing environment.

Priscilla says their philosophy includes "organic wherever we can," "feed people well," and "keep bread affordable." She is proud to be a significant employer on the island, and enjoys buying organic products from many on- and off-island growers. Ron Pither of Mayne Island supplies vegetables, and Flora House of Saturna Herbs supplies herbs. Four local wine connoisseurs advise on the store's selection.

There's an impressive symbiosis between the store, the bakery and the café. The café produces pesto and other things for the store's deli. Priscilla says when the café recently had a corned beef sandwich on the menu, the bakery produced "really big rye bread." Leftover crumbs from the bakery go into Hubertus' famed Go-Nut Burgers that are sold in the store.

I stock up on spelt bread, whole-wheat croissants, giant Loon cookies and Date Crunch Cereal, before following Priscilla by car to the bakery. Those exceptional Loon cookies and many of the Haggis Farm Bakery breads are available in Victoria at Seed of Life, Lifestyles Markets and Planet Organic.

Saturna Herbs

The 25-acre Breezy Bay Farm is located in a sheltered valley, just across the road from the Saturna Lodge & Restaurant. The property is mainly in forest with about 10 acres of pasture for sheep, together with greenhouses and an acre under cultivation. There's also a bed-and-breakfast, where guests stay in the pretty 1892 farmhouse, surrounded by orchards and scented lindens. I learn that the farmhouse was built by Gerald Fitzroy Payne, the grand-father of Noël Richardson of Victoria's Ravenhill Herb Farm.

It's a co-operative farm, owned by members of the Saturna Freeschool Community Projects (SFCP). The SFCP was named for a freeschool that operated on the property in the early 1970s. Member Flora House says: "Since then the farm has been run by members and a number of 'newcomers' — that is, you've only been on Saturna for 20 years or so!"

Flora and some of the others grow culinary herbs including thyme, sage, oregano and basil. The basil greenhouse is a beautiful thing to look at, and I stand inside a long time just inhaling. All drying and packaging of the herbs is done on-site, and they're sold through the farm's website, and at the Saturna General Store. You'll also find them on the menus at the Saturna Lodge & Restaurant and the Saturna Café.

Flora says the SFCP members have farmed organically for over 25 years, feeling "it's better to feed the land to feed ourselves." They have recently also become organically certified.

Saturna Island Vineyards

A relative newcomer to Saturna Island, the vineyards have made a big impact on 60 acres of south-facing waterfront, and their wines made quite an impact both regionally and nationally. At the 2000 Northwest Wine Summit winemaker Eric von Krosigk won a Crystal Rose award for the 1997 Vancouver Island Riesling Brut and a silver award for both the 1998 Gewürztraminer Rebecca Vineyard and the 1997 Okanagan Valley Riesling Brut. At the 2001 All-Canadian Wine Championships, the vineyard won "Best Dry Riesling" for its 1999 vintage.

In some ways, it's all happened very quickly for the Page family of Vancouver. Larry and Robyn Page had been looking for a retirement property on Saturna when this spectacular property became available. They bought it and, with encouragement from their friend and viticulturist Jean-Luc Bertrand, decided to grow grapes in 1995.

Daughter Rebecca is the general manager, and I chat with her between tastings in the winery. She loves Saturna and is used to a small community, having lived in Pemberton, BC, where she ran the gas station and deli. She is delighted to have her young son in the local school. She tells me the vines have been planted to take advantage of sun trapped on the property by vast sandstone cliffs. The cliffs act as a sort of heat radiator that "keeps the soil warm — several degrees warmer than the rest of the island." The land slopes, so it's ideal for drainage, and the soil is well fertilized "from nearly a century of sheep farming."

Michael Vautour is the cellar master who runs the convivial wine tastings and tours of the vineyards. It's a fairly hot day, so he suggests a tour by air-conditioned van. A former Vancouverite himself, he tells me how much he enjoys living in a small community now: "I feel everyone is family on Saturna."

The vineyards are magnificent. The Rebecca Vineyard produces the award-winning gewürztraminer, as well as pinot gris, pinot noir and merlot. The two Robyn Vineyards produce chardonnay and pinot noir. The Long Field Vineyard also produces pinot gris, and in the Falcon Ridge Vineyards, 14 experimental varieties include muscat, cabernet sauvignon and syrah. Because of its age, the vineyard has been using some grapes from the Okanagan, but it will eventually be self-sufficient. Eric, "the flying winemaker," actually lives in the Okanagan, so he is able to make the grape selections personally.

I stand in the Rebecca Vineyard and catch my breath. The sun beats down. The grapes hang heavy with mellow fruitfulness on the vines. At the end of each row there is a pretty rose bush that "attracts aphids and provides early warning signs of any mould or mildew." Eventually, the Pages will plant olives and produce oil, but for now, their days are full with the vineyard, the winery and the casual bistro.

I enjoy a nice antipasto plate and glass of riesling on the patio and take my time leaving.

MAYNE ISLAND

Deacon Vale Farm

Shanti McDougall asks: "Have you ever had the divine pleasure of eating a sun-warmed tomato fresh off the vine?" and picks me a handful of her best cherry tomatoes. We're touring her greenhouse, and she's pointing out some of the special varieties that she grows for her famous (but still only in small production) tomato sauce: San Marzanos (she brought the seeds back from Italy); Alicante (considered the best tomato by the British Horticultural Association); and the heritage variety, Brandy Wine.

Shanti will harvest as many as 3,500 pounds of tomatoes, and then go into serious sauce production in her commercial kitchen. Her tomato sauce is in hot demand, mainly from private customers in Vancouver who buy it by the caseload. Local Mayne Islanders can buy it, and her jams, chutneys and relishes, at the Saturday Farmers' Market and Tru-Value store; in Victoria, they're available at the Market on Yates and Planet Organic. Shanti says she will move beyond direct marketing once her production levels are higher. Eventually, she would like to be able to hire local residents because she believes the island needs more small-scale industry.

When the McDougalls started out, tomatoes were their main crop, but they now produce more of a variety. They grow 800 pounds of Spanish Roja garlic, pinot noir grapes, raspberries, artichokes and greens. There are Damson plums and yellow plums, from which Shanti makes jam. They harvest 500 chickens a year, and sell 20 to 24 sides of beef. Shanti says some people buy a whole year's supply of chicken from her and freeze it.

Deacon Vale is a magical, certified organic farm of 95 acres, co-owned by the McDougalls and the Abbotts (Shanti's brother is Vancouver doctor Bill Abbott). About half of the land is in hay or pasture, and another large section is in woodlot. There's a large, 20-foot-deep pond in the centre of the property, surrounded by fruit trees. Closer to the McDougalls' house is a one-acre market garden, and another half acre of new plantings, including the grapes. Shanti is thinking about putting in some hazelnut trees because organic nuts are hard to find. Saltspring Island breadmaker Heather Campbell had told me that she couldn't find organic hazelnuts for her bread, so I introduce them — the grower and the baker — and, perhaps, organic hazelnut bread will one day be coming out of Heather's oven.

The farm operates on a closed-cycle system, producing what it needs to operate. To keep the soil viable, the McDougalls maintain a hot compost that measures about 25 feet by 8 feet by 6 feet and is turned four times a year. The soil gets a good dose of micronutrients from local seaweed that is collected by the Village Bay Improvement Association and scattered over their plantings.

Mayne Island Farmers' Market

Shanti and Don McDougall were instrumental in starting the farmers' market on Mayne Island "to forge a closer bond between people and the food they eat." It's held at the "Ag Hall," built around 1900, the place where things happen on the island. The hall and grounds offer an ideal setting. In the middle of the grounds, the McDougalls have built a quaint pole structure, used as a stage for local performers.

The market offers a stunning array of the island's bounty: goat cheese, produce, sauces and chutneys, jams and jellies, pies, soft lamb pelts and yarn made from mohair goats. It's a great day when Peter Renner has come across from Galiano with his superb wood-fired breads to sell. Deacon Vale Farm cooks up a delicious lunch (homemade sausages, hot beef sandwiches, salmon burgers, etc.), so many people spend the morning shopping, eating and chatting with their neighbours. The lunches are delicious, not surprising when one discovers they are prepared by a chef trained at London's Dorchester Hotel — that's Don McDougall! Market organizers hope to develop a complete food court in future.

Shanti says she values the quiet and privacy of her farm, but also enjoys the social aspect of the market. There are usually ten vendors, and this increases to 20 stalls for the annual Fall Fair. The market runs from the Victoria Day long weekend in May to Thanksgiving.

Oceanwood Country Inn

Romance and food are always a good combination, and English country house gentility provides a relaxed setting. I arrive alone to find a lovely, rambling home set in the caress of the aptly named Dinner Bay, and ring the doorbell. Jonathan Chilvers, looking dapper in khaki shorts, greets me with: "Are you planning to come in, or have you just missed the bus?"

Jonathan is a long way from his birthplace "in the shadow of Wandsworth," but his dry, particularly English humour is fully intact. An ex-pat myself, I take an instant liking to my host and ask him how he happens to own this charming place.

He and his late wife, Marilyn, were living in Vancouver, working in advertising and public relations respectively, when the idea emerged to have a weekend place in the Gulf Islands. The couple bought a low-maintenance cottage on Mayne Island and escaped for long, Friday-to-Monday weekends as often as they could.

In 1989, a realtor friend suggested they look at a property that had just become available, and Jonathan agreed on the understanding that he and Marilyn were only looking. When they returned to see it a second time, they took friends. Their friends said: "All you could do with this property is open a bed-and-breakfast," so they did.

While Jonathan excuses himself to change for dinner, I take a leisurely tour of the grounds. There's a prolific vegetable-and-herb garden overlooking the bay, and comfortable nooks and seating areas, all situated to take in the view. An impressive flagstaff sports the British Columbian, Canadian, American and British flags. Through an open window, I can see the kitchen in the full flutter of preparations for dinner.

Sorrel and Spinach Soup

 Serves 4. "The green leaves of sorrel give a lemony zing to this spring soup. Though not usually found in the regular supermarkets, sorrel is easy to grow from seed. In early spring, the tender young leaves are delicious in a salad or can be cooked like spinach as a vegetable. The secret to success with sorrel is not to cook it too much or it becomes brown and unattractive — although it will still taste delicious." — *Chef Kruse*

2 tbsp	unsalted butter	30 ml
1/2	medium yellow onion, thinly sliced	1/2
2	carrots, peeled and thinly sliced	2
2	stalks of celery, thinly sliced	2
1 c	white wine	240 ml
4 c	chicken or vegetable broth	1 L
2 c	spinach leaves, washed	480 ml
2 c	sorrel leaves, washed	480 ml
2 tsp	finely chopped fresh thyme leaves	10 ml
	salt and pepper to taste	

Sweat the onion, carrot and celery in the melted butter for 3 minutes over medium heat. Add the white wine and allow to reduce for a further 3 minutes. Add the chicken or vegetable broth and the spinach and bring it to a boil. Turn the heat down to a low simmer and let cook for 40 minutes. Turn the heat off. Add the sorrel, stir it in, then immediately purée well in a blender in small batches. Return the purée to the pot and reheat but do not boil. Serve in warm bowls. Garnish with a drizzle of cream that has been steeped with roast garlic and some finely chopped lemon zest.

As I wander around the side of the inn, I chance upon Chef Steve Kruse taking a brief coffee break before service. He worked extensively in restaurants as both waiter and dishwasher before "getting serious and going to school in 1994." A graduate of the Stratford Cooking School, he worked at Sooke Harbour House and owned his own bistro, the Miner's Bay Café on Mayne Island, before landing the big job at Oceanwood.

He loves living and working on the island, and appreciates the opportunity to use high quality, refined ingredients in the Oceanwood kitchen. He says he tries to keep his cooking "straightforward and honest" and that the best food is "pulled out of the ground."

He relies on the inn's own gardens for much of the spring and summer, but also buys from some of the local cottage growers including Helen O'Brien and Naralaya Farm's Ron Pither. While the menu is planned a week in advance and posted on the inn's website, it can change daily, such as last Thursday when no fisher had caught the anticipated skate that day. For chefs working on these somewhat remote islands, menu planning is both a challenge and a joy (the joy is when something fresh and inspiring arrives unexpectedly at the kitchen door).

Jonathan greets me again in the library with: "Would you like a beautiful martini or a nice, delicate sherry?" As I settle onto chintz with a glass of Harvey's Bristol Cream, Tony Bennett croons in the background and a kitchen helper passes by the window with a bowl of fresh-picked salad greens from the garden. An American couple joins us for a drink while their teenage daughter "completes her makeup" in their room upstairs. Returning guests, they ask Jonathan to recommend a local chardonnay, "something we haven't tried before."

Jonathan later tells me that the British Columbia wines are in great demand, and he is pleased to be supporting the local economy. I enjoy his comments on the restaurant's wine list, such as that against the popular Venturi Schulze Millefiori: "Enjoy it here because it is unique and you won't find it back in Kansas, Dorothy."

We all head downstairs to the oceanside restaurant for dinner, where a window seat has been reserved for me, although I can see that every table in this dining room commands a sea view. There is a rather large yacht in the bay tonight, the owners of which are dining at the table next to mine. When I mention that I will be overnighting on Pender Island, they point to it across the bay and we contemplate whether or not it's within swimming distance.

When the *prix fixe* menu is presented, I drift away into foodie heaven. One can choose from two appetizers and two mains, and the rest of the menu involves no effort on the part of the diner, other than emitting a few ooohs and ahhhs when the food arrives.

This evening's *amuse bouche* is a simple (or "honest," as Chef Kruse would say) cucumber slice topped with Smoked Sooke Trout Mousse. What follows is an amazingly good soup: Mayne Island Lamb Broth with White Beans, Zucchini and Tomatoes. A fresh sage leaf from the garden adds to the delicious, earthy taste. The lamb was delivered from the island's Iredale Farm. The accompanying breads, Calendua (edible marigold) and Whole Wheat Walnut, are both excellent.

I have chosen the Pacific Octopus in Carrot Broth with Thai Basil, Daikon and Nasturtiums, a brilliantly coloured presentation that reminds me of a Chagall painting. I ask for a soup spoon to finish every last drop of the broth. A raspberry and fennel sorbet cleans the palate, and then I move on to Albacore Tuna Loin seared rare served on Lemon Couscous with Rosemary-Caper Butter Sauce. Jonathan has paired this with a Tinhorn Creek merlot.

My waitress, Candida, is a charming woman who also looks after the inn's gardens and paints and decorates in the off-season. Like many Gulf Islanders, she has embraced the necessity of employment diversity. Working two or three different jobs is the way many are able to sustain life on the islands.

Alas, the ferry calls, and I take my leave. Jonathan opens the big gates and waves me off into a dark night. I foolishly tell him I know the way. With no sense of direction and only the moon to guide me, I somehow avoid all three deer that leap across the road en route, and find myself the only passenger boarding the 9:10 P.M. ferry from Mayne Island.

GALIANO ISLAND

Daystar Market and Market Café

Since *An Edible Journey* was first released, I have had the good fortune to spend extended periods of time on several of the Gulf Islands. During a three-month sojourn on Galiano, I did my grocery shopping at the Daystar Market — store, café and community gathering place all in one. I was always impressed by the quality of ingredients that were available on what is arguably one of the least populated and remote of the Slow Islands in the gulf.

Stopping by before the place opened one morning to meet the sisterhood that runs it, I began to understand the difference passion can make to business. Tahirih Rockafella is a 25-year-old beauty who could easily walk the Milanese fashion runways if she was the least bit interested in that lifestyle. She isn't. In fact, she tells me she "could easily fall into the easygoing lifestyle" that her parents originally shared at Primal Point Commune on Galiano in the 1970s. Her boyfriend, Gabriel, a carpenter on the island, who has joined us for the interview, smiles at this.

Indeed, the lifestyle of Tahiri's parents, Lony Rockafella and Johanna New Moon, was in many ways idyllic in those early days. They picked fruit in the Okanagan and trucked it to the

125

Lower Mainland. Later, they started Wild West, an organic-food-distribution company, before selling out and moving to Galiano Island. From their nine-acre property, they cut the trees that would be used to build their house and the Daystar Market store.

The café came later, and was actually built around the four-ton reefer truck that they had originally used to transport fruit. Tahirih tells me that when she and her three sisters were younger, they "used to hang out in the truck's cubby above the café." The truck is now the café's cooler — seeing is believing!

Although their parents eventually divorced, they remained a tightly knit family. The girls lived with Johanna in Cobble Hill on Vancouver Island, but "we came home faithfully to our father every weekend." Tahirih worked at Capers in Vancouver for a year, returning to Galiano to run the Daystar Market with her sister, Josli, 23, for two years. They leased out the café, but Tahirih also did a waitressing stint there.

Gradually all four sisters took on specific areas of responsibility in the store and café. Cecia, 14, comes across from Cobble Hill in the summer to wash dishes; Oleann, 20, runs the produce department; and Josli works in the office. Tahirih runs the Market Café with great enthusiasm. From her work at Capers and in the Daystar Market, she "got a good front-end idea of what people like to eat and what they are willing to pay." She attracted to the café Martine Paulin, a terrific island chef, whose wholesome cooking is a big draw.

My sister and I, still on the urban clock, stopped in for coffee and fresh cranberry muffins one morning. We were joined by islander John Scoones, who was just taking a break from excavating a nearby building site to tuck into the Farmer's Lunch, a hearty vegetarian pie with whole wheat crust, served with salad. There is a great community feel in the café. It's commonplace to share a table, and interesting conversation is always on the menu.

The store and café depend on a wide range of suppliers, with "as much organic as possible" from local growers like Erik Nelson, Sutil Lodge and Doug Lhatta and from Mayne Islander Ron Pither. Tahirih says "we grew up organic because of our parents," and what better gift to pass on to one's children?

Donna Marben

Just when I think I've met most of the dynamic organic farmers around these parts, Donna Marben invites me to enter paradise. Her farm, located way off the road on the north end of Galiano Island, has an amazingly diverse topography, allowing her to grow almost anything from kiwi to kamut.

Donna and her life partner, Hans Bongertman, met at the Primal Point Commune on the island in the early 1970s. Disillusioned about the Vietnam War, she had left her home in Minneapolis "to find a wilderness, a quiet space to live and work." Hans is a carpenter from Holland, who Donna says has farming in his blood; his surname alone means "man of the orchard." I learn that Hans is the linear planter; Donna the free-form artist who plants all over the place.

They both loved the communal life, but in 1984, with their two children in tow, they set out to carve their own piece of paradise out of a five-acre forested property. Their farm began as a way to sustain their family. When Donna realized she was buying a box of fruit every week, she quickly began to plant her own. Today, their orchards alone comprise 400 apple, pear and plum trees.

My tour begins at the upper bench, the property's rockiest area, where Hans and Donna have established raised beds. There are leeks, French heritage pumpkins and prolific grapes for making wine and raisins. A small greenhouse holds 25 varieties of tomatoes. Says Donna: "The important thing is to diversify. That way, if one kind doesn't take, another will."

The property dips way down into a three-acre valley that is naturally boxed in by huge trees, creating a micro-climate. As we climb down what feels like hundreds of steps, Donna tells me she goes "up and down six times a day," often accompanied by her black Lab, Lucy. There are two vast, 25-foot-deep ponds in the valley, one of which is covered with the most fragrant lotus plants. From the valley's upper garden — the sandiest part, and therefore the first tilled every spring — Donna often gets two or three successive crops. Today, there is a profusion of lettuce, corn, potatoes, sunflowers and squash. The latter has been planted around the perimeter so it can wander. There are also echinacea and St. John's Wort that Donna makes into tinctures. She picks me a few delicious raspberries and tells me the local goldfinches visited here a couple of nights before, "learning to sing and eating the seeds of the sow thistles."

What Donna calls her mid-garden contains onions, broccoli, cauliflower and cabbages. Here also are the many grains that she hand-grinds into flour: Tibetan barley, kamut, golden flax and Mandan corn. The garden in the lowest part of the valley is given over to winter carrots, parsnips, potatoes, turnips, beets and several kinds of radish. These are the crops she digs out to trench under a foot of soil in the upper bench area for winter storage. Last year, the family was still eating trenched carrots in June. Donna lifts some of the floating vegetable row covers to harvest arugula and a host of Oriental greens. The tenting provides warmth and acts as a great bug barrier.

From a garden designed to sustain one family, this property has grown to feed many in the Galiano community. Donna rises at dawn every day to prepare brown boxes, each one made to order. As with many other brown-box programs, her customers choose from a daily "menu" of fruits, veggies, preserves and juices. Donna tells me that some people are very specific ("too specific, and they run the risk of being cut off from paradise!") and others love getting a box full of surprises.

During a sojourn on Galiano, I loved the adventure of receiving a box from Donna. Ordered the night before, it was waiting for me in the morning, having been tucked behind a rural mailbox by her son on his way to work. Being a greedy foodie, I couldn't wait to open it: a just-picked bouquet of Oriental greens, four succulent varieties of tomatoes, tiny, jewel-like beets, spicy arugula, small new potatoes, hard heads of the season's first garlic and a big bottle of mellow apple cider. Breakfast never looked so good.

Max & Moritz

Christian and Lucy Banski are the smiling faces behind the little red catering cart with the German fairytale characters painted on its side that parks at the Galiano ferry dock in the summer. The intoxicating aromas of Indonesian (her background) and German (his) foods are hard to resist, no matter what time of day it is. I have often picked up a portion of *bami goreng* (stir-fried noodles with vegetables, tofu and peanut sauce) for breakfast, particularly if my ferry is about to leave and I know I won't be back to the island for a while! Even though Lucy cooks a great all-day breakfast omelette, it didn't take much convincing from her to get me to try the noodles before 9:00 A.M.

The service is fast and friendly, and the lineups first told me that this was a good place to eat. The Indonesian side of the menu offers either rice or rice noodles with delicious combinations of veggies, chicken, beef, sausage or tofu. The house-made spicy sauce is so popular that Christian and Lucy now sell it by the bottle. German fare includes bratwurst with sautéed onions and sauerkraut on a toasted bun, and *schaschliktasche* — grilled beef or chicken with green peppers and onions in a pita-bread pocket.

Good coffee, cookies made by the Haggis Bakery on Saturna Island and Mario's gelati bars are also on offer. There are seats scattered about, which make this another of the important "meet-and-greet" spots on the island.

WINE ROUTE

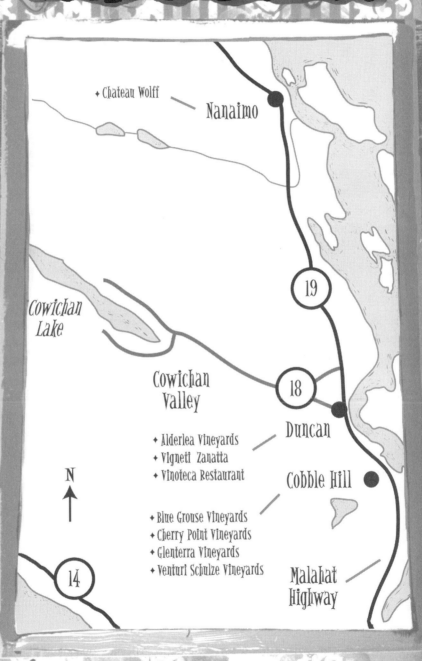

Chateau Wolff

Nanaimo

19

Cowichan
Lake

Cowichan
Valley

18

Duncan

✦ Alderlea Vineyards
✦ Vigneti Zanatta
✦ Vinoteca Restaurant

Cobble Hill

✦ Blue Grouse Vineyards
✦ Cherry Point Vineyards
✦ Glenterra Vineyards
✦ Venturi Schulze Vineyards

N
↑

14

Malahat
Highway

*S*omewhere along the way, I knew I would have to admit a weakness; it's about wine. I love the stuff and drink a glass of vin rouge every day. I know exactly what I like, but I'm no expert. So it seemed appropriate (and also turned out to be fun) to invite not just oenophiles but also professional sommeliers to accompany me on the wine route. That route loosely includes vineyards in the Cowichan Valley and Cobble Hill area, a destination that might not yet be Napa North, but, as vintner Roger Dosman says, is "something like Mendocino."

My experts of choice are Daniel Beiles, sommelier and wine importer with Vinifera Wine Services based in Toronto, and Frances Sidhe, sommelier at Zambri's restaurant in Victoria. Both are not only knowledgeable, they're patient with me!

Daniel was certified as a sommelier by the International Sommeliers Guild in Toronto. He first trained as a chef, working at The Royal York Hotel and Scaramouche in Toronto, followed by a stint at The Wickaninnish Inn. With both family and business on Vancouver Island, he maintains a bi-coastal existence, and I was delighted to meet up with him for visits to Blue Grouse and Vigneti Zanatta vineyards, as well as Sooke Harbour House. Daniel's unpretentious enthusiasm for his craft make him an ideal wine-tasting companion.

Frances achieved her certification from the International Sommelier Guild in Vancouver. She now designs the Zambri's wine list, which is 90 percent Italian. Both intellectual and gracious, Frances is a pleasure to learn from. She tells me she "has a problem with big descriptions of wine," and tends to comment more on weight and sensation than aroma.

Frances says she is interested in adding some Vancouver Island picks to Zambri's offerings. So, if we had a mission at all, it was to discover what was on offer at some of the local wineries, and possibly find out what Vancouver Island wine really is. So, we set out early one morning to visit Alderlea, Cherry Point and Glenterra vineyards with a road-trip picnic of Wild Fire Bakery's walnut and raisin loaf, chèvre and a couple of bottles of water, and the great anticipation of finding some winning "weights and sensations."

130

Percy Bojanich creates a perfect cappuccino at Mirage Coffee Shop in Victoria.

Kathy McAree of Victoria's Travel with Taste Tours checks the clarity of a local wine.

Mermaid mosaic, designed by Karen White, in the gardens at Sooke Harbour House.

Chef Edward Tuson of Sooke Harbour House happily displaying a rockfish — will this catch wind up on your plate tonight?

Reawaken your taste buds at Sooke Harbour House with skate wing with alaria and sea lettuce.

Gastronome Sinclair Philip of Sooke Harbour House exhibits a choice vintage.

"Mead is the oldest art of fermentation. Consumed by all, from kings to peasants, mead has gained a reputation as a giver of life, wisdom, courage and strength down through the ages."
— Tugwell Creek Honey Farm, Sooke

Chef Angelo Prosperi-Porta in his garden at Cooper's Cove Guesthouse and Angelo's Cooking School in Sooke.

Jerson Hernande'z and Tamara Koltermann, of Hernande'z in Victoria, dish out food, love and philosophy.

Chef de Cuisine Christophe Letard surrounded by the bounty at The Aerie Resort, located on the scenic Malahat.

These tidbits at The Aerie Resort are as artfully presented as they are scrumptious.

Darren Cole flambés while dinner guests warm to the atmosphere at Steeples in Shawnigan Lake.

Hilary and Patty Abbott offer a tasty sample of the wares at their cheese shop in Cowichan Bay.

Clipping herbs in the gardens at Hastings House on Saltspring Island. Tall fences surround the garden to keep out bold deer.

A palatable plate at Hastings House.

The Community Farm Store in Duncan is a wonderful source of local, seasonal and organic produce.

Jonathan Knight has brought organic baking to Cowichan Bay at his True Grain Bread bakeshop.

The gardens at Fairburn Farm in the Cowichan Valley — described by Sinclair Philip of Sooke Harbour House as "one of the most beautiful farms in the world."

Chef Mara Jernigan of Fairburn
Farm slices freshly baked pizza.

Chickens roam free at Fairburn Farm.

Alderlea Vineyards

Frances and I find vintner Roger Dosman pruning the canopy ("the curtain of leaves and shoots that is formed by the grapevines," Frances tells me). He agrees to give me a lesson. As it's January, he first removes the clips that attach the vertical shoots to the wire fencing — there are some 100,000 clips among his eight acres of vines. Then, aiming to keep the shoots separate so that when the clusters of grapes appear, they won't touch each other and create rot, he choses two or three of the shoots to salvage, and clips the rest. The tiers will come along after him and tie the shoots down. Ideally, one wants to leave two vertical shoots from the previous year for renewal (Roger sometimes leaves a third as the shoots are susceptible to breakage when they are tied down).

He explains that it's all about allowing sunlight and air to get to the fruit. Mid-June to the end of July is the heavy-labour period when he and his workers will be "deleafing in the fruit zone" of each vine. Roger is a lot like the Venturi Schulze clan: he does everything the hard way, beginning with propagating his own plants. Says Roger: "Higher quality canopy management gets a better fruit."

Roger had an automotive shop in Vancouver, but didn't want to live in a big city any more. He took note when the provincial government passed legislation in 1989 to allow small farm wineries. Frances jokes about how to make a small fortune in the wine business ("Start with a large fortune," she and Roger agree, "and wait a few years."). Roger did not start with a large fortune but, after searching in the Okanagan and on Vancouver Island for two years, he found a lovely, sloping, 10-acre parcel that faces southwest in the Cowichan Valley, and set to work.

He has stuck to his mandate: "to produce wine only from grapes grown in our vineyard." Beginning with 30 varieties, he has narrowed them down to 15 that perform well.

The vines are heavy with grapes at Alderlea Vineyards.

Roger describes the business as "slow as you go," meaning that you don't know until you try if things will work or not.

What certainly has worked for Roger and his wife, Nancy, who runs the wine-tasting room, is that they have created a viable business and healthy (all that hard work and fresh air) lifestyle. They are contributing to the local economy by providing jobs for five workers in season, and they are giving wine connoisseurs and even amateurs like me the benefit of their considerable skill.

We stopped to taste the talk of the town, the vineyard's fruity, ruby-style port called Heritage Hearth. Roger set out a nice piece of Stilton and some fresh filberts from a farm down the road, and we quietly imbibed. Frances declared the nectar "rich and lush, with good acidity," and immediately ordered a case for the restaurant. I bought a bottle that I have practically hidden at home to enjoy with my cheese course.

Other offerings at Alderlea include Bacchus (a riesling/sylvaner cross), Angelique (a blend of optima and siegerrebe), pinot auxerrois, pinot noir, pinot gris (partial French oak barrel fermentation) and a claret that Frances describes as "a big, fat, juicy, fruity" wine.

We talk about defining Vancouver Island wine, and Roger suggests that "it will take at least another 10 years to see what the island industry really is." He points out that, even within the Cowichan Valley, the locations of vineyards "vary greatly in their ability to grow grapes." One day, say Frances and Roger, it will be nice to see a flavour profile, to be able to say what's typical of the area.

For now, we can enjoy the journey from vineyard to vineyard and winemaker to winemaker, and make our views part of the exciting evolution of this area's style.

Blue Grouse Vineyards

It's one of those heart-stopping, big-blue-sky days in the Cowichan Valley, as Daniel Beiles and I pull into what is arguably Vancouver Island's prettiest vineyard. In the tasting room, we are warmly greeted by Sandrina Kiltz, who introduces herself as the "DOB — daughter of the boss."

The boss is Dr. Hans Kiltz, microbiologist, biochemist and former veterinarian for the United Nations, who brought his family to the Cowichan Valley in 1989. The timing was ideal; provincial legislation was just changing to allow small farm wineries to operate commercially. The Kiltz family began to test different varietals for suitability, eventually settling on Ortega, Bacchus, pinot

Sandrina Kiltz offers wine tastings at her family's Blue Grouse Vineyards.

gris, siegerrebe, pinot noir, gamay noir and others suited to the relatively cold climate. They planted in earnest in 1992 and 1993.

The vineyard is truly a family affair: Hans and his son Richard, both European-trained winemakers, make the wines; Hans' wife, Evangeline, lovingly tends the vines by hand; and Sandrina, a graduate in international business, is responsible for the marketing and daily public wine tastings. Now 27, Sandrina tells us it was wonderful growing up at Blue Grouse: "My brother and I did the weeding, thinned out the grape clusters and learned how to drive a tractor before a car. I think it's given us a really good work ethic, and the kids at school thought it was cool that we lived in a vineyard."

Before we turn our attention to the business at hand — wine tasting — we catch a parade of white swans on one of the lower slopes. Then, a couple from North Carolina drops by, and all eyes and ears are fixed on Sandrina, who pours the first selection: Ortega 2000. Daniel notes the "tropical fruit in the nose — lychee, as well as fresh, ripe peach; low acidity on the palate; and a clean fruit-driven finish."

Next up is the winery's Müller-Thurgau 1999, a relation of riesling, from which Daniel gets "soft, white peach and Bosc pear on the nose; petrol [typical of fine riesling] on the palate, and a faint herbal, lemon-balm finish." He tells

me it would pair perfectly with a light fish (Sandrina recommends halibut) or shellfish.

The Pinot Gris 2001 is a big hit, and the entire tasting group appreciates what Daniel declares its "floral aspects and figginess." He identifies geranium, white peach, ripe cantaloupe and even a slight nuttiness, and suggests its low to medium acidity would pair well with lamb or fatty fish such as salmon. We learn that Blue Grouse was the first winery in the valley to produce pinot gris and they have been winning awards for it in the prestigious Oregon wine festival ever since. This is the wine we stock up on before reluctantly saying our goodbyes.

Cherry Point Vineyards

Helena Ulrich apologizes for not being available the day Frances and I are going to visit. She's off to Alberta for a week with the grandchildren, and her daughter has already persuaded her to jet-set back for a day in the middle of her holiday to accept the Lifetime Achievement Award from the British Columbia's Institute of Agrologists that she and her husband, Wayne, have won. So, Frances and I pull up chairs at the kitchen table with Wayne and ask how he came to be running a 34-acre vineyard that produces some 5,000 cases a year — the largest operation on Vancouver Island.

He'd always kept a decent cellar of mainly Italian wines. When he and Helena married, he pulled out several cases and his reds went first, before the whites and hard liquor that the caterer had recommended. He worked as an agricultural engineer, and Helena was a lab technician and co-owner of the well-known 17-Mile House restaurant (on the road to Sooke) when the couple decided to follow their entrepreneurial spirits.

They moved to Victoria and ran the Victoria Lampshade Shop. However, having a small farm had always been a dream for Wayne. While he was still working for the federal agriculture department, he had been sent to the Okanagan to evaluate a request for funding from a fledgling winery. He visited several vineyards at that time and figured "those guys were enjoying life more" than he and Helena. Like many Vancouver Island vintners, he points to 1989, when the government allowed farm wineries to start up, as the pivotal year in his decision to follow his dream.

They bought the Cowichan Valley property in 1990 and intended to be selling wine by 1993. However, their business plan hadn't factored in the birds that descended in 1992 and put the whole operation back a year. By 1994, Cherry Point was fruitful and fully licensed.

There's a lot going on at this vineyard. In addition to the grape growing, wine production and wine tasting, there are a well-stocked gift shop, outdoor patio wine bar, tours with lunch and wine tastings, catered private parties including a recent dinner for the Confrérie de la Chaîne de Rôtisseurs (Helena and a neighbouring chef are the talent behind those events) and fabulous summer concerts in the 160-seat pavilion. People are encouraged to attend the concerts with their own picnics or buy a casual meal at the vineyard. The concerts are regularly sold out, so it's advisable to call well ahead for tickets.

Wayne has learned to make wine "just by doing it." He has recently been assisted in the winemaking by Hilary Abbott of neighbouring Hilary's Cheese, and has help in the vineyard. Wayne tells us that, as an engineer, "so much of the vineyard is in my head that I frustrate new employees because not much is written down."

We sample the well-received new blackberry port, which Christie Eng of the Shady Creek Ice Cream Company in-cluded in her Blackberry Lavender Trifle recipe (I found it hard to save some for the trifle!). Made with wild blackber-ries from the Cowichan Indian Reserve, it's not the sweet, cloying drink one might expect; Frances praises its dryness and tanginess. The Cuvée de Pinot, a blend of pinot blanc, pinot gris and Auxerrois has "a spicy nose, with acid from the pinot blanc and a nice long finish;" the Pinot Gris 2001 won a People's Choice award at the island's wine and oyster festival; the non-vintage Valley Sunset is notably fruity; the Pinot Noir 2000 has "less fruit, more structure and length," and Frances suggests it would match well with our West Coast salmon. With all of these tastings under our belt long before breakfast, we make our next stop Black Coffee at Whippletree Junction for a couple of Moriss' serious Americanos. Cherry Point Vineyards was recently sold to the Cowichan Tribes, with Wayne and Helena Ulrich now consulting to the winemaking process.

Glenterra Vineyards

John Kelly was a traffic-safety signmaker and his wife, Ruth Luxton, a Dubrulle-trained chef who cooked for the fabulous Meinhart food store in Vancouver when the couple decided to make a move. John had been commuting for two years to Okanagan University College to take a diploma in viticulture and oenology and had also volunteered at several Okanagan vineyards to learn the trade. When a 17-acre parcel became available on Vancouver Island, they moved the family across the pond.

Ruth does catering with her good friend Connie Papin of Cumberland's Chez Cuisine Kitchen, and also cooks at Livingstone's restaurant in Duncan. John tends the 4.5 acres of vines and makes the wine. They are both involved in the promotion of their vintages; I first met Ruth at the Harvest Bounty Festival where she turned me on to their pinot noir. Even though the property was originally a vineyard, John has done his share of experimentation. Early on, he determined that the Alsace varieties would do best: gewürztraminer, pinot blanc, pinot noir and pinot gris. He tells me about the Duncan Project, a practical research project in the early 1980s in which vintners from the island's first wineries did a range of test plantings to determine the suitability of grape varieties.

It's a very cold day when Frances and I visit John in his tasting room, but we are soon warmed up with good conversation and samples of his Vivace 2002, a blend of Ortega, Auxerrois, Bacchus, Siegerrebe, Schonberger, et al. that Frances finds to be "almost sweet at the start with a kick of acidity." We

Owner John Kelly pours for two Seattle samplers at Glenterra Vineyards.

both enjoy the Gewürztraminer 2002 straight from the barrel with its lychee, rose petal and grapefruit notes. Frances is impressed with the acid in the wine, as she is always looking for a good structure to stand up to Peter Zambri's dynamic cooking. Another tasting is of the Brio 2002, again from the barrel. John says its herbaceousness comes from the Dunkelfelder grapes. He will add some cabernet sauvignon to round off the flavour.

My ears perk up when John says he is applying for organic certification for his vineyard. He has stopped spraying, started controlling weeds with organic fertilizer mulch and will be switching to metal posts. It's a long road, and one that winemakers seem slower to travel than farmers. John says he's "trying to get there because the wine tastes better, cleaner." He also points out that he is working in the vines and doesn't want to be around pesticides and herbicides.

Glenterra has already won a silver medal for its Pinot Noir 2000 at the prestigious North West Wine Summit. John says they are producing 400 to 600 cases now, and will eventually increase production to 10 acres and 1,200 to 1,500 cases. John and Ruth are also hoping to add some type of food service on their property — possibly barbeque, which I've told them would be well-supported by urban hunter-gatherers like myself.

In addition to the estate-grown vintages, a visit this spring will be rewarded with tastings of the Meritage 2001, a classic blend of cabernet sauvignon, merlot, cabernet franc, malbec and Petit Verdot.

Venturi Schulze Vineyards

We all know that there's balsamic and then there's balsamic. Venturi Schulze produces Accto Balsamico, a nectar that attracts calls from all over the world. I first sampled it with a group of travel writers one overcast day, and I swear the sun came out.

Michelle Schulze tells us that the family's vineyards were originally planted for vinegar, and "then we found we were able to make wine. You see, for vinegar, we need to use grapes that are as high, if not higher, quality than for wine. If you have faults or a mouldy taste, it is so huge after 12 years that you have to throw it away. You can't use pesticides, or the poisons end up in the vinegar. We like to do things the difficult way, and if there's a harder way, well, we'll find that too."

She passes around samples of the vinegar on silver spoons, and tells us: "You're looking for sweetness, and you have to have some acid in there. These can be fairly high in acid, say 5 to 6 percent, but you won't be able to tell because they're so sweet. This one can be almost 50 percent sugar. A lot of people expect something quite acid, but they say: 'Wow, it's so good. It's sweet!'" I find it delicious — a dessert in itself. We all want to buy bottles to stash in our purses.

Michelle says they like their balsamic vinegar because it maintains some flavour of the grape. "We really enjoy a lot of the Italian ones, but they don't taste quite as alive. Our woods are younger than theirs. You're looking for some wood flavour, and often people don't recognize that. If you put your nose in there, you can smell cherries."

Michelle recommends serving it over strawberries or on really good ice cream. If you're going to use it in a sauce, she advises adding it at the end, as it's already so concentrated. One doesn't want to boil it down and destroy the flavour. We also learn that the Venturi Schulze vinegar is not as black as some of the commercial vinegars because there is no added colouring.

We wander out to the vines to admire the healthy clumps of Madeleine Sylvaner, a white-grape variety used for the vinegar. Says Michelle: "We'll go through there seven times in a certain season. You can basically tell by July how your fruit is set and how it's going to ripen. Sometimes you can pick everything at once in one or two days; sometimes it's over three weeks. You get in there, and start picking those

Barrels of the famed Aceto Balsamico in the vinegary at Venturi Schulze Vineyards.

Balm

"Balm is good for your health. Mix together with some ice and feel it cure all!" — *Michelle Schulze*

glass of club soda
drop of Venturi Schulze's Aceto Balsamico

bunches that have ripened first. Giordano [Giordano Venturi, her stepfather], will say, 'I need more acid,' so sometimes we even pick portions of bunches."

Sometimes they have to let the grapes overripen because they need higher sugar and lower acid to make it work. Once picked, the grapes are crushed as they are for wine, and the juice is simmered in 60-gallon pots for about three days. Michelle says: "It's really kind of a fun process. It's like making a broth, and the proteins come to the top. They have to be skimmed off or they'll turn brown and have a bitter flavour. We're looking for a clear product."

When Michelle opens the door to the vinegary, the aroma pulls us inside. The neat rows of barrels represent more than 30 years of work. Giordano made his first barrel of vinegar in 1970. He comes from a very poor family and had never had the real stuff. His first batch went mouldy and had to be thrown out. Michelle tells us: "He ended up going back to Italy and bringing back a live culture. He put it in a barrel and basically forgot about it. It was many years later that he tasted it and that was it! It was just sort of a fluke that it happened that way, and it took off from there. That's the little barrel right there — the mother barrel. We didn't make another vinegar until 1986." Although they've slowed down the evaporation from that original barrel, basically, the whole stock comes from it.

Michelle laughs as she points to the flowerpots on the property, barrels cut in half with geraniums in them. "Each represents $30,000 in lost revenue. When there's mould, you just have to throw the vinegar out and that's all they're good for. It's hit and miss, really."

Michelle's mother, Australian-born Marilyn Schulze, received a National Research Council grant to obtain certain Italian documents regarding vinegar

production. She was able to make sense of them, and worked side by side with Giordano to create their special vinegar.

The current release is a blend of vinegars between 6 and 32 years old from the various barrels. Barrels are laid on their sides, side by side, and holes are cut in the top for evaporation. It gets fairly warm in the vinegary, so there is intense evaporation. They lose up to 30 percent volume a year, depending on how hot it is.

Each barrel gets topped up from the barrel beside it. That's why each barrel is slightly larger than the one next to it; it's also a year younger. The vinegar moves down the whole line, which is why they have to keep the grape production up. It takes a long time.

Vinegar barrels are traditionally made from mulberry wood, but it's a protected tree so it's now unavailable. Venturi Schulze uses oak, acacia, cherry, chestnut and ash barrels.

Michelle puts the whole production into perspective: "If you start with 1,000 gallons of juice, in 12 years you will have between 25 and 30 gallons, which is why it's so expensive. This is Giordano's dream, and it's working out. We're the only ones who are doing this commercially in North America."

Venturi Schulze is also highly regarded for its wines: a Brut Naturel that was chosen for the Queen's 1994 visit to the Commonwealth Games in Victoria; Millefiori, the ultimate tropical fruity siegerrebe; and Brandenburg No. 3, a rich dessert wine that pairs perfectly with my favourite course, the cheese course. They are all estate-grown, and Marilyn is adamant that this is the only way to develop a regional identity for wine. She is concerned that some local winemakers are buying their grapes from other parts of the province and not declaring their origin. She sees huge potential for the Cowichan Valley wine area, and just wants it to be true to itself. Venturi Schulze has become the exclusive distributor of an amazingly authentic grana cheese that's made in Alberta. "This natural, aged cheese gives off explosions of flavour that we have found in the past only with fully aged Parmigiano Reggiano," says Marilyn. Leoni Grana Cheese is available in 2.5 kg and 300 gr pieces.

Vigneti Zanatta

A visit to Vigneti Zanatta should properly be combined with a meal at the vineyard's farmhouse restaurant, Vinoteca, so Daniel and I, together with friends, make time to do both.

Loretta Zanatta is the kind of thoughtful, intelligent vintner you want making your vino. The care and pride she takes in what she does and her obvious depth of knowledge are inspiring. We ask how she got into the business in the first place.

"We're an Italian family," she tells me, "so we have always grown grapes and made wine." Her parents emigrated from Treviso, which is north of Venice, in the 1950s. They found a 120-acre dairy farm just south of Duncan and decided it would be "a great place to raise kids," so they raised dairy cattle and their own children. The family always grew their own vegetables and grapes.

By 1981, Loretta's father was experimenting with grapes in earnest. The family turned an acre of land over to the Duncan Project, a government-sponsored effort to determine which grapes would really grow well in these parts. Loretta says she spent a lot of time "testing the acids and sugars" of what was planted. She and her husband, Jim, had acquired degrees in plant science from the University of British Columbia. Loretta had also obtained a master's degree in winemaking from the university in Piacenza, Italy. They were more than prepared when the provincial government introduced legislation that enabled farm wineries.

In 1992, Vigneti Zanatta became the first licensed commercial vineyard on Vancouver Island. Loretta is known for her sparklers that she makes "in the champagne style." She calls sparklers "the cleanest wines," because they contain no sulphur and are based on un-adulterated wine fermented only with naturally occurring yeast and sugar. At Vinoteca, you can enjoy a champagne tasting of Loretta's three sparklers paired with an appetizer plate, and I can think of no merrier way to begin a leisurely afternoon on its veranda.

Daniel tastes but, as I'm driving, I opt to take the three sparkling beauties home and make a dinner around tasting them — one of my more delicious excuses for a party. So, at a later occasion, my friends and I happily imbibe Glenora Fantasia Brut (made from 100 percent Cayuga grapes, aged up to six years); Alegria Brut Rosé (Loretta's personal favourite, a light rosé made from pinot noir and auxerrois grapes);

and Taglio Russo (made from cabernet savignon grapes, a deep red sparkler that's based on the still wine Loretta used to make for her grandmother). All of us are most taken with the Fantasia Brut, the sparkler Daniel describes perfectly as having "a fine, light pale yellow complexion with thin, persistent streams of bubbles; a nose of fresh bread and Granny Smith apple; followed by a medium mouth feel with a crisp and tangy citrus finish." The Zanatta winery also produces pinot grigio and Damasco, an appetizer or sipping wine that's made using auxerrois wine refermented on Ortega skins.

Loretta is proud of what her family vineyard produces. They only make wine from their own grapes and will not bring in product from other grape-growing areas like the Okanagan. She recognizes that wine is a new industry in the Cowichan Valley, but would prefer to see more estate-based operations. "Ideally," she says, "all vintners in the valley will grow all their own grapes or buy them from other Cowichan Valley growers, and then we'll have a true sense of what Vancouver Island wine is."

Vinoteca at Vigneti Zanatta

Chef Fatima da Silva sleeps with her menu. "No, really," she tells me, over a cup of tea in the restaurant. "I often think of something in the night, switch on the light and scribble it down."

Chef Fatima da Silva gets a helping hand in the kitchen of Vinoteca.

Fatima's Famous Flourless Chocolate Cake

FATIMA DA SILVA, VINOTECA AT VIGNETI ZANATTA

Serves 8. Fatima is too modest to name her cake "famous," but I took that liberty because it *is* famous!

8 oz	dark chocolate (Bernard Callebaut)	227 g
8 oz	butter	227 g
8 oz	white sugar	227 g
8 oz	eggs	about 4
5 oz	coarsely ground, toasted nuts (hazelnuts or almonds)	142 g
2 tsp	vanilla extract	10 ml

Melt chocolate and butter together in a double boiler at medium heat and set aside. In a mixing bowl with the beater set on high, beat the eggs and sugar together until double in volume. Turn mixer on low and slowly stir in the chocolate mixture and vanilla. Fold in the ground, toasted nuts. Bake in a lined spring-form pan at 275°F for approximately one hour. The cake should be slightly soft in the middle when you take it out. Let it cool in the pan. Serve the cake with ice cream or whipped cream.

On the day I visit, the restaurant is two weeks away from opening for the season, and that menu is still a work in progress. Fatima is expecting the delivery of a sample of smoked duck, which she is keen to offer to customers. She will use Cowichan Bay Farm's duck. "I'm planning to serve a smoked duck open-face sandwich with fig and caramelized onion chutney for lunch, and smoked duck and arugula risotto finished with goat cheese and toasted pine nuts for dinner."

In the meantime, there's lots of preparation afoot to ready the restaurant for its opening. Everything is being cleaned and polished around us as we chat about what brought Fatima to this magical place. She arrived in Quebec City from Portugal in 1997, worked as an au pair and studied French at Laval University. She often cooked for her host family, and they offered to send her to cooking school, but Fatima thought that sounded like "too much of a girlish thing."

Instead, she followed her sister to Victoria, where Fatima studied English at Camosun College and worked at the old French Connection restaurant in James Bay. "I began as a dishwasher, but was soon cooking the lunches." Then, she made a career change from the food industry to the home-care field. All the while, she and her friends would have wonderful dinner parties at which they'd try new wines. At one party, someone brought a bottle of Glenora Fantasia Brut from Vigneti Zanatta, and everyone loved it. Fatima loved it so much that she decided to visit the winery. She and her friends tasted the wines and ate at Vinoteca, the charming restaurant in the Zanatta family's 1903 farmhouse. They returned many times to eat at Vinoteca, and one night overheard someone say the chef was leaving. Fatima's friends encouraged her to apply, and she is now running the place.

She loves being able to work with some of the finest local ingredients the Cowichan Valley has to offer: produce from the restaurant's own gardens and from Engeler Farm, chicken and duck from Cowichan Bay Farm, venison from Broken Briar Fallow Deer Farm and lots of other wonderful things that simply arrive at the kitchen door from local growers. Fatima offers a select menu based on what's in season.

Says Fatima: "We've noticed in the past year that people are eating more and staying longer." The reasons are obvious. I can think of no better fare — fresh, and cooked with an ample dose of the chef's good humour — and cer-

tainly no better setting. On a beautiful day, nothing beats a table on the restaurant's large veranda with its expansive view of the vineyards, and a bottle of house-made wine and trademark Vinoteca antipasto platter between me and my husband.

Château Wolff

Harry von Wolff pulls up a chair in the late fall sunshine and welcomes me to his "little piece of paradise." He'd had the local women's Francophone association here the night before. They come every year, bringing cheeses and pâtés to enjoy with Harry's wines. The evening had ended, as always, "with a great deal of singing."

This afternoon, he's relaxed. The day's work is done. We range over many topics, from modern parenting to late marriages, but central to our conversation is the wine. The vineyard has been a long time coming for Harry.

Harry von Wolff in his tasting room.

Born in Latvia, he immigrated to Canada in 1953. He'd been fleeing west towards "a society of democratic freedom" since the outbreak of the Second World War, and working on his uncle's Peace River ranch was a good place to land. He soon sponsored his mother and grandmother, who began their new life in Vancouver.

Harry moved about a lot — 59 jobs in 11 years. From fixing fences, picking rocks and threshing in the Peace River district, he moved on to become an apprentice typographer. When lead poisoning sidelined him from that trade, he worked as a compass man on the railway on Vancouver Island. He always had his eye on hillsides, and began looking for one with southwestern exposure, but several more careers came up before he would finally have his vineyard.

Stints as a wine steward and then barman at some fancy golf clubs in Vancouver got him thinking about proper training. He attended hotel school in Switzerland, then took positions running hotels in Haiti, the Queen Charlotte Islands and Jasper. His next venture was a shoe-repair and western shop in Nanaimo, where he met his future wife, Helga.

After he married, Harry began growing grapes and experimenting with winemaking. Friends raved about his apple and blackberry wines, telling him he "could sell them to the public." When eight acres came up with what Harry considered the right combination of latitude, climate and soil, he began his current venture.

Describing his vineyard as "my 40-foot, mahogany yacht in Hong Kong harbour" really puts it into perspective. It's a hobby for Harry. People come to the winery for tours and tastings on the weekends. Some enjoy their picnics in the vineyard and everyone buys the wine, but Harry really just wanted to prove he could do it. "It's about living and having fun," he tells me.

I leave with a bottle of Harry's "new wine for the world," his Grand Rouge Demi-Sec, the Viva! pinot noir and a bottle of Grand Rouge dessert wine, which he advises me to enjoy with someone I love. It's late September, but Harry is not picking his grapes just yet. This year, he will wait until the last week of October so he can bottle late harvest wines.

The expansive vineyards at Château Wolff — Harry von Wolff's successful hobby.

Mid-Island

Denman Island
Hornby Island

19

4

Qualicum Beach

Nanoose Bay

Parksville

Lantzville

Gabriola Island

Nanaimo

Cedar

Cowichan Lake

Ladysmith

Chemainus

18

Cowichan Valley

Duncan

Cobble Hill

N

14

The Malahat

he Mid-Island is truly the tummy of Vancouver Island — a noticeably warmer and contented stretch from Shawnigan Lake in the south to Hornby Island in the north that is blessed with unique farms, vineyards and eateries. Of late, this area has attracted a number of significant gastronomes from across the pond, including chef (and now farmer) James Barber; host of CBC's *Pacific Palate* Don Genova; and chef, author and mushroom expert Bill Jones.

SHAWNIGAN LAKE

Steeples

I cannot believe it's taken me this long to discover Steeples, the stylish yet cozy restaurant in the heart of Shawnigan Lake Village. When I finally step through the door, I feel a sense of déjà vu — based on the many reports I'd read and the good things I'd heard, I must have been here before.

Steeples was born just four years ago, when locals Daphne and Michael Francis realized the village needed a proper restaurant. They're not restaurateurs, but they had the vision necessary to renovate the former Sylvan United Church. Despite a change in the nature of its business, the building has somehow retained a sense of spirituality. The dining room soars with light and colour. The altar is now a modern open kitchen and the pews have been replaced by tables and chairs at which patrons can dine on divine creations like roast duck breast with blackberries, grilled vegetable and goat cheese torta and prosciutto-wrapped filet mignon.

Partner and manager Darren Cole describes the renovation and decoration of the former church as "one big art project." Experienced in starting restaurants from

Chef and co-owner Darren Cole in the dining room at Steeples.

scratch (including Mill Bay's Fridays and Sidney's McGinty's), he clearly enjoyed the process. His cooking experience has come in handy, too — from stints at Victoria's Fogg 'n' Suds, Six Mile Pub and the short-lived but brilliant Classical Pig Café. Before Darren worked in the restaurant industry, he was a motivational speaker, and I ex-

The dining room at Steeples was once a church.

pect that training stands him in good stead in a business where not everyone knows what to order.

Like Brasserie L'École in Victoria, this is a very social room. I always enjoy dining by myself when a dining room is a-buzz with interesting conversation and table-hopping around me. I can feel part of the action without actually having to engage in conversation. All the more time, I gleefully think, for enjoying my food and drink.

What impresses me immediately is Darren's commitment to showcasing local producers. Chicken comes from Cowichan Bay Farm, greens and pears from Engeler Farm, free-range turkey from Kilrenny Farm, vegetables from Apple Bear Farm, mussels from Saltspring Island and oysters from Fanny Bay. The wine list reads like my wine route for this book: an entire section is devoted to the best of Alderlea, Blue Grouse, Cherry Point, Glenterra, Godfrey Brownell, Vigneti Zanatta and Venturi Schulze vineyards. And Darren has gone one important step further: he has noted on the menu which wines are produced entirely from grapes grown in the Cowichan Valley (versus those that have been made with grapes imported from the Okanagan). Darren tells me he loves selling the Vancouver Island wines, and I take great pleasure hearing him turn other diners on to a new merlot from Alderlea and the refreshing Millefiori from Venturi Schulze.

I start with a fabulously flavourful thin-crust pizza with duck confit, goat cheese and red onions and then try Darren's favourite, the grilled prawns and Digby scallops atop avocado with a summertime salsa of pineapple, mango and cilantro. The ultimate filet mignon served with a portobello mushroom topped with meltingly sinful Cambozola and mashed potatoes, whole carrots and asparagus spears is one of the restaurant's most popular entrées. I end with a chocolate pâté with orange custard from local pâtissier Gerald Billings' significant repertoire.

There's a lot to like at Steeples, including the heated deck where it was warm enough for dinner on Valentine's Day; the enclosed garden with its pretty pond and kiwi vines where diners can play croquet before or after their meal; and the sense of occasion that seems to permeate every table in the place. I particularly like the fact that servers actually serve the excellent house-made focaccia one beautiful, warm slice at a time, and don't need to be asked to bring more, and that they take the time to prepare Caesar salad and a host of dessert flambés tableside.

Steeples may no longer be a church, but food is sublime here and the service is appropriately divine.

THE MALAHAT

The Aerie Resort

The drive up to The Aerie feels like a turn off the autobahn, and suddenly one is in a romantic, almost fairy-tale setting. Yet this is more than a *haus* on the hill; an exclusive European destination resort awaits. A member of the prestigious Relais & Châteaux group and recently voted top resort in North America by the readers of *Condé Nast Traveler*, The Aerie is sitting pretty.

I check into my vast room, which, for one person, seems hugely extravagant until I begin to use and then appreciate every indulgence. In the sunken living room, I sink into the couch to take in my surroundings and find a bowl of strawberries and freshly baked organic oatmeal cookies within handy reach. The cookies are made with Millstream flour from the organic mill in Victoria's James Bay. I decide to put on the kettle and savour tea and biscuits while enjoying the view across Finlayson Arm. After tea, I need no encouragement to run a deep bath in the round Jacuzzi by the window. Keeping my eye on that view, I slip in to soak and dream until dinnertime.

The dining room is set dramatically high above Finlayson Arm, and the views are spectacular from every table. From across the room, Brad Prevedoreos, the internationally renowned guitarist and recording artist, strums softly. I'm dining this evening with 10 people, including Alicia Richardson of Williams Sonoma's *Taste* magazine; Paige Herman of *Gotham and Hamptons*; Emily Benson of the American Food Network; Markus Griesser, the resort's general manager; and Mara Jernigan, of Engeler Farm at that time. It's a convivial group of people who are knowledgeable about and appreciative of good food.

We begin with Spiced Red Wine Cured Chicken Breast and Foie Gras Spring Rolls with Sesame and Ginger Tossed New Zealand Spinach and a Thyme and Spring Morel Mushroom Infusion. Markus tells Mara that he wishes someone in the valley would produce foie gras, so great is the demand from their guests and,

"What inspires us is the curiosity of our guests. People are now very curious about what they are eating, what goes into their food."

—Markus Griesser,
The Aerie

naturally, they would prefer to buy local. The meal continues through many inspired courses, finishing with Torrefazione coffee, a 10-year-old tawny port and one of the most inventive desserts I've encountered: "Trio" includes Tangy Grapefruit Jelly and Dark Chocolate Tart with Minted Fromage Blanc Sorbet; Long Pepper and Coconut Sorbet with Fresh Strawberry on a Spiced Wild Strawberry Syrup; and Chicory Root and Dried Candied Fruit Nougat Glacé with Licorice Sauce. Had I not known the chef, I would have guessed its maker to be Titania, the Fairy Queen.

As a food writer, I've learned that the best stories are found right in the kitchens or on the farms — in other words, where the action is. When Executive Chef de Cuisine Christophe Letard invited me to don an apron during dinner preparation one evening, wings couldn't have carried me there faster. I quickly discovered that backstage at The Aerie is a well-choreographed, happy set. And all the players are unbelievably (to me, anyway) young, talented and dedicated.

Letard is a wiry, handsome, 30-something Frenchman who operates in perpetual motion for the three hours I'm at his side. I join him just as he begins to prepare the Pommes Anna for tonight's tasting menu. Never have I seen a chef so cleanly and exactly peel a potato, slice it into mere breaths and then create perfect rosettes from those slices. The rosettes are lightly brushed with olive oil, and sprinkled with salt, then popped into the oven to come out golden and crisp. I ask about his knife. "Ah, this. Everyone uses it. It's just a knife I'm comfortable with,

Author Elizabeth Levinson is recruited to make potato rosettes in The Aerie's kitchen.

that I started with in France." No lock and key here, no one assigned to carry the chef's knives. Later, Letard takes a moment to sharpen his knife before filleting some Arctic char. He uses his father's stone ("Actually, my father usually sharpens it, but I haven't been back for three years").

Back to the rosettes. Three will be stacked with Summer Truffle Tartufo and Grain Mustard Beurre Blanc to form a base for the Grilled Ling Cod Pavé. Letard turns the rosette-making over to me, and deftly prepares the truffle paste. In the middle of his work, he stops briefly to give me a taste, and a comment about three oils: huile de truffe ("fantastic"); huile d'olive Provence ("for cooking"); and certified organic golden olive oil from Greece ("for taste!"). Finally, I taste the truffle tartufo, which is deep with truffle and garlic. Letard notes that the garlic will mellow with cooking, but says the paste "is me; that's my flavour."

While some chefs are shying away from the labour of tasting menus, Letard is planning to stay the many intricate courses. He loves "the little dishes — they're beautiful, like tapas," and he has a clientele that appreciates the small-plate experience.

Organics are very big in this kitchen. Letard reckons he is cooking with 80% organic produce (including meat, poultry and dairy) in the summer months. He is delighted to be cooking a menu that "happens with the seasons," and has come to depend on his local and on-site suppliers — from a monk who brings fiddleheads, sorrel and stinging nettles to his kitchen door, to David Groves who produces the meltingly tender fallow deer meat, to Wendell Curry who runs the resort's vegetable and herb gardens. Asparagus are feverishly anticipated every year from The Asparagus Farm, as are morels, chanterelles, figs and artichokes. The restaurant uses all locally raised meat except beef, which comes from the Nicola Valley.

Initially, the location of The Aerie meant they didn't have the luxury of farmgate shopping; it was a challenge to seek out quality ingredients. But many producers come to the door now, and Letard says his challenge is to space out the deliveries, so he is not overwhelmed with, say, mushrooms. He preserves as much as possible of the summer fruits, including some 20 types of heirloom tomatoes.

I ask Letard what the differences are between his work in Europe and in Canada. He says the training he received in France was more extensive and the equipment was more sophisticated, but he speaks highly of the cooking experiences he's had in this country (The Inn at Manitou and Langdon Hall, both in Ontario).

Letard was raised on his family's farm in Normandy. They had a bit of everything and were largely self-sufficient. There were cows, vegetables. His father made his own calvados. Letard took an early interest in "the science and the art of cooking," helping his mother prepare meals for his father and six older brothers. He went on to Hotel Savoie Leman, France's oldest cooking school, where he trained for four years. He says of that time: "I was small, and they didn't think I would last, but I came out with a degree of server."

He then focussed on pastry, working at establishments in Les Deux Alpes. When he landed the job of pastry chef at La Réserve in Albi, he was starting to think about becoming a chef. He made a deal that he would teach pastry to the chef, and the chef would teach him to cook. After that, he went back to Normandy to become chef de partie-saucier at La Ferme Saint Simeon, where he "worked so hard under an old-school chef" that he really respected. "I had 13 sauces to finish every night, but that was a great learning experience." While he was at Saint Simeon, the restaurant was awarded its first Michelin star.

Feeling he should travel and have some new experiences, Letard came to Canada, spending a couple of seasons at The Inn at Manitou in McKellar, Ontario, under the tutelage of Jean Pierre Chalet, the chef he holds up as his mentor. He credits Chalet for teaching him to cook using styles from many countries but incorporating local flavours.

After that, he worked at the Normandie Hotel in Manchester, which was awarded England's first Michelin star (and where he served the Queen Mother for a week). Then, a stint cooking on a luxury cruising barge in Burgundy and the Upper Loire, where he met his wife. The two came to Canada, where Letard was the working chef at The Domain of Killien in the Haliburton area. Someone told him he should see British Columbia, so he headed west.

Letard and I are standing in the dining room, inhaling that big, blue view. He tells me when he came to The Aerie with his wife, he stood in this very place and thought to himself: "One day, I would love to work here." He didn't introduce himself at that time, but sent in a résumé after returning to Ontario.

Today, he is executive chef. His sous-chef is Michael Minshull, formerly of Victoria's Empress Room. They are a formidable pair, with the talent and drive to keep The Aerie's restaurant on the world's gourmet trail for a long time. At the same time, Letard is charmingly self-effacing: "I'm not a genius. Sometimes it goes well, sometimes not. It takes a lifetime to put everything together to make sense."

A Day in the Life of an Executive Chef

At noon, Letard is in the kitchen, seeing that breakfast went well and noting any concerns. From there, he checks the evening's reservations, the fridges and the day's supplies. He confers with head gardener Wendell Curry to see what's available from the resort's herb and vegetable plantings. He orders tomorrow's supplies, returns calls, sets the tasting menu and determines what needs to be prepped for the evening meal.

In the early afternoon, he has meetings with hotel management (and pesky food writers!) and helps to prep and instruct prep for the evening menu.

At 4:30 P.M., he leads a menu discussion for guests dining that evening, often passing around samples of fresh ingredients. He is joined by Markus Griesser, who presents the evening's recommended wine pairings. Says Letard: "You learn a lot about the people you are cooking for, so you can change a dish to suit what you think they would like."

By 6:00 P.M., Letard is on the line and I am in gastronomic heaven, sitting in the luxuriously appointed dining room and enjoying his creations all the more now that I have seen up close his impressive devotion to the food he prepares.

Salon du Thé

Chef Letard took a rare holiday in his native Normandy recently and returned with the idea of offering "afternoon tea with a French twist at The Aerie Resort." With fewer sweets and more savouries on offer than the traditional *thé à l'anglaise*, and an impressive offering of teas from T, the luxury line based in Vancouver, these are afternoon teas worth pulling over for.

Villa Cielo

Owner Maria Schuster welcomes a small group of foodmeisters and journalists to view her "summer palace in the heavens" one afternoon in late spring. And how does one reach heaven, you might ask? By golf cart, of course, expertly manoeuvered on my visit by James Kendal, who returned to The Aerie Resort as its general manager after a stint at Jasper Park Lodge. We climb to "the highest point on southern Vancouver Island," and stop at a

villa that could be in Monaco or Cannes. Its graciousness looms large and its views are, as at The Aerie, indescribably expansive and beautiful.

There is a sense of great privacy, of discretion, of giving guests their well-deserved luxury. The five rooms are opulent yet comfortable. There is a little wedding gazebo, should the occasion arise. Best of all, there is a small, first-class demonstration kitchen, where Chef Letard and Sous-Chef Minshull offer private cooking classes followed by lunch in the sea-facing dining room.

MAPLE BAY

Grapevine on the Bay

Several years ago, chef and food consultant Bill Jones recommended a tiny restaurant in Genoa Bay to me. When I was finally able to check it out, it had moved to the next bay over! Grapevine on the Bay had a huge reputation for seven years in Genoa Bay, then reopened in Maple Bay in December 2003.

One cold afternoon that month, my husband and I had a long wait for the Crofton ferry to Saltspring Island and decided to take a drive, which happily brought us to the Grapevine. Daniel and Ruth van den Wildenberg were in the throes of opening their restaurant in a space no bigger than a breadbox, but there were enticing pastries and organic coffee on offer and a takeaway dinner menu from which many locals were popping in to order.

Fast forward to the summer of 2004, when my parents and I were heading to Qualicum Beach for a little break and decided to see what was cooking at the Grapevine. In that incarnation, the restaurant had expanded into a back room with breathtaking sea views and we had a marguerita-pizza-and-salad lunch that my very dear but very particular mother is still raving about.

"Now," says Daniel, when I drop in to see the fully renovated space in 2005, "we have what we want: a nice sunny feel, a restaurant where everyone can be comfortable, whether you've jumped off your boat in shorts or feel like dressing for supper." The transformation is impressive. Walls have been knocked down and larger windows installed to capture "those picture-postcard orange moonrises in summer." There's a large, open kitchen positioned so that both diners and cooks can enjoy the view, unique driftwood furnishings and a revival of the full, seafood-focussed menu of Genoa Bay days.

Local customer Liv Finch, who has dined every month at the Grapevine (on both bays) drops in for coffee and tells me: "Nobody cooks seafood like this guy." Although Daniel describes himself as "old school," having been formally trained under the European hotel and restaurant management style in Bruges, Belgium, he also admits to "breathing some fresh air into the basics." Ahi tuna, salmon, halibut and Arctic char appear on the menu — as do oysters, but only those from Union Bay, which he claims "have the lightest beards. The farther you go up the island, the cleaner the water, the cleaner the beards, so the cleaner the oysters," he tells me.

Ruth is a chocolatier, also trained in Bruges. When they came to Canada, Daniel worked front of house in Vancouver at the William Tell and Hy's at the Mansion. In those days, there was more tableside cooking involved, "but then nouvelle cuisine came in and the cooking and presentation went back inside the kitchen." Ruth reminisces about the days when "dessert and specialty coffees were prepared at the table," and says the couple hopes to introduce some of that style at the Grapevine.

Big supporters of the local food producers, Daniel and Ruth buy from farmer David Weibe, Engeler Farm, Providence Farm and Hilary's Cheese Company, and also go slightly farther afield to Saltspring for David Wood's cheese and Parksville for Little Qualicum Cheese. A customer grows their herbs, and they offer several wine selections from nearby Alderlea and Blue Grouse vineyards. Ropey Fish on Saltspring custom cold-smokes halibut and tuna for the Grapevine, which is presented in a Nordic plate along with smoked salmon, herbed cream cheese, garden greens and horseradish dressing and appropriately served with akvavit.

DUNCAN

The Community Farm Store and Corfield's Coffee Shop

For those who believe that there are no coincidences in life, consider the gray day in February when I decided for no particular reason to pull off the highway at Duncan and see what might be new in town. Surely the Duncan Garage was put there for me to find.

The bright yellow building across from the railway station caught my eye and the sign on its side ground me to a halt: The Community Farm Store — a name from the past, a whole-foods store that I'd written about in *Getting Fresh in and Around Victoria* (TouchWood Editions, 2001) when it was located in Glenora, just outside of Duncan. I instantly remembered its notable baker, Susan Minette, and the ginger scone recipe she had so kindly parted with, and I went in to investigate.

The old Duncan Garage, now beautifully restored, houses Ulla's bookstore; an outlet of The Udder Guy (the original ice cream shop is in nearby

Cowichan Bay) that's been designed to look like a 1950s-style diner; Long John's musical venue, which hosts all kinds of performers; and The Community Farm Store and its offshoot, Corfield's Coffee Shop. What a find! Nourishment for stomach and soul all under one roof!

The Community Farm Store is just as it was, only larger and with a more extensive stock of organic fresh and dry goods. This time, there were things I'd never tried before, like goat's-milk butter, refried bean mix and black japonica rice. A great cheese selection includes Mountain Meadow sheep feta, several Quebec cheeses and Courtenay's Natural Pastures cheeses. Cowichan Bay Farm's chicken pieces and sausages, candied chum salmon from Cortes Island and organic French chocolate truffles were only some of the new offerings. Since I was heading north for the weekend, I couldn't shop for groceries, but I had no difficulty buying "road food" from the selection at Corfield's Coffee Shop next door.

With a commitment to organics and many vegan selections, the deli offers irresistible snacks like a Brie, tomato and sweet red onion sandwich; a yummy hot strata of eggs, cheese and vegetables served with what appears to be just-picked salad; and millet, cheese and herb croquettes with a creamy curry dipping sauce. There are heavenly treats (again, many are vegan or made with alternate grains like spelt or rice and sweetened with rice syrups or orange juice) such as Double Dutch chocolate cookies, spelt carrot cake, caramel nut squares and a pineapple cheesecake topped with fresh and candied pineapple slices that I tried very hard to share but just had to polish off myself.

I look forward to returning for breakfast when the offerings include cheesy scrambled eggs with veggies and organic toast; a fried egg sandwich with onion, cheese, mustard and mayo; and rice or oatmeal porridge with raisins, cinnamon and cow's or soy milk. The mention of that porridge alone takes me back nostalgically to a shack on Hermosa Beach, California, in the 1970s — a restaurant whose porridge I still crave. After eating her pineapple cheesecake, I'm convinced Susan's porridge will at last provide Hermosa Beach's match.

COWICHAN VALLEY

The Asparagus Farm

Charles Ford and his dog, Asta, are just returning from picking up mail at the end of the road as I pull in to The Asparagus Farm. It's still a little early in the year, but my visit is partly designed to add to my own anticipation of the short, six-week asparagus season. Standing at the farmgate, I visualize myself right at the front of the long lineups that occur here every day from about mid-April through May. People travel from as far as Vancouver to buy the Fords' asparagus, and Charles says it's not unusual to have 50 cars parked at the gate before he opens it at ten o'clock in the morning. One man, crossing the Atlantic on the *Queen Elizabeth II*, complained to his tablemate that he couldn't find white asparagus in North America. The tablemate sent him to Charles.

What is all the fuss about? To me, it's two things: you can't get any asparagus any fresher (these are picked daily in season and only hours before the gate opens), and you can buy white asparagus here. Freshness and the way the asparagus is handled mean everything to the connoisseur: the tenderest shoot can become woody from being stored too long or stored in the wrong conditions. That "woodyness" can actually climb up the stalk after it has been picked, and if the asparagus is not chilled immediately after picking, its sugars turn to starch.

The white asparagus is a whole other story. Long prized by Europeans, white asparagus or spargel arrives with great fanfare every year. It is traditionally served with a white sauce and boiled potatoes. Charles has answered the prayers of many here who grew up in Europe with a taste for white asparagus.

We take a walk across the 10-acre property. Asta bounds ahead and has a wonderful time chasing the California quail out of the asparagus patch (Charles encourages the quail, as they eat many of his weeds). I ask how he got into this much-sought-after product in the first place.

Charles has always farmed, but mostly cranberries in Pitt Meadows on the mainland. He says he was lucky to be growing cranberries "during the

White Asparagus with Balsamic Vinegar Mayonnaise
Carole and Charles Ford, The Asparagus Farm

During asparagus season, I'm always looking for new ways to enjoy the king of the lily family. This presentation is always well received.

White asparagus requires different preparation and cooking methods than green asparagus. While it is not necessary to peel green asparagus and cooking is minimal (three to five minutes) so as to produce a bright green, tender-crisp product, this is not the case with white asparagus. Raw, (it has a sweet nutty taste, and crunchy texture) white asparagus may be eaten as is. If cooked, white asparagus MUST be peeled first, so that no skin remains, and steamed until completely tender (20 minutes or more).

To peel, begin lightly at the tip and peel deeper as you get toward the butt end. If peeling is done too timidly or cooking time is inadequate, the asparagus will be stringy. While there are special white asparagus peelers available in Europe, a potato peeler works fine. As with green asparagus, the more fibrous portion on the butt end should also be removed. Snap at its natural breaking point. Do not despair — the peeling goes quickly!

Make a mayonnaise substituting good quality, traditional balsamic vinegar for the regular vinegar and lemon juice. Peel and cook white asparagus as detailed above, then chill. Serve mayonnaise with the chilled white asparagus tips. The balsamic mayonnaise will lose its flavour within a day so do not make it too far in advance.

boom time when Ocean Spray was buying tons of fruit." When his wife, Carole, accepted a teaching position at the University of Victoria in 1989, the couple decided to look for land on Vancouver Island. The Cobble Hill farm fit the bill, and Charles planned to grow asparagus and apples. He planted the apples first, but they got blight, and he focussed on the asparagus.

Charles is also experimenting with growing the coveted black truffle, as well as black elderberries, which are known for their health properties. As he collaborates with a botanist on the truffle project, Vancouver Island chefs are holding their collective breath.

Black Coffee and Other Delights

Okay, it's true. Coffee is what fuels the urban hunter-gatherer, which is probably why the people who know me best know to find me in the

Black Coffee beckons just before Duncan at Whippletree Junction. Don't forget to order a cinnamon bun!

island's cafés. One favourite re-fuelling stop is Black Coffee and Other Delights at Whippletree Junction, south of Duncan. Even when I'm pressed for time, I still stop for a takeout giant cinnamon bun and an Americano — such is my addiction.

Located in Cobble Hill's former general store/post office building, which was moved to the Whippletree Junction site along with buildings from Duncan's old Chinatown, Black Coffee has been in business since March 2001. It's run by baker Andrew Simonson, coffee maven Morris Cleveland and Morris' wife, Corrine Wilson, a local pharmacist who is involved "behind the scenes."

Andrew and Morris are brothers who grew up in Calgary. As teenagers they worked for Heartland, a busy general store/bakery/café in Kensington, a well-established coffee district there. Corrine tells me it was at Heartland that Andrew began to hone his baking skills "under the watchful eye of Alice Kichik," the cook who, it seems, really kept him in line ("No soup served before 11:30 A.M. even if it is ready! No cutting out the centre cinnamon bun before the side ones!"). Andrew bakes all those amazing "other delights" — hearty food made from scratch like the soup, chili, muffins, date squares, big cookies and even bigger (and quite sinful) cinnamon buns. Morris is the coffee guy, using the great Caffé Fantastico beans from Ryan and Kristy Taylor in Victoria.

In summer, the place hums with tourists who love shopping at Whippletree Junction's antique and curio shops. Part of the attraction of

Black Coffee for me is that you can also stop there in the middle of winter, early in the morning when most Whippletree shops are closed, and have a coffee with the locals and the truckers. It has great warmth and charm.

Corrine says they support local producers for dairy, berries and produce in season, particularly Engeler Farm, which is just down the road. They have copies of the cookbook Andrew contributed to during his time at Heartland: *Heartland Country Store Cookbook* (Centax Books, 1995) by Alice Kichik and the restaurant's owner, Nonie Sundstrom. And let me know if you've ever tasted a better cinnamon bun! Black Coffee to Go, the kiosk that has recently opened on the south side of the highway, means I can get a buzz coming and going.

Broken Briar Fallow Deer Farm

The very first fawn David Groves raised was called Briar, and she became a family pet. Unfortunately, she lost her life to a careless hunter, but her name lives on.

The farm, originally called Barkley Farm, was a whistle stop on the Canadian Pacific Railway line. David's father, Tom, bought the farm from

David Groves offers an afternoon snack to one of his fallow deer at Broken Briar Fallow Deer Farm.

Kitty Barkley. Tom's father, whom David describes as "a genuine remittance man," also had a farm in the area. "He did anything for sport, including logging and fox hunting." He used to say to Tom: "No Englishman ever got up at 4:00 A.M. to milk cows."

Tom wasn't afraid of milking cows, but he ended up taking a degree in forestry engineering at the University of British Columbia, then built bridges all over the country.

Later, David took a Ph.D. at Purdue and became an animal nutritionist. He began to study protein synthesis and mammary tissue culture, and taught animal physiology and biochemistry at both the University of Alberta and the University of Victoria. He'd always been interested in farming and enjoyed applied research.

David believes in raising animals in conditions that are as natural as possible. The number of fallow deer he raises "are in direct proportion to the capability of the land to produce feed." While their ancestors came from the Middle East, these hundred or so fallow deer are offspring of David's original herd, which were brought from Sidney, James and Saltspring islands. His neighbour had trapped some of the deer on those islands and sold them to both David and the Douglas Ranch near Merritt.

I tasted David's venison at The Aerie, and liked venison for the very first time. The meat is very tender and mild tasting, without that strong gamey flavour. Other restaurants have standing orders, including Saltspring Island's Hastings House, the Inglenook in North Cowichan and the Mahle House in Cedar. The First Nations buy hides from him, and "there are always roasts in the freezer for people who just drop by."

With the restaurants demanding the saddles for ribs, Dave says he and his wife eat a lot of bone-out shoulder. He barbeques it, always serves it medium rare, and only sometimes adds a glaze such as maple syrup and garlic. It's delicious meat on its own, so he doesn't advise marinating or drowning it in sauce.

David and I take a walk out to see the deer. He picks a bunch of burdock, and only has to wave it once before they come leaping over for their "candy."

Cowichan Bay Farm

Mara Jernigan loves the fact that she can grocery-shop by "just going from farmgate to farmgate" in the Cowichan Valley. This doesn't mean only fruit and veggies, but also local wines and cider, and top-quality pastured chicken, chicken sausage and duck at Lyle and Fiona Young's Cowichan Bay Farm.

When we arrive at the farm, we are treated to the sight of a movie being shot. The juxtaposition of actors in Second World War attire and crew running around against the original farm buildings on a pastoral 43-acre backdrop is quite fun. We stop to chat and discover that this is a locally based production company of young people who are shooting their first pilot, which they hope to sell to Hollywood.

The farm buildings are fascinating. There is the 1920s butcher shop, erected by Lyle's grandfather, Nigel Kingscote, to process his own pork. It has a wooden walk-in fridge, sloped tables for ease of

One of the rustic farm buildings at Cowichan Bay Farm.

cleaning after he rolled the pork into sausages, and earthenware urns for immersing special cuts of meat in brine. Behind is the wooden smokehouse where the hams and bacon, as well as Cowichan Bay salmon, were cured. The butcher shop is still in operation, and this is where local customers come to pick up the farm's pastured poultry, lamb and beef.

There's the newlywed cottage, where Lyle's grandparents lived after their marriage in 1935. Across the way is Nigel's workshop, where Lyle spent many hours straightening and sorting bent nails for his grandfather. He says he "remembers fondly the subtle lessons of an old man passed on to a young boy, simply by being fortunate enough to be there." Other original buildings include the Chinese labourers' shack, the granary, the horse barn, the dairy and the cow barn. The creamery boasts Lyle's grandmother's interesting collection of milk bottles.

Every Father's Day, the Youngs host a wonderful art show, with over 30 local artists represented. It's always thrilling to walk through the old farm buildings, their walls laden with the impressive talent of painters like Grant Leier, Adam Noonan and Wendy Bradshaw, and to sample delicacies such as gelato from Victoria's Italian Bakery and sausage dogs containing Cowichan Bay Farm's own chicken sausage.

Duck Breasts with Blackberry-Chocolate Sauce

DON GENOVA, HOST OF CBC'S *PACIFIC PALATE* AND COWICHAN VALLEY IMMIGRANT

Serves 4. Don Genova figures in many of our lives through his culinary radio broadcasts and magazine articles. His enthusiasm for the local food and wine scene is reflected in the recipes he creates in his own kitchen — always fresh, always seasonal and always bold, as in this rich and delicious presentation for duck breasts.

4	boneless Cowichan Bay Farm duck breasts	4
	salt and freshly ground black pepper	
2 c	fresh or frozen blackberries	454 g
1/8 c	water	30 ml
1/4 c	sugar	57 g
2 tbsp	balsamic vinegar	30 ml
1/2 tsp	cinnamon	2.5 ml
2 tbsp	cold butter, cut into cubes	30 ml
1 oz	orange liqueur such as Cointreau or Triple Sec (optional)	30 ml
1 tbsp	semi-sweet dark chocolate, roughly chopped	15 ml

For the sauce:

Put the blackberries, sugar and water in a heavy-bottomed pot over medium heat. Bring to a boil, stirring occasionally, and simmer until the berries have completely broken down. Remove from the heat and let cool for a few minutes. Strain the berry mixture into a bowl to remove all the seeds, then return the juice to the pot. Add the balsamic vinegar, the cinnamon and the orange liqueur and simmer over medium heat until reduced by half. Remove from heat, and whisk in the chocolate a little at a time. Then whisk in the butter, a half-tablespoon at a time, until fully incorporated. Add salt and pepper to taste. Keep warm while you prepare the duck breasts.

Preheat oven to 450°F. Heat until very hot a cast-iron or oven-safe heavy-bottomed frypan large enough to hold the breasts in one layer. With a sharp knife, score the skin of each duck breast, without cutting through to the flesh, in a diamond-shaped pattern. Season the breasts all over with salt and pepper and lay them skin side down in the frypan. When the skin has become crisp and golden and the fat has rendered out of it, remove the duck to a plate and carefully drain most of the fat from the pan. Put the duck breasts back in, skin side up, and roast in the oven for about 5 to 7 minutes for medium-rare. Remove from the pan, cover loosely with foil and let rest for a few minutes. To serve, place each breast on a plate and pour a little pool of sauce around it.

NOTE: Don says: "This dish goes well with some sautéed pea tips and some steamed couscous."

We trek out to the fields to see the pastured-poultry operation and run into Jerry, one of the farm hands. He used to work for Lyle's grandfather and still enjoys his work on the farm. He shows us the method the Youngs use to raise their birds. First developed by Joel Salatin, a Virginia farmer, it's a model that Lyle chose to use for its humane practices. The chickens are housed in large moveable pens that are set out in the pasture. Jerry demonstrates how the pens are moved every day, thereby giving the birds an always-fresh source of food. They stay together and behave in a natural way, in contrast to chickens caged indoors. Whereas many chicken farmers follow the modern agricultural model of getting the animals to market as fast as possible, the Youngs are focussed on taking the animals to their own food in a natural environment. Birds that are allowed to develop naturally turn out happier, healthier and tastier.

The Youngs' chickens and ducks are featured on some of the area's top restaurant tables including Victoria's Herald Street Caffé, Cafe Brio and Brasserie L'École and Tofino's Long Beach Lodge. They can be bought from the island's better butchers, including Victoria's Fourways Meat Market and Slater's First Class Meats. Mara Jernigan calls Cowichan Bay Farm "simply the best for roast chicken, clean healthy liver, delicious handmade chicken sausages with no mystery meat or additives and pasture-raised duck, which many chefs consider the best they have ever had."

When the Youngs first took over the farm, they raised veal calves in addition to the poultry, but they felt they were looking for something else. On a trip to England some years back, they began to take an interest in rare breeds of livestock, and when they returned to the farm, decided to invest in a few San Clemente goats, Navaho Churro sheep and Dexter cattle. The goats were brought by explorers from Spain to the coast of California, and left there as a food supply for whenever they returned to that part of the world. In Spain, the goats became extinct, but they lived for another 200 years on San Clemente Island until the American army used the island for bombing practice. Most of the stock was moved, and the Youngs ended up getting theirs from Boston. Today, there are probably only a hundred San Clemente goats in the world.

Deerholme Farm and Cottage

Bill Jones has been busy since we last crossed paths in the forest. He and his wife, Lynn, have renovated their five-acre property in the rolling hills

Mustard Greens and Tomatoes with Warm Bacon Dressing

BILL JONES, DEERHOLME FARM AND COTTAGE

Serves 4. Bill Jones says: "The best food in the world is produced at the shortest distance to the plate." If you grow your own mustard greens, onions, tomatoes and parsley and forage for the mushrooms, you'll have better taste and nutrition and probably more satisfaction in making his lovely, Moorish salad.

4 slices	smoked bacon, minced	4 slices
1	medium onion, peeled and diced	1
½ c	diced mushrooms	120 ml
2 tbsp	balsamic vinegar	30 ml
2 tbsp	olive oil	30 ml
1 lb	mustard greens or spinach	455 g
2	medium tomatoes, seeded and chopped	2
1 tbsp	chopped Italian parsley	15 ml
1 tbsp	grated Parmigiano-Reggiano cheese	15 ml

Sauté the bacon in a large, non-stick pan over medium high heat. Add the onion and mushrooms, and cook until soft and just beginning to brown. Remove the excess fat with a spoon or soak it up with a paper towel, and stir in the vinegar and oil. Place the mustard greens and tomatoes in a salad bowl, top with the warm bacon dressing and toss well to coat. Garnish with the Parmesan cheese and parsley and serve immediately.

*Reprinted with permission from *Chef's Salad*, Whitecap Books, 2003.

south of Duncan to accommodate her vast production gardens and his workshop and demonstration-cooking facility. It's taken two years to create, because they've done most of the work themselves and "want it to look like it has been here forever."

I visit in the middle of a rainstorm when Bill is excited about the Douglas-fir cabinets he's just been sanding and the stencilled art nouveau-style motifs of fungi on the walls. His goal of making Deerholme Cottage "feel comfy and natural" has been realized from the highly polished concrete counters in the kitchen to the Charles Rennie McIntosh-inspired furnishings throughout. Bill says his concept of offering workshops on mushrooms and other local seasonal foods as well as professional chef-training classes was influenced by Michael Stadtlander, whose eclectic farm and restaurant outside Toronto, Eigensinn Farm, regularly garners international attention.

The Jones' goal is to provide "a beautiful space to think about agriculture and food — where it comes from and what the difference is in growing organic." Lynn offers tours of her gardens and Bill has a regular schedule of workshops that can be followed by barbeques in summer and cosy meals in the kitchen in winter.

The farm is situated above Glenora Creek on the Trans Canada Trail, which "goes from here all the way to Newfoundland." Bill and Lynn are actively involved in the stewardship of the creek through the Community Land Trust.

Fairburn Farm

Who said you can't roller skate through a water buffalo herd? It was Darryl Archer, whose dry humour came in handy through a very difficult time at Fairburn Farm. A few years ago, Darryl and his wife, Anthea, imported 18 Bulgarian Murrah River water buffalo from Denmark. Their dream was, and still is, to launch a buffalo dairy that would sustain their farm and "create local jobs and new opportunities from the many spinoffs" of that dairy.

An unfortunate, and largely political, intervention by the Canadian government has put them back two or three years. Because their animals were imported just prior to the first outbreak of Bovine Spongiform Encephalopathy (BSE) in Denmark, the Canadian Food Inspection Agency ordered them destroyed. The pertinent facts were largely ignored: worldwide, there have been no cases of mad cow disease in water buffalo, and the Archers' animals had been quarantined and monitored on a Danish farm prior to export and had never eaten feed with any animal by-products.

Anthea and Darryl, with the local farming and restaurant communities, fought a long, hard battle to keep their water buffalo. Support poured in from all over the world and there were major fundraising events to help defray the legal costs. On July 28, 2002, they lost their fight and the original 18 animals were destroyed. Subsequent tests of the buffalo showed they were not contaminated with BSE.

The light is beginning to glimmer from the end of that long tunnel. The Archers' Canadian-born buffalo have been released from quarantine, and they are now continuing with their plans. When I visited the herd with Darryl, I could see how hard it must have been for them to have parted with the other buffalo. The animals are incredibly loving and each is named. Of the herd, I met Ferdinand, Kimberly, Teresa, Ashley, Karina and Murray. The Archers have now built their milking parlour and look forward to producing milk, ice cream and the much-anticipated bocconcini. Their dairy, and the water buffalo-milk cheese, will be unique in Canada.

My first visit to Fairburn Farm was on a wild, windy December night. My husband and I, with many other members of Vancouver Island's Slow Food convivium, had gathered in the 1894 farmhouse to celebrate the season. The storm was so severe that we drove from Victoria with most of the highway traffic lights out, and arrived to find the 130-acre farm in complete darkness.

We inched our way into the house, where we were greeted with much merriment. The kitchen had been lit with candles. Mara Jernigan and Peter Zambri were joyfully preparing a feast, seemingly oblivious to the lack of electricity and water. Within an hour, Darryl had managed to start the generator and the crowd began greeting each other in earnest. We spent that night in one of Anthea's cosy bed-and-breakfast rooms, and woke to see what Sooke Harbour House's Sinclair Philip describes as "one of the most beautiful farms in the world" through our window.

Fairburn Farm was originally settled in the 1880s by John and Mary Jackson. Mary, who hailed from Scotland, named the farm Fairburn, which means "beautiful stream." Most of the 1,200-acre farm was sold to MacMillan Bloedel in the late 1940s by Mary's son, Edwin. In 1955, Jack and Mollie Archer, Darryl's parents, bought the remaining 130 acres.

Mollie founded the Vancouver Island Organic Vegetable Co-operative in 1955, and the family learned to farm the hard way. Fairburn Farm went through many incarnations (in the 1960s, Mollie ran a children's summer camp there), but has stayed in the family. Today, Darryl and Anthea, with help from their children, are beginning to realize their dreams of self-sufficiency at the farm.

Chicken Liver Pâté with Blackberry Port and Saskatoon Berries

MARA JERNIGAN, FAIRBURN FARM, COWICHAN VALLEY

 Mara says: "Generous quantities of butter and pristine livers from healthy animals are the key to delicious liver pâté. This recipe has converted several friends who did not eat liver at all!"

2 lbs	chicken livers*	907 g
1 lb	unsalted butter, cold and cubed	454 g
6	medium-sized shallots, finely diced	6
1	clove garlic	1
2	bay leaves	2
2 ounces	blackberry port*	59 ml
	salt and black pepper, to taste	
2 tbsp	fresh lemon juice or verjus	30 ml
1/4 c	coarsely chopped Italian parsley	57 g
1/4 c	saskatoon berries (fresh or frozen)*	57 g
2 tbsp	honey	30 ml

*Mara uses Cowichan Bay Farm's chicken livers, Cherry Point Vineyards' Blackberry Port and saskatoon berries from the Saskatoon Berry Farm

Using a paring knife, clean the livers by removing veins, blood spots or connective tissue. Chop the shallots and mince the garlic. On high heat, sauté the shallots and garlic in an ounce of the butter. When the shallots become translucent but before they brown, add the livers and the bay leaves. Continuing on high heat, sauté the livers and season with salt and pepper. It is important not to overcook the livers. They should be moist on the inside and seared on the outside — tender and pink but not bloody. When the livers reach this stage, deglaze the pan with the blackberry port, remove from heat, discard the bay leaves and transfer to a bowl to cool. While the livers are cooling, place the saskatoon berries in a small saucepan on the stove with the honey and 2 tbsp (30 ml) water. Cook at high heat until the berries barely burst (just a couple of minutes). Once the livers have cooled to room temperature, place them in the work bowl of a food processor and purée until smooth. Add the cold cubed butter through the processor chute and continue to process. When the mixture is smooth and all the cubes of butter are well incorporated, turn the machine off and taste the mixture for salt, pepper and acidity, which can be adjusted with the lemon juice or verjus. Transfer once again to a bowl and fold in the cooked, cooled saskatoon berries with a spatula. Pour the mixture into loaf pans lined with plastic wrap. Generously coat the top with the chopped parsley. Cool in the fridge at least 6 hours. Unmold the loaf pans and transfer to a decorative plate surrounded by crackers or thinly sliced whole-grain bread.

Mara Jernigan at Fairburn Farm, Culinary Retreat and Guesthouse

"This year will see more change at Fairburn Farm than there has been in the last hundred years," says Mara Jernigan, who is wielding a paintbrush and flashing her characteristic impish smile. It is now February, and by April she "will have given this *grande dame* a facelift" and will begin receiving farmstay guests. The *dame* in question is the 111-year-old family home at Fairburn to which Mara has moved her agritourism operation (previously, she and Alfons Obererlacher owned and operated a similar agritourism operation, Cobble Hill's Engeler Farm). Fairburn's owners, Darryl

and Anthea Archer, have already relocated into a new home on the property and will be focussing their energies on the *mozzarella di buffala* production.

Mara, a chef who parlays her considerable knowledge and talent into educating people about eating well, practises what she preaches. She has always been proud to "do everything the Slow Food way — I can say where everything on my table comes from." As Slow Food's Canadian coordinator of the Ark of Taste and coordinator of southern Vancouver Island's Feast of Fields, she is well known for her strong advocacy of our local food-security system and sustainable agriculture.

What people may not realize is that she is also known for her aesthetic taste and decorating abilities (don't forget that gorgeous red dining room at Engeler Farm). Those bold colour schemes and attention to details like fine linens, silverware and china reflect her goal "to give Fairburn Farm's accommodations and dining room elegance paired with down-to-earth hospitality."

Fairburn has offered farmstays for over 50 years, and Mara is honoured to be continuing that tradition. She tells me the Archers were the first people she met when she came to the Cowichan Valley and "they are very special people to me." She says that between them, they now have the potential "to take the farm to the next level, from both a culinary and a farming point of view." Mara says she is excited to be working with the buffalo products from the Archers: "While the products will be in very small supply in the first few years, I will be the first to get my hands on them, so look forward to buffalo-milk pannecotta, ricotta for ravioli and ice cream on my menus."

Mara's guests will be able to participate in cooking classes taught by her and her coterie of distinguished guest-chefs (at Engeler Farm, these included James Barber, Karen Barnaby, Peter Zambri, Sean Brennan, Edward Tuson, Christophe Letard, Michael Stadtlander, et al). Not to be missed will be "Sunday lunches on the farm," when Mara will present six-course, leisurely lunches in the European tradition, but using all local ingredients. Served on the verandah, these "events of the day" will encourage urbanites to take a drive into the country and experience both the cuisine and the farm itself.

"What always appealed to me about agritourist accommodation in Italy," says Mara, " is the emphasis on dinner," and I couldn't agree more. The North American focus on bed and elaborate, five-course breakfasts may look great on the websites, but often those breakfasts can be excruciating. Mara is excited to be offering bed-and-dinner ("of course, farm-fresh breakfasts are on offer every morning, but there is more focus on the occasion of the evening meal").

In addition to the Sunday lunches, cooking classes and farmstays, Mara will continue to offer Cowichan Valley farm tours with Alfons Obererlacher, which will culminate with lunch at Fairburn Farm. On Saturdays in season, people can arrive at Duncan's Farmers' Market by train (the train from Victoria stops right in the middle of the market at 9:30 A.M.), where they will be met by Mara to gather produce for lunch later at Fairburn. After spending the day on the farm, they will be returned to the train station for the pleasant journey home. In the shoulder and quiet seasons, Mara will offer more cooking classes as well as her popular culinary tours of Italy.

Feast of Fields

Vancouver Island's foodie event of the year highlights the strong links between our local growers and chefs, and dishes up some of the best food you may ever eat. Set at a different island farm each time, the event is the ultimate gastronomic walkabout. Ticket-holders are greeted with a plate, a wine glass and a large linen napkin and invited to stroll from stall to stall to eat (all items are designed to be eaten by hand) and imbibe over the course of a long, leisurely afternoon.

The area's best chefs and vintners purvey their wares: one moment, you are savouring ostrich kebabs straight off the grill from Sidney's Dock 503 restaurant; later, you are enjoying the bouquet of a lively pinot gris from Cobble Hill's Glenterra vineyard or cooing over an almond Johnny cake drizzled with poaching sauce, enhanced with a dollop of cinnamon crème fraîche with lemon verbena and a rosette of slivered caramelized poached pear, and sprinkled with candied ginger and a confetti of pansy blossoms, created by David Feys of Feys & Hobbs Catered Arts.

Feast of Fields is a fundraiser for Farm Folk, City Folk, a non-profit organization that recognizes and promotes "the connection between those who grow our food and those who eat it, and the interdependency of all living things." Among its many projects, FFCF is active in the development of food policy around food security, supports sustainable agriculture and conducts a broad public-advocacy campaign to project awareness of food issues in British Columbia.

The indefatigable Mara Jernigan is Vancouver Island's representative for FFCF. She has organized successful Feast of Fields at many of the island's stellar farming operations including Oldfield Farm and Ravenhill Herb Farm in Saanich, Cowichan Bay Farm and Duncan's Providence Farm. It's a sell-out event every year, so if you are planning to be on the island in mid-September, call for tickets well in advance.

Merridale Ciderworks

In the tasting room at Merridale Ciderworks, I join an extended family from Mexico to sample six of the cidery's eight beverages. I discover that what owners Rick Pipes and Janet Doherty say is true: there is "a taste for every palate" here. From the very dry Cidre Normandie to the award-winning, strong and sharp Scrumpy to the sweet and velvety port-style Winter Apple, we all find something to enjoy.

As Andrea Butler pours, she describes the qualities of each style of cider and expertly advises on food pairings. For example, Scrumpy, the robust blend of crab apples and cider apples, "pairs well with strong-flavoured meats and blue cheese"; Winter Apple, with its aroma of baked apples and brown sugar, "is great with melon, dark chocolate and aged cheese."

After the tasting, I sit down to chat with co-owner Janet, who was named Rural Woman of the Year for 2004 by the Women's Farmers Institute of southern Vancouver Island. Recognized for her contributions as chair of the British Columbia Agritourism Alliance and her tireless efforts to promote the Cowichan Valley's culinary tourism, Janet says she was "deeply honoured" to be chosen by women whom she herself admires for their own hard work and commitment to the rural life.

Janet previously worked in the construction industry, as a realtor and accountant; her husband, Rick, is a lawyer specializing in commercial real estate law. They bought the existing cidery five years ago "because we were looking for something to do together and a change in lifestyle. This opportunity came across Rick's desk and we said to each other: 'How hard can it be?'" She laughs as she tells me that, as the cidery has turned out to be both idyllic and a lot of hard work, but she "loves creating things and loves the people aspect" of the cider business.

From where we sit in the tasting room, we can see across to the experimental orchard where they are growing some apples on the vine using the Swiss *dispelier* method, which has never been done here before. A self-guided tour takes visitors through that orchard and down to the pond, where they learn not only about apples but also about the indigenous flora and fauna in the orchard. Woven into the tour of both the orchard and the plant is a story about apple-blossom fairies and their involvement in the process. I was charmed by the fairy-sized doors and portals, the mining village and even a Mad Hatter that have been placed around the cidery to "bring the magic into the orchard" and captivate visiting children.

There are guided tours as well that are particularly interesting during the autumn harvest when it is possible to view the massive picking, sorting, washing, pressing and fermentation process. Merridale Ciderworks "makes all of our cider for the coming year when the fruit ripens." They do not use concentrates, which allow commercial ciders to make cider on demand. They believe that using estate-grown, cider-specific fruit, following the seasons and "letting nature control the cidermaker" is the way to make great cider. Soon, visitors will also have the opportunity to book a tour that "unlocks the vault door to our barrel room" and includes sampling the new releases.

The cidery has a stunning reception room and extensive covered and open decking where weddings and meetings can be held. In season, lunch paired with ciders can be ordered for groups of up to 100 people. Designed by chef and restaurant consultant Bill Jones, these meals showcase many of the Cowichan Valley's culinary delights, from Fairburn Farm water buffalo sausage and True Grain Bread to The Udder Guy's special apple sorbets and the Hardy Boys' candied smoked salmon. Janet makes sure their business supports other culinary ventures in the Cowichan Valley because she believes "we've got something special here." A welcome addition to the cidery in 2005 is La Pommeraie bistro. John and Tracy Waller, formerly of the popular Sunflower Cafe in Shawnigan Lake, are cooking up a storm. So you can now make a great day of it, with a tour of the cidery, followed by lunch or dinner in the bistro.

Even more adventurous and great fun are the master-chef dinners that Bill Jones and James Barber, celebrity chef of Urban Peasant fame, television personality and cookbook author, stage at Merridale several times a year. From their duck and mushroom feast in November to a cornucopia of aphrodisiacs for Valentine's Day, these are always very cheerful and a wonderful way to sample the area's bounty expertly prepared.

Cowichan Bay Winter Pork Chops

JAMES BARBER FOR MERRIDALE CIDERWORKS

 James Barber has now made the Cowichan Valley his home, where he teaches "imaginative, simple-cooking classes using locally sourced ingredients" to groups of six to eight people in his kitchen (classes are offered year-round by appointment). Writes James: "Summer in the Cowichan Valley is soft and warm. The fields are green, the skies are blue and the cows are chewing in that gentle, ruminating way they always do, like country philosophers. If they had rocking chairs they would sit in them. The tourists love it: the Saturday market, the roadside stands, eggs, tomatoes, salads, new potatoes, cheese, honey and pots of jam.

"I'm writing this in the middle of January. For breakfast I had poached eggs from Madame Daugenet at Cali Farm, big brown eggs with brilliant big orange yolks in them, on toasted slipper bread from True Grain Bread in Cowichan Bay. For lunch I had soup, made of kale from my garden, garlic from the same place, potatoes from Helma down on Lakes Road and sea salt from Tofino. For supper there were more potatoes, roasted crisp-skinned in fat from the Christmas goose (also from Helma), brilliant fresh salad greens from Lynn Jones at Deerholme Farm and thick-cut pork chops from the Quist Farm cooked in cider from Merridale.

"Here's tonight's supper."

2	thick pork chops	2
1 tbsp	olive oil or duck fat	15 ml
1 tsp	ground pepper	5 ml
1 tsp	salt	5 ml
2 cloves	garlic	2
1	medium onion, sliced thin	1
1/2	green cabbage, sliced thin	1/2
1 tsp	dried thyme	5 ml
2	Yukon gold potatoes, peeled and sliced thick	2
4 1/4 c	Merridale Ciderworks Traditional Cider	1 L

Heat a frypan with a lid over medium heat. Add the oil and fry the pork chops light brown (about 2 minutes each side). Push the chops to the side of the pan (stand them on their sides). Turn the heat to medium-high. Fry the onions, add the cabbage and garlic, sprinkle with pepper and salt and stir well together. Flip the chops back over the cabbage and sprinkle with thyme. Lay the potato slices on the chops and pour about a quarter of the cider into the pan. Bring to boil and put the lid on, turning the heat to low. Simmer 20 minutes. Eat with fresh bread and the rest of the cider.

The Mushroom Guy

I'm heading into the hills behind Shawnigan Lake with Bill Jones, geologist, former chef at Sooke Harbour House and other superb restaurants from Alsace to Vancouver, author of six cookbooks (watch for *Salmon: The Cookbook*, edited by Bill, in summer 2005) and busy food consultant. We're going way off-road to stalk the much-lauded chanterelle, a trumpet-shaped wild mushroom that emerges after the rains from mid-August through mid-November or until the killing frosts start. Not being too specific about our location is all part of the adventure: once a picker has found good foraging ground, he is not about to tell the world. I agree to keep the code.

It's a beautiful day in the woods. We've waited the requisite three days since the last rain to ensure there will be lots of new mushrooms, so we grab our bags and Swiss Army knives and make our way through the underbrush. It's fun, and a highly aerobic process. Bill steers me toward mossy beds where the chanterelles are most likely to be found, telling me that when I find one, I'll certainly find more. The yellow-orange ones (*Cantharellus cibarius*) are fairly easy to spot, and today there are white ones (*Cantharellus subalbidus*) as well — a real treat. I'm quickly hooked.

This is perfect territory for chanterelles, which, it turns out, are one of the hardiest mushrooms. Bill tells me that pharmaceutical companies are looking at the chanterelle's composition in their antibiotic research as they are almost never attacked by insects or worms, and don't tend to rot.

Picking mushrooms, I discover, is a tactile, organic experience. Once the specimen has been identified as edible, you knock off any debris that may have settled on it. Then, firmly holding the stalk, you pull the whole plant out of the ground, cut a small slice off the bottom of the stalk to perfect it, and pop the plump, spongy mushroom into your bag. It feels like a grown-up Easter egg

Mushroom expert, chef and author Bill Jones.

hunt. With the retail price of chanterelles in my head, and the prospect of a mushroom feast that evening, I have no problem staying out in the woods for the rest of the afternoon — eyes roaming the forest floor, knife at the ready.

By the time our bags are full, we've spotted at least two dozen of the 2,000 or so varieties in the world including the Zellers bolete (*Boletus zelleri*) and honey mushroom (*Armillaria mellea*). On an old nurse log, we spy a bouquet of angel wing mushrooms (*Pleurcybella porrigens*), so named because of their shape. We eat them right away, their disarmingly fresh, nutty taste bringing the beauty of the forest to our palates.

At the end of our hunt, we climb back to the logging road and snack on organic apples from Bill's farm before heading to Engeler Farm. Later that day, Bill will cook up Phyllo Packets of Roast Chanterelles, Farm-cured Bacon and Leeks; Mushroom Risotto with Saltspring Island Cheese Company's Montana Cheese; Cured Salmon on Three Kinds of Kale and Porcini Mushrooms in Tomato Sauce; and a grand finale of Heritage Apple Tart with Vanilla Rosemary Ice Cream.

With a menu like that and a chef like Bill, I'm devastated to be double-booked and miss the meal. Still, I have a bag of fresh chanterelles and within hours they're merrily sautéing in a little olive oil with garlic and a

Grilled Oyster Mushrooms on Mixed Greens with Balsamic Vinaigrette*

BILL JONES, MAGNETIC NORTH CUISINE

Serves 4 to 6. "The slight charring of the mushrooms works well with the sweetness of the balsamic vinegar. You can buy a pre-made salad mix like mesclun and have good results. Make sure the greens are crisp or refresh them in a bath of cold water. A salad spinner works well to rid the leaves of excess moisture. Place in the fridge for 5 to10 minutes after washing and even tired greens will be revitalized." — *Bill Jones*

Mushrooms:

1 tbsp	minced fresh ginger	15 ml
1 tsp	sesame oil	5 ml
1 tsp	hot sauce	5 ml
2 tbsp	extra-virgin olive oil	30 ml
1 lb	oyster mushroom pieces	454 g
	salt and pepper to taste	

Salad:

6 c	mixed salad greens, washed (lettuce, mustards, radicchio, arugula, etc.)	1.4 L
2 tbsp	balsamic vinegar	30 ml
2 tbsp	light soy sauce	30 ml
2 tbsp	extra-virgin olive oil	30 ml
	toasted sesame seeds for garnish	
	shredded nori for garnish	

In a bowl, combine ginger, sesame oil, hot sauce and oil. Stir to mix well and add the mushroom pieces. Season with salt and pepper and toss well to mix. Place on a hot grill and cook until soft and slightly charred at the edges. Transfer to a salad bowl and set aside. Add the salad greens and drizzle with vinegar, soy sauce and oil. Season lightly with salt and pepper and toss to coat. Serve family-style or transfer to four plates and garnish with a sprinkling of sesame seeds and nori.

*Reprinted with permission from *The Savoury Mushroom* by Bill Jones, Raincoast Books, 2001.

splash of wine. Since I'd picked them myself, they were of course the best I'd ever eaten.

Bill has done extensive renovations to his heritage farmhouse where he caters for private parties. His real love, though, is everything mushroom, and his company runs foraging tours and cooking demonstrations in season. In addition to the chanterelle run, there are morels from March through April (Bill says the first crocus in spring is a sign the morels are out) and pine mushrooms in the cold season.

Saskatoon Berry Farm

On a summer Sunday, I join one of the popular farm tours offered by The Aerie. I feel like a real tourist as the van pulls out and host Mara Jernigan begins to tell us about the day's program. "We'll stop by a cidery, a vineyard, a pastured chicken farm and how about a mystery stop this morning?" Naturally, we all agree. The mystery stop is one Mara hasn't been to yet, either, and it turns out to be a highlight.

Saskatoon Berry Pie

CONNIE DYRLAND, SASKATOON BERRY FARM

Serves 8. I took my first saskatoon berry pie to a dinner party in Youbou on Cowichan Lake and was immediately invited back. Make the pie yourself, and you be the judge: was it my scintillating company or the irresistible pie?

Pastry for a two-crust pie:

3 c	saskatoon berries	720 ml
3/4 c	sugar	180 ml
1/4 c	uncooked minute tapioca	60 ml
1 tsp	lemon juice	5 ml
4	drops of almond flavouring	4

Line a 9" pie plate with pastry. Combine all ingredients in a bowl and mix until slight juice forms. Pour into pastry shell and cover with other pastry, cutting openings in crust for steam to escape. Bake 450°F for 15 minutes, then 350°F for 45 minutes, until pastry is golden.

It's the Saskatoon Berry Farm, a relative newcomer in the area. Alwin and Connie Dyrland moved to the Cowichan Valley from Edmonton, thinking it would be a great hobby to grow the berries of their native prairies, but the farm's popularity has exceeded their expectations. With so many prairie folk having moved to British Columbia and the annual influx of "snowbirds" every winter, the berries are in high demand. "On any weekend, you can meet most of Alberta and Saskatchewan at our farmstand," Alwin says.

The Dyrlands bought the farm six years ago and started the six-acre orchard with 14,000 to 16,000 seedlings from southern Alberta. The plants take eight years to fully mature. Alwin shows us the extensive drip-irrigation system he's devised for the fields ("That was about the fourth mortgage," he jokes). Connie keeps busy producing jams and the best saskatoon berry pies this side of Edmonton. Every weekend, they sell from their farmstand, and the cars never stop pulling in. Even though the season is short, it's a year-round operation and, as Alwin says: "We don't get off the farm much."

Across Canada, saskatoon berries go by a variety of other names including chuckleberries or Indian plums. As Alwin says: "They don't like wet feet, so that's why you don't usually see them out here [on Vancouver Island]." He is lucky to have land with a 20-foot slope from one end to the other. Also, the land has been covered with weeping tile to ensure good drainage.

Alwin takes us straight to the fields where the berry bushes are ripe with fruit, and invites us to "eat and enjoy." We are like kids in a candy store, and soon our mouths and hands are stained from the succulent, dark purple fruit. Mara suggests picking a quantity, promising us sabayon to go with the berries, which she later prepares in her farmhouse kitchen. We pick with gusto, everyone thoroughly enjoying this real hands-on farm experience.

The fresh saskatoon berries are available from early July for three to four weeks. While they last, frozen berries are available direct from the farm.

COWICHAN BAY

Hilary's Cheese Company

I've been invited into the ageing room at Hilary and Patty Abbott's Cheese Pointe Farm to see for myself the many monastery-style cheeses they produce. Stacked up are their well-known St. Clair, a cow's-milk, Camembert-style cheese with a white rind bloom that was named in honour of Vancouver Island's sultan of Slow Food, Sinclair Philip; St. Michel, the goat's-milk version of St. Clair with a similar creamy texture and nutty, mushroom-like rind; Red Dawn, a French-style *tomme* whose rind has been washed and massaged in Merridale Ciderworks' traditional cider to break down and ripen the cheese from the rind toward the centre; and Belle Ann, another French-style *tomme* that has been bathed in Cherry Point Vineyard's blackberry port.

That ingredients from neighbouring farms and vineyards show up in the Abbotts' cheeses reflects their strong commitment to being part of a regional culinary identity in the Cowichan Valley. As members of Vancouver Island's Slow Food convivium, they believe in actively promoting the regionality of their products — their milk comes from local dairy farmers David Lestock-Kay and Joan Wilkinson of Shin Cliffe Farm, whose cows are pastured and allowed to graze naturally.

Hilary and Patty haven't always been in cheese. He was a school administrator and fundraiser; she, a banker and gardener. When Hilary's father had a client who wanted to open a cheese factory, the Abbotts thought it sounded interesting and got involved. The Cowichan Cheese Company was founded in 1998, but it eventually fell victim to too many investors with different visions. However, the Abbotts had caught the bug of taking their cheese to farmers' markets and meeting their customers face to face. They decided to continue on their own and eventually bought the 10-acre Cheese Pointe Farm in the bucolic Cowichan Valley.

A visit to the farm provides the opportunity for a tour and viewing of the cheese-making process (due to provincial sanitation regulations, visitors watch through a window) and to purchase artisan cheese at source. For those with limited time, the Abbotts' cheese shop in Cowichan Bay is a delightful stop. There, they sell both their own labels and cheese from other parts of Canada such as maple-smoked Canadian cheddar and blues from Quebec, Swedish vodka kasse, Spanish manchego and aged Italian asiago. Hilary's Cheese Company also supplies many Vancouver Island restaurants, including Long Beach Lodge and Clayoquot Wilderness Resort in Tofino, Dock 503 in Sidney, Steeples in Shawnigan Lake and Sooke Harbour House.

The Mellow Side Arts Lounge & Café

"Every musician has a mellow side," I'm told by John Androsky, the "soul proprietor" of Cowichan Bay's new Mellow Side Arts Lounge & Café. A drummer and percussionist, John honed his own talents in Vancouver for several years before moving to the bay to work for old school chum Jonathan Knight at True Grain Bread.

When the café next door to the bakery became available, John moved his drums and coffee machine in and now offers a full menu of coffee beverages along with his homemade soups and sandwiches. The menu even lists a "two-minute drum roll for $5.00," but the main attractions are the jazz ensembles, storytellers and Argentine dance lessons. It's a funky, relaxed place that's packed with locals at the end of the day, and now you know about it, too!

True Grain Bread

It seems to me that Cowichan Bay's thriving new retail food district could be attributed to the arrival of Jonathan Knight, a sort of modern-day Pied Piper. He introduced real bread to this sleepy little fishing community and attracted not only loyal customers but also other food purveyors and artisans who have set up shops around his. Now, one doesn't go to the bay just for The Udder Guy's natural ice creams (although that is still a delightful destination in its own right), but for breads and pastries, fine cheeses, coffee and even superb jazz and ceramic vessels.

I stopped by to chat with Jonathan just as he was winding up his last day of baking before a well-deserved winter holiday. As he showed me around the bakery, I loved the slightly slippery sensation of flour under my feet, the evocative aromas as one last batch of whole-wheat bread with apples and cranberries was taken out of the oven.

In the middle of the room there is a large wooden table, "where everything happens." All loaves are hand-shaped here, pastry is rolled out for the fine apple strudel, *chocolat* is added to croissant dough to make the exquisite *pain au chocolat*. The dividing-arm mixer takes pride of place nearby. Jonathan tells me he found it in New Brunswick and shipped it out. "It's the perfect size to hold two bags of flour." He has also recently acquired an Italian dough sheeter for making his already-famous croissants.

When the bakery opened, there was a queue outside every morning for the few croissants he was able to make by hand. I remember the great excitement of my foodie friend, David Beiles, on being able to buy three croissants one summer's day. The dough sheeter has now allowed Jonathan to make enough of the heavenly pastries to meet his demand. And finally, there are the three ovens, which labour from 4:00 A.M. every morning.

Jonathan always knew he would work with his hands, but initially thought his profession would be carpentry. He came to baking by tasting the great loaves of Europe, where he "discovered what bread was all about." After many years of travelling, on a flight from India to Vancouver he "knew it was time to settle down." He took his journeyman baker's certification through Vancouver Community College, apprenticing with master baker Katharina Dittus, who owned the Artisan Bakeshop.

Later, he biked all the way to Cape Breton, WOOFING (Willing Workers on Organic Farms) as he went. In Bay St. Lawrence, "an end-of-the-world type of place," he opened a small bakery, Cullin Bakery, in a community centre. Introducing natural, organic breads to the Cape Breton diet was challenging but ultimately successful. Eventually, though, Jonathan returned to the west coast where he began to look for a location to open "a real, storefront, full-on bakery instead of a wood-fired oven down a dirt road."

As chance would have it, Katharina had moved to Cowichan Bay to raise horses and laying hens (her eggs are now used by True Grain Bread) and he paid her a visit. On a blustery day, "in the middle of a snow storm," Jonathan discovered that a space in the old fish market was for lease. He "quietly opened the door" a year ago and has been overwhelmed with the response. He tells me that baking suits him well. "I can create something new every day, and having my own bakery means I get to be involved in the whole process, not just be an 'oven man.'"

Vienna Strudel

JONATHAN KNIGHT, TRUE GRAIN BREAD

Makes 2 strudels of 10 to 12 servings each. My friend Phyllis Remple had never made strudel before, so she was the ideal candidate to test this recipe. She achieved sweet success. She said that to get that paper-thin quality, it helped to let the dough rest for several minutes before rolling it out.

Pastry:

1.7 fl oz	eggs, beaten	50 ml
1/4 c	vegetable oil (Jonathan uses sunflower)	59 ml
1/3 c	water	80 ml
1 1/3 c	untreated white flour	312 g

Mix together and knead WELL to form a smooth dough. It will have a silky feel. Rest the dough in the fridge for at least one hour (or up to a week).

Filling:

5 c	peeled, sliced, and cored apples (preferably local Gala apples)	1.4 kg
1/2 c	sugar	113 g
1/2 tsp	cinnamon	2.5 ml
1 cup	coarse bread crumbs (Jonathan uses his organic baguette)	227 g
1/4 lb	melted unsalted butter (amount approximate)	118 ml

Mix the filling ingredients together quickly. Roll out the dough to almost twice the length of your biggest cookie sheet, then roll the width until it is almost transparent (says Jonathan: "Thin enough to read a Viennese newspaper through!"). Cut in half lengthwise and brush liberally with the butter. Leaving a couple of inches on the sides and bottom of the dough, spread both halves evenly with the apple mixture. Without pulling too tight, roll up both logs with the end on the bottom, and tuck the two sides under. Place the strudels side by side on a slightly greased cookie sheet, and brush liberally with melted butter. Bake at 350°F for 1 hour, brushing with melted butter every 20 minutes. When cool, sprinkle with icing sugar and slice into 1" servings.

The shelves are lined with such irresistible loaves as Vollkornbrot, the naturally leavened German rye with whole rye kernels; ciabatta, the Italian hearth loaf with a long fermentation; bay loaf, the hearty naturally leavened hearth loaf unique to Cowichan Bay; and baguette and ficelle ("the baguette's slender sibling"), along with pretzels, granary buns, French buns and that always-tempting apple strudel. I leave with a poppy-seed challah to share with my parents and a bag of cheese whirls and sweet swirls, which I wisely lock in the trunk of my car so they make it back to Victoria "safely."

Jonathan's bread can also be found on the menus at Amici's and the Lake House restaurants in Cowichan Bay and Vinoteca restaurant, Merridale Ciderworks and Godfrey-Brownell Vineyards in the Cowichan Valley.

CEDAR

Cedar Farmers' Market

The Cedar Farmers' Market features mainly organic growers from the surrounding area including Yellow Point Orchards, Bensons' Olde Tyme Farm, Limberlost Orchard, Golden Maples Farm, Big D Emu Farm and Munro Creek Farm. There are some crafts and great bread and baked goods from the Cedar Women's Institute.

To make a wonderful day of it, combine your visit to the market, which is located on the field next to the Crow and Gate Pub, with a nice pub lunch and afternoon visit to the nearby Barton Leier Gallery, featuring the paintings of Grant Leier and Nixie Barton, and their magical, whimsical garden and giftshop.

Mahle House Restaurant

I arrive early for dinner, and Maureen Loucks bounds out of the kitchen to greet me. "You must see our gardens first," and she walks me around the colourful vegetable and herb beds, stopping to show off various plants ("Look, have you ever seen white borage? Juliet tomatoes. Aren't they just perfect? Every kind of carrot, Maxibell French filet beans, Florence fennel"). She shows me zephyr, Costa romanesco and pale green pattypan squash, saying: "A chef can't create something wonderful out of inferior products."

Maureen established the kitchen garden to ensure she would always have high-quality organic veggies. The garden has been tended by Kate White, who also gardens for the folks at Hazelwood Herb Farm. She's off to Arizona to take an herbalist course, and in her absence, Scott, a local orchardist, will take over.

We wander over to the house itself, a Queen Anne beauty built in 1904 and surrounded by immaculate flower beds. These gardens are cared for by Maureen's sister-in-law, Ginny Horrocks. In July, Mahle House holds its Summer Wine and Garden Party. Maureen's brother and partner in the restaurant, Delbert Horrocks, organizes a dozen or so wine reps to proffer their wares, and a huge alfresco brunch is set out for guests. I immediately mark my calendar for the second Sunday in July.

Once inside, I am impressed by the hominess of the restaurant and the clubbiness of its patrons. Fine dining takes on an appealing friendliness in the country, and the air is vibrant with greetings. It really is a close-knit place. Not only is it run by a brother and sister, but the next generation is involved. Delbert's daughter waits tables; Maureen's daughter worked in the restaurant before moving to Victoria where she now runs the venerable Bengal Lounge in The Fairmont Empress.

I take a seat by the window with a lovely view of Ginny's flower beds, and then count six of Grant Leier's richly textured food paintings on the walls around me. One can only hope that food emulates art here.

It seems I've timed my visit well because tonight is the famous "Adventurous Wednesday," when ordering from a menu is thrown out the window, and the chef gets to surprise diners with things they might never have considered ordering before. The concept took off from day one. People come from all over the island with friends and family, and everyone at the table is served something different for each of four courses.

Even though I'm dining alone, I can vicariously enjoy the reactions from tables around me. The two couples opposite are obviously thrilled as the appetizer is set down: prawns with cannellini beans for one man; Kataifi-wrapped prawns with wasabi

Chef Maureen Loucks of The Mahle House proffers freshly picked tomatoes at the Harvest Bounty Festival.

sauce for another; steamed mussels and calamari Dijonnaise for the women, one of whom says: "I can see a food fight coming."

I've given Chef Loucks a bit of a challenge with my request for "no pork or shellfish," but she certainly rises to the occasion. I begin with a salad of tomatoes from her garden, topped with melted fontina and shredded basil and follow with a delicately flavoured carrot-ginger soup. The accompanying molasses bread is locally made for the restaurant.

My main course, lamb tenderloin with a basil and Dijon mustard sauce, is served with some of those beautiful baby zucchini and red cauliflower from the garden. Delbert, winner of a whole wall full of wine awards, gets to have fun on Wednesdays, pairing new wines with the food. I enjoy Lang Pinot Auxerrois 2001, Hogg Fumé Blanc from Washington State and Wolf Blass Yarra Valley Pinot Noir 2000 and Yellow Tail Shiraz (all in very small amounts, as I'm driving myself back to Victoria).

The pièce de résistance is a chocolate triple sec pâté with raspberry purée and a good cup of coffee. Earlier, Maureen told me: "I am really happy when I'm cooking," and her food is a winning reflection of that.

LADYSMITH

Hazelwood Herb Farm

Sitting under the arbour with the heady fragrances of clematis, ahebia, cidergum eucalyptus and passion flower lulling me, watching the fantastical mating dance of hummingbirds and looking over a gentle lily pond to the herb gardens beyond, I am transfixed. This peaceful place is a dream come true for Richard White and Jacynthe Dugas. He is originally from Leeds, England, and was a maintenance mechanic for the local sawmill; she hails from Val d'Or, Quebec, and worked for the federal government. Richard says he had fixed every piece of equipment at the mill many times, and it was time to find a new challenge.

It was his idea to start growing herbs for the local restaurants, but that didn't work out. In those days, the restaurants were only looking for a little bunch here and there, so the venture didn't pay. Not one to be deterred, Richard quit his job and the couple began growing herbs in earnest, improving the gardens and buildings as their budget allowed. Jacynthe soon

Owners Richard White and Jacynthe Dugas and their delightful gift shop at Hazelwood Herb Farm.

left her job, and the two have thrown themselves into creating a multi-faceted business whose success, they say, is sometimes overwhelming.

By the end of May, there are over 400 different culinary, landscape and medicinal herbs proliferating, from what Richard calls the Simon and Garfunkels (parsley, sage, rosemary and thyme) to some very unusual varieties. Many people come looking for alternative health cures, and what the couple don't already grow, they are always game to try. Richard says if a medicinal herb hits the news, they are flooded with requests; evening primrose, St. John's Wort and milk thistle are in constant demand.

Word of mouth brings people from all over Vancouver Island, and there are many out-of-country visitors in the summer. It is not unusual for people to bring in plans for herb gardens, to seek Richard's advice and stock up on plants. Everything is conveniently labelled to help people orient themselves to the many types of herbs. There are historical herbs like germander to treat gout; camphor for the stomach; every imaginable variety of thyme; Tucson blue rosemary; calamint; lemongrass; angelica; sweet cicely, a sugar substitute appreciated by diabetics; red bugle, a styptic; bloodroot, a native plant

for medicinal purposes; red-flowered comfrey to rejuvenate skin cells; and lavender, which finds its way into Jacynthe's soaps and soothing eye masks.

The formal garden is just the beginning. Beyond are raised beds of herbs and a lath house — an open-slatted nursery with a plastic roof that allows watering to be manually controlled. The building is full of herbs, lined up row on row. We are joined at this stage of the tour by Saffron, the resident golden lab who politely leads us to the first greenhouse. Here, many plants begin their growing cycle heated by the wood-burning stove. The greenhouse's thermostat is set at 60°F, and when the stove cuts out, the oil furnace kicks in. Richard says this hothouse is also a wonderful place to hang out in winter with a glass of brandy.

In addition to their generous free advice, Richard and Jacynthe have hundreds of potted herbs for sale, and there is a fabulous gift shop brimming with all things herbal.

Kiwi Cove Lodge

When I arrive, Peggy Kolosoff is saying goodbye to some of her bed-and-breakfast guests. They are six women who have been kayaking down the coast for two weeks and are singing the praises of her bathtubs and showers. There are 12 rooms at the inn, all facing the orchard, and beyond it, Ladysmith Harbour.

It's a lovely fall morning, so we take a walk through the vines. Peggy and Doug Kolosoff bought this 10-acre property in 1994 with the intention of making it into a campground. The rezoning didn't happen as planned, so they built a lodge and planted a thousand Christmas trees.

Owners Peggy and Doug Kolosoff of Kiwi Cove Lodge.

Kiwi Salsa

PEGGY KOLOSOFF, KIWI COVE LODGE

Makes 2 cups. This tasty salsa is good for dipping, for use in wraps or as an accompaniment to grilled fish or chicken.

5 or 6	kiwi fruit, puréed	5 or 6
1/2 c	diced red onion	113 g
2 tbsp	lime juice	30 ml
2 tsp	packed brown sugar	10 ml
1/2 tsp	oregano	2.5 ml
1	avocado, finely chopped	1

Mix all ingredients together. This salsa keeps for several days in the refrigerator.

They gave a lot of thought to producing a crop that "would be fairly low-maintenance and would create a nice ambiance on our property." Kiwi fruit vines came to mind, and the result is seven varieties on a three-quarter acre vineyard of immaculate design. Doug, a forestry worker who has kept his day job, chose the site wisely and has developed an irrigation system that waters the plants while ensuring that the leaves don't get wet. He created slight valleys between the rows of vines and the whole orchard slopes toward the shore, which is essential for run-off during heavy rains.

There is no spraying and very little threat of predators. Peggy says the deer don't like kiwis (finally, something they don't like!), and the birds could care less about the fruit. Only the rabbits are interested, but Doug wrapped the bottom of the vines in chicken wire to prevent any major damage.

The Kolosoffs grow the well-known Hayward variety of kiwi as well as other "fuzzy" varities like the Elmwood and Saanichton and three Arguta (smaller, grape-like) Kiwi. Yellow Kiwi will be available in the future. The Arguta ripen on the vine and are available in October. The fuzzies are handled differently. They are picked unripe in the first week of December, then placed in cold storage.

When Peggy needs some for use at the inn or for a buyer, she simply brings them to room temperature and lets them slowly ripen. Guests enjoy a variety of "kiwi cuisine," from kiwi glaze on homemade yogurt and pancakes to kiwi cheesecake, jelly rolls, chutney and salsa. The night before my visit, Peggy's kiwi jalapeño topping received rave reviews from the kayakers.

Page Point Inn

The best food experiences are often revealed, not anticipated, and such was the case at Page Point Inn. I'd heard about the 1940s charm of the place, the classic cooking of John Grove and the friendliness of the staff. I enjoyed it all, but was blown away by a sailboat — or more specifically, by the prospect of dinner on a sailboat under a starry sky.

The inn has a long and colourful history, dating back to 1873, when David Page homesteaded 160 acres at Page Point. Page raised oysters in Oyster Bay (now Ladysmith Harbour). It's amazing the chap lasted as long as he did, given the cougar dens on his property and the Natives who regularly threatened his life, but he lived at Page Point until 1911 when he moved to Ladysmith. The property was bought by an American doctor who leased it to the Krjivitsky family. The family's daughters, known as the "Russian Marys," rowed across the bay every day to attend school in Ladysmith. Their father planted asparagus, flowers and fruits: cherries, peaches, currants and apples. When he died in 1938, the family moved to Vancouver and Page Point fell into disrepair.

Harry and Zella Olmstead bought it in 1947 and built Manana Lodge the next year with help from a local artist, Ron Grouhel. Grouhel was responsible for the totem pole art still on display in the older guest rooms and an interesting rolled copper mural that was uncovered in 1999 during a renovation of the dining room. Zella Olmstead had a pet deer called Bambi that had the run of the lodge's dining room, and it was Zella who claimed there were singing fish in the bay.

Fortunately, much of the colourful past lives on in Page Point Inn's new incarnation. Owners Lawrence and Lexie Lambert were former next-door neighbours who had their eye on the property and were able to purchase it in 1998. They've made some improvements, like new docks for the many boaters who come to stay or eat at the inn, and they've introduced first-rate dining, but happily, they're keeping the rustic, original guest rooms and the leisurely pace of yesteryear.

Grand Marnier Chocolate Mousse

Serves 12. John Grove's much-requested signature dessert recipe is now in print. Thank you, John!

1 c	dark chocolate	250 gr
2 c	36% cream	500 gr
1/4 c	Grand Marnier	50 gr
1 tsp	orange zest	5 gr

Melt chocolate over a water bath until hot to the touch. Whip the cream and Grand Marnier until soft peaks form, and stir in the orange zest. Whisk half of the whipped cream into the chocolate to temper, then fold in the other half. Pipe into small bowls and chill until ready to serve.

I arrived in the middle of the night, having dined in Nanaimo, and was shown to one of the original guest rooms facing the marina. I took a welcome hot bath and a tipple of the sherry that is thoughtfully put out in the bedrooms, and went to sleep to the gentle clink of boats' masts in the bay. Rose, a neighbour and Page Point's morning waitress, served me a continental breakfast in the oceanside Harbour Room, and then I was off to explore the grounds. Just as I headed around to the hot tub, Rose called out: "Lexie has something to show you down on the dock."

That something was something else — the 65-foot Australian *Dame Pattie* that had competed in the 1967 America's Cup. It seems that Lawrence, an avid sailor, had found the boat in bad shape in Victoria and brought it home to Ladysmith to restore. I climbed aboard and swooned at the quality finishings inside and the prospect of returning in summer for a dinner cruise. This big, beautiful sailboat can be chartered for an afternoon or several days and comes equipped with staff and chef.

Back on shore later, I was offered the best seat in the house — stoveside in Page Point Inn's kitchen. Chef John Grove, who aims to cook "simple,

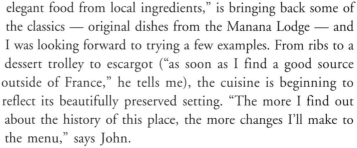

elegant food from local ingredients," is bringing back some of the classics — original dishes from the Manana Lodge — and I was looking forward to trying a few examples. From ribs to a dessert trolley to escargot ("as soon as I find a good source outside of France," he tells me), the cuisine is beginning to reflect its beautifully preserved setting. "The more I find out about the history of this place, the more changes I'll make to the menu," says John.

He's certainly got my attention as he whisks a classic brandy-horseradish cocktail sauce for a prawn cocktail. In just the right glass bowl with sloping sides, he places crushed ice, then shredded lettuce. He next hangs six large, succulent-looking prawns from the rim, then takes out his reamer to gut a lemon half. Into the lemon goes a good measure of cocktail sauce. John presents the starter with a slice each of lemon and lime. My culinary memory goes back to Victoria's Princess Mary Restaurant in the early 1960s, when shrimp cocktails and banana cream pie ruled — a happy place for me.

John's next presentation is grilled and sliced breast of duck with a grapefruit reduction and seven (count them!) vegetables, served with a phyllo pastry beggar's purse filled with potatoes that have been mashed with roasted garlic and truffle oil. This fine dinner is followed by a simple yet rich chocolate mousse ("a recipe I've made for 10 years") using his favourite Belcolade Belgian chocolate and cream. It's served close to room temperature with a sprig of pineapple mint and a delicate chocolate cigar that he's tipped with 24k gold leaf. For me, it's a dinner that's hard to beat in a setting that is both nostalgic and freshly attractive.

John apprenticed at The Aerie Resort and was pastry chef at The Wickaninnish Inn for three and a half years before coming to Page Point Inn as chef de cuisine. His interest in food began at Esquimalt High School in Victoria, where he took the cook's training program with Jason Hoskins, now sous-chef at The Wickaninnish. They've worked together many times, been roommates, gone fishing. This is John's first crack at all-out cheffing, and he is enthusiastically yet respectfully embracing the role.

He enjoys the inn's proximity to local ingredients. Andrew Dryden drops off indigenous oysters daily from the family-run Evening Cove Oysters, which is just down the road. John buys produce from Russell's Farm near Chemainus, cheese from Hilary's Cheese Company, herbs from Hazelwood Herb Farm. He makes a point of visiting the herb farm personally when he has a wedding cake to design, to hand-pick edible flowers to decorate it. I saw his portfolio of cakes and was impressed with their diversity, from a tree-shaped chocolate buttercream with varigated bark made of chocolate to tiny vegan cupcakes no larger than pears that are decorated with intricate fondant icing patterns. Alderlea, Venturi Schulze, Blue Grouse and Saturna vineyards figure on the wine list here, although I was, as usual, not able to sample as I was back on the road straight after dinner.

I've interviewed surfing chefs, show-jumping chefs and chefs who aspire to tap dancing. John Grove is a sailing chef who lives "out there" aboard the 30-foot yellow-and-cream sloop, *Maria Mhaoi*, which he named for his great-great-grandmother. She and her husband came from Hawaii for the fur trade and lived for many years on Russell Island. It seems Maria was quite a sailor and John has always had sailing in his blood. I ask if he feels he's too close to work. "Not at all," he tells me, "and besides, I can sail away and drop anchor whenever I want to." One day he hopes to get a bigger boat and sail around the world, but for now he's very happy cooking the classics from quality, local ingredients and taking the time to greet diners after dinner, often taking dessert orders and enjoying the repartee with fellow sailors.

NANAIMO

Carrot on the Run

Nanaimo's Island Natural Markets acquired a new neighbour when Carrot on the Run took over from Green Jeans Deli about a year ago. Cynthia Eyton and I dropped in one cold winter morning and were rewarded with hot coffee and freshly baked chocolate-mint cookies. We loved the giant paper mâché carrot over the display case that was created for the deli when it participated in Bite of Nanaimo (the city's annual culinary event in September) by Richard Berlingette, husband of co-owner Alexandra.

"Nanaimo is overrun with fast-food restaurants on every corner," says the deli's other owner, Melissa Hamilton, when we sit down to chat, "so we find that locals and travellers appreciate being able to pop in for a quick and healthy lunch or for takeaways." She and Alex are best friends and have worked together for many years in the food industry. She sees the deli as a natural meshing of their compatibility and talents.

Tuscan Potato Salad

ALEXANDRA BERLINGETTE, CARROT ON THE RUN

Serves 10 to 12 as a side dish. Alex's new twist on potato salad will be a big hit at your next picnic — the addition of cheese makes this practically a meal in itself.

3 lbs	red potatoes, cubed	1.4 kg
2/3 c	Parmesan cheese, grated	170 g
1 c	ricotta cheese	227 g
4	garlic cloves, minced	4
1/2	onion, thinly sliced	1/2
1/2 c	olive oil	120 ml
6 tbsp	apple cider vinegar	90 ml
	salt and pepper to taste	

Cook the cubed potatoes in boiling water until just tender. Drain and set aside. Mix the remaining ingredients and toss with the potatoes while still hot. Garnish the potato salad with ½ cup (113 g) of chopped parsley.

NOTE: This salad can be served warm but improves with chilling.

Melissa is Nanaimo-born and -raised. She originally worked as a waitress, and credits Alex with teaching her how to cook. Alex is from Sussex, England, and received her chef's papers through Vancouver Community College. When I caught up with her a few weeks later, she told me she took those papers and headed out to the bush, working for many years in camps and fishing lodges near Bella Bella, BC.

Returning to Nanaimo, she ran the kitchen at Filthy McNasty's, which was where she and Melissa connected. Alex said that whenever she was in town, she was "always hankering to get back to the bush, but as I got older and the work got harder on the body, I started to think about nesting." So, eight years ago, she settled down in Nanaimo and launched 24 Carrot Catering from a commercial kitchen in her house.

When the deli came available, it seemed like "a natural progression for me and it has become a great creative outlet." The day we spoke, she'd created quinoa salad with corn, fresh greens and a light lemon vinaigrette; cashew-nut pâté for vegans; and a yummy vegetable-ricotta cheesecake with breaded tomatoes on top. Alex also makes time to teach a hospitality management course at Malaspina University–College. "I teach the restaurant part of it, and the students actually open a temporary restuarant at the college that serves 100 covers a night."

The deli and Island Natural Markets share customers, and Alex and Melissa say they're enjoying the challenge of catering to people with allergies or on special diets. Their "treasure of a baker," Ian, even creates a wonderful range of healthy cookies from things like spelt, soy and potato to satisfy sweet teeth that shouldn't have sugar.

Glow World Cuisine

With so few see-and-be-seen dining rooms around, I was thrilled to find one had opened in Nanaimo — in a 110-year-old, well-preserved brick building that used to be the city's fire hall. The main dining room exudes stage-set decor: bright, high-ceilinged and lavished with gauze curtains and banquettes in appetite-stimulating colours like tomato, violet and lime green. A sweep of stairs made of plexiglass and dotted with tiny lights takes customers to a smaller, mezzanine dining room.

One sunny day, my parents and I opted for a window table in the main room, with views across the city. We came with good appetites, having heard that the tapas brunch was more than worth the drive from Victoria. At $21 for eight selections per person, we were impressed with the value, and we had fun choosing and sampling from each other's plates. Our all-round favourite was the classic eggs Benedict in a novel form. The eggs and hollandaise topped light, home-baked scones, and a drizzle of balsamic vinegar and sprinkling of chives were nice, modern additions. The chef's *hor d'oeuvres* was a pretty composition of local quail eggs stuffed with pâté and rolled in ground pistachios, foie gras piped into choux pastry, salmon tartar, a king prawn and caviar on a slice of cucumber. Among 12 other choices were a grilled lamb chop over yam mash, local organic greens from Nanoose Edibles dressed in a pesto and truffle vinaigrette, a gyoza of Cowichan Bay Farm chicken and vegetables with ginger dipping sauce and a substantial slice of leek, apple and fennel tart topped with pear confit.

Glow World Cuisine's glowing interior.

We finished with pumpkin cheesecake and black cherry kirsch trifle, and asked to meet the chef.

Luke Griffin has brought a new, Jamie Oliver-style enthusiasm to Glow. He has what is to me the passion of youth combined with the skills of a seasoned chef, and he "gets it" about *terroir* — about creating a sense of place in his cuisine, about linking field to feast. He takes his staff on working field trips, to make sure they see and touch and understand — "and work!" At Bea Graf and Dirk Keller's nearby Sloping Hills Farm, staff picked beans, and "we're heading back soon to help with the re-seeding." He plans another trip to Alderlea Vineyards in Duncan, and will keep the field trips going in an effort to share his belief that "the availability and freshness of product is incomparable" in the mid-island region.

Luke hails from Toronto where he trained at George Brown College and cooked for the Oliver & Bonaccin Group of restaurants. He "began to hear about organics in BC and came to see what was going on." That journey led him to Glow to work as sous-chef when it first opened, then to The Wesley Street Café, and finally back to Glow when former chef Gerd Voigt left to return to catering.

Sitting at the Glow bar before prepping begins for the dinner service, Luke tells me his idea at Glow is to represent many different cuisines, while still keeping some classics going for local tastes. Personally, he "really likes playing with Asian ingredients," and regularly runs fusion specials that are starting to turn people on to new tastes, new ingredients. Yes, Virginia, there is a lot more in Nanaimo these days than meat and potatoes.

A case in point is Luke's signature albacore tuna presentation, which is one of his own favourites. He whips up the chili-and-granola-rubbed tuna loin with green beans and sultana raisins in a sweet and spicy sauce that is so fresh and flavourful, I almost lick the plate afterwards. Luke suggests that a glass of gerwurztraminer would pair beautifully with this dish, and I'll certainly try that when I'm not driving.

Prawns with Red Pepper Jelly

LUKE GRIFFIN, GLOW WORLD CUISINE

Serves 4. This piquant appetizer literally glows with freshness and colour on the plate, and sings on the palate.

2 lbs	red bell peppers, seeded	907 g
1 tsp	crushed chilies	5 ml
1 oz	chopped shallots	28 g
1 oz	chopped garlic	28 g
1 oz	chopped ginger	28 g
3 oz	pectin	85 g
1/2 c	fresh lime juice	120 ml
2 tbsp	chopped fresh mint leaves	30 ml
2 tbsp	chopped fresh cilantro	30 ml
1 c	granulated sugar	227 gr

You will also need:

12	large black tiger prawns, peeled and deveined	12
1/4 lb	fresh arugula, washed and stems removed	113 g
	roasted garlic croutons (purchased or made by rubbing roasted garlic over bread cubes and baking in a hot oven for about 5 to 8 minutes)	

Purée the red peppers in a food processor until slightly chunky. Sauté the garlic, shallots, ginger and chilies in a little vegetable oil. Add the pepper purée to the sautéed mixture and cook for about 5 to 10 minutes on medium heat. Add the granulated sugar, lime juice, mint and cilantro, and simmer for about 15 minutes. Add the pectin and cook for another 20 minutes, stirring to ensure the bottom of the pot doesn't burn. Let the mixture cool overnight. In a frying pan on medium heat, add the peeled and deveined prawns with about 1 tablespoon (15 ml) of butter and cook until they are about half done. Add the red pepper jelly and finish cooking. In a stainless steel bowl, toss the arugula and garlic croutons with a little freshly squeezed lemon juice and olive oil. Add the prawns (taking care not to add too much of the jelly from the frying pan — only the coated prawns) at the last second and toss all together. Plate three prawns per plate in a tower fashion and serve immediately.

CHEF'S NOTE: "This recipe is one of my favourites. The spice from the chilies and the sour taste from the lime juice create an amazing combination."

Chef Luke Griffin and dining room manager BJ Bates at Glow.

Another change at Glow since I first visited is BJ (William Joseph) Bates, who replaced Mark Wachtin as dining-room manager when Mark moved to the Arbutus Grille at Brentwood Bay Lodge. BJ was raised in Nanaimo, took the hospitality management co-op program at Malaspina University-College, and then worked as a wait captain at the Aerie. Responsible for the wine list at Glow, he is "looking to increase the Vancouver Island offerings," and currently buys from Alderlea, Venturi Schulze, Vigneti Zanatta, Marley Farm and Saturna Island vineyards.

The dining room is still gorgeous, made even more so by the replacement of white tablecloths with bold yellow, red and blue ones. The tapas brunch is still the most amazing deal around; and new this year is a prolific rooftop herb garden that, along with those invigorating field trips, will ensure the cooks stay in touch with their ingredients.

In recognition, Glow was named 2004 Restaurateur of the Year by the BC Restaurant and Foodservices Association, continuing a Vancouver Island triumph: in 2003 Victoria's Cafe Brio won the award.

The old Nanaimo fire hall now houses Glow World Cuisine.

Island Natural Markets

I suppose I've always been under the impression that it takes a large population to support large, full-service organic grocery stores. I am now happy to admit that's wrong. Courtenay has Edible Island Market, there's a Lifestyles Select Market in Sidney, and in the middle of sprawling mall country just north of Nanaimo, Island Natural Markets has been doing a booming business for three years.

The store has a very open, almost tropical feel to it (although there are four walls and a ceiling). Shelves are lined with all things organic and there's a bustling deli serving veggie and fruit juices (wheat grass is optional), fruit smoothies (with or without protein powder), yummy energy balls made by Trish Vet of Hornby Island and homemade gourmet pizzas by the slice.

I enjoy my first Creekmore's BuzzRight coffee of the day and watch the locals shop.

McLean's Specialty Foods

I can never decide what brings me back to McLean's more — the food or the humour. But of course, it's both. Nowhere outside of England have I found the range of foods near and dear to my homeland except here, where Baxter's soups, Bird's custard and Rose's lime marmalade share shelves with pickled fish, rémoulade, fried onions and lingonberry jam from Scandinavia and passion fruit pulp, rooibos and beef biltong from South Africa.

There are over 100 cheeses and smoked meats. In the fall, Eric holds convivial wine- and cheese-tasting evenings. As early as July, people like me start ordering whisky and cherry brandy Christmas cakes and deluxe puddings that are brought in specially from the Old Country. Says Eric: "Our customers tell us they eagerly await the phone call to tell them, 'your cake is ready!'" The selection of German stollen and English chocolates, jams and chutneys is remarkable. As I ooh and ahh my way around the store with

"If we don't have it, you don't need it."

— Eric McLean, McLean's Specialty Foods

Owners Sandy and Eric McLean always have a smile and often a good joke for their customers at McLean's Specialty Foods.

Eric one December afternoon, he keeps darting to the back room to replenish things that he can't keep on the shelves.

My road trips are never quite complete without a stop at McLean's for a cup of tea and an excellent, house-made "bap," a white English roll that's slightly crunchy on the outside and soft inside, filled with cheese, salad cream, lettuce and tomato. There are delicious made-from-scratch soups and popular sandwiches like the prosciutto with Camembert and sweet chutney, and salads such as bocconcini with tomatoes, fresh basil and quality balsamic vinegar and olive oil. The teapots have handknit cosies and the china has roses on it. For fleeting moments, I'm back in Britain as I chat with Eric ("The Big Cheese") and Sandy McLean, the seriously fun owners.

The couple had lived in Maple Ridge on the mainland where Eric was an account representative for Cadbury-Schweppes, and Sandy was an office manager for the provincial government. Fifteen years ago, their Nanaimo friends invited them across for a look around. "They took us to the pub, and we liked the feel of the town — less anonymity." They were fed up with big-city living and wanted to be near the ocean, so they made the crossing permanently.

Eric worked for a food distributor for a while, but became frustrated: "That was when you couldn't get grocers to stock extra-virgin olive oil, good-quality Italian pasta, Parmigiano-Reggiano or balsamic vinegar." From years of doing business with grocers, he realized: "Few people actually knew what they were selling." His frustration led to the opening of McLean's Specialty Foods, a cornucopia of food and sociability. The shop's much-anticipated wine- and cheese-tasting evenings are regularly sold out.

Eric was raised in a little Scottish town. The family didn't have much money, but he remembers things like the fishmonger apologizing to his mother if there were still bones in the fish. He appreciated the interest that people took in what they were eating. He believes people need to be educated about

Cullen Skink

ERIC McLEAN, McLEAN'S SPECIALTY FOODS

Serves 4 to 6. This is Eric's mother's recipe for a traditional Scottish seafood soup. He cooks it from memory, but kindly worked out the quantities for this book.

6.5 oz	smoked haddock or smoked cod	182 g
4 c	light cream	1 L
2 oz	butter	60 g
1	large onion	1
3	medium to large potatoes	3
4 c	vegetable stock	1 L
2 tsp	flour	10 ml
2 c	water (approximate)	1/2 L
1 tsp	chopped parsley	5 ml
	salt and pepper to taste	

Peel the potatoes, boil and drain. Peel and dice the onions. Sauté in a little olive or vegetable oil till soft and golden, but not brown. Flake the fish. Drain the potatoes and very lightly mash them. Mix them in a large pot with the cooked onions and the butter, flour and fish. Add the vegetable stock and water. Bring to the boil, then reduce heat to medium and simmer gently for 10 minutes, stirring often and adding the light cream to adjust the consistency (consistency should be reasonably thick, not runny, with small pieces, not chunky). Adjust seasoning. Sprinkle with the parsley and serve.

their food, and he and Sandy love helping their customers find more interesting alternatives. He doesn't sell mozzarella, which "you can buy everywhere," but recommends something new for a pizza: fontina, asiago, pecorino. And customers keep coming back.

McLean's picnic hampers are still a bit of a secret, but those in the know (such as chef James Barber) rely on Eric and Sandy's creativity and quality foods whenever they want to venture forth into nature or need provisions for the ferry ride back to the mainland or a long-haul flight. How do the McLeans know what to put in a hamper? "We ask a lot of probing questions," says Eric: "Are they wanting food of a particular ethnicity? Is this a special occasion? Are they serious foodies?" Ah, serious foodies. You're home.

Shady Mile Farm Market

Before the Shady Mile Farm Market sprang up, small farms in the area never had an outlet, beyond the farmgate, to sell what they grew. Bill and Sharon Earthy have changed that with their open-door policy of buying surplus fresh produce from the locals.

Bill is a former welding instructor and landscaping contractor; Sharon managed a wholesale food company. They both wanted to open a country nursery, but recognized that it wasn't a year-round proposition. They could see a growing interest from urban dwellers in the "country experience," so when the opportunity came up to lease seven acres of the historic 118-acre McClure Farm, they decided to combine a nursery with a food market and café.

You can pet the deer at Shady Mile Farm Market near Nanaimo.

Their big, sunny establishment includes a couple of production greenhouses

Pick a peck of peppers at Shady Mile Farm Market near Nanaimo.

and a 5,000-square-foot greenhouse selling annuals, perennials and hanging baskets. Indoors, there is a butcher shop, and dry-goods and fresh-flower sections. The cosy café serves small-batch, custom-ground coffee and treats. There's a fireplace and lots of good gardening-related reading material, which makes the café a perfect spot to relax.

The café doubles as a demonstration kitchen and seminar room where Bill offers popular cooking classes. Drawing on local ingredients and wines, the classes are given over three nights, and participants learn to cook six complete meals. He recently "graduated" a group of six men who are now planning to cook dinner for their wives. Sounds good to me!

Out in front is the large produce area, protected from the elements with a courtyard wall and heaters in winter. It's an inspiring place to shop on a cold day and still enjoy the ambiance of an outdoor market.

The McClure Farm was first homesteaded in 1892. Bill is in the process of bracing the original farmhouse and adding a few heritage elements, like a replica hand pump, so children can learn about how the place used to operate.

The Wesley Street

Gaetan Brousseau studied political science at university, but decided he didn't want to be a starving student, so he learned how to cook. He took his chef's training in Lausanne, Switzerland, and his sommelier training in Bordeaux. He and his wife, Linda, worked in the wine-distribution business, then in a restaurant in Arizona. Keen sailors, they ended up in Vancouver where they ran the successful Granite Café, which was awarded best restaurant status in Vancouver two years running. From their sailing jaunts, they learned of an opportunity at Silva Bay on Gabriola Island and ran their restaurant, Latitude, there for five years.

"And then," says Gaetan, "we decided we were ready to take the boat to Mexico." What changed that plan was another opportunity to take over a restaurant, this time in Nanaimo. The Wesley Street is relatively new to the scene, but has established itself quickly as the place to dine well on the mid-island, for both lunch and dinner. I arrive early for dinner, in order to spend time with Gaetan and his charming chef, Daniel Caron. Daniel is formerly of the Château Laurier in Ottawa, and Vancouver's Waterfront Hotel and the Vancouver Club. He tells me he is thrilled to

The charming Wesley Street restaurant and co-owner Gaetan Brousseau.

be cooking on a more intimate scale now. Daniel's wife, pastry chef Tammy Deline, is working at Nanaimo's Scotch Bakery.

My first question, as always, is about their ingredients. What are they sourcing locally? The answer puts The Wesley Street on the same page as restaurants run by the chefs of the Island Chefs Collaborative (ICC) that "emphasize locally grown, organic, seasonal and minimally processed ingredients." Says Daniel: "We all have our own conscience to answer to. It is our preference to serve locally grown and raised foods in the restaurant." He's known about the quality of Vancouver Island ingredients because "when I worked in Vancouver, we ordered many things from the island."

The menu features pork from nearby Errington, chicken from Cowichan Bay Farm and venison from Qualicum Farms. Greens are supplied by Nanoose Edibles, and the cheese course showcases Courtenay's Natural Pastures cheeses. Gaetan has put his sommelier training to good use on the wine list, which is garnering a lot of favourable attention. I'm pleased to see featured selections from Alderlea, Glenterra, Blue Grouse and Saturna Island vineyards.

Gaetan pours me the Victoria Estate Vineyard's Madeleine Sylvaner 2000, and presents the house-made warmed egg bread as I consult the evening's menu. There is a good choice, pleasingly French-leaning, with some personal favourites of mine like bouillabaisse and grilled rack of lamb. I start with delicate slices of venison carpaccio served with mustard aïoli, Nanoose Edibles' mesclun and toast points and then two large ravioli filled with peas and mascarpone and served with small, sweet scallops and seared prawns, finished with basil and chili oils. Both appetizers are first-class.

Gaetan and I have a lively discussion about eating wild versus farmed fish (he favours wild, and serves wild salmon). Hearing he has a good supply of sockeye from Barkley Sound, I decide to go for the salmon baked on a cedar plank, and served this evening with a warm citrus chutney, a nice slice of eggplant, zucchini and onion tart, carrots and perfect rice. I realize I have eaten everything on my plate and can't even contemplate dessert or cheese. That momentary catastrophe is soon remedied; I will just have to come back, and soon.

As Gaetan attends to other diners, I reflect on my excellent meal and think how fortunate Nanaimo is that he and Linda postponed their journey to Mexico.

GABRIOLA ISLAND

Gabriola Gourmet Garlic

Anyone who plays continuous classical music to his chickens is all right with me. As Ken Stefanson gives me a tour of his tranquil Gabriola property, I am particularly taken with his animals: those sophisticated Araucana chickens, a dear miniature horse named Peter and two Angora goats who vie with each other to have their photo taken. Then there are the prize-winning schnauzers. I lose count of how many there are as they frolic around me. Ken's wife, Llie Brotherton, is a professional dog groomer, and the couple has always raised show dogs.

It was Llie who found their Gabriola property. The couple had been living in Vancouver when she paid a visit to the island with a girlfriend. Says Ken: "She came home and reminded me that I'd once said I could live on an island." They are now happily settled in their island home. Llie has a prolific vegetable garden and makes beautiful baskets. Ken, who had previously sold computers, furniture and real estate, and bought and sold 18 restaurants, has found a new profession in garlic and chocolate.

The garlic was his doctor's suggestion. After Ken had suffered four strokes, she told him to get his blood pressure down by eating more garlic. That led Ken to grow garlic, which led to his growing a lot of garlic — more than 6,000 pounds a year. He grows it mainly on the southern, warmer part of the island and has a barn over on Vancouver Island for drying it. Ken tells me he'd always enjoyed garlic, but "I didn't know how much I liked it until I started growing it." Also on Vancouver Island is the

Mr. Gabriola Gourmet Garlic, Ken Stefanson.

chocolate factory where he and his business partner, Ille Jocelyn, produce their amazing array of chocolate bars and truffles.

The chocolate was Ken's own idea. He'd been experimenting with garlic dipped in chocolate. He met Ille, a chocolatier, and they launched The Original Gabriola Bar made of dark chocolate and garlic. The range of Gabriola Gourmet chocolate bars now includes The Exquist Gabriola Bar (ginger and garlic), Red Hot Chili Bar, Gabriola Island Orange, Gabriola Island Mint and Gabriola Island Espresso. I arrive just as the mint and coffee bars are being launched, and add my praise to the mix between orgasmic bites of each flavour.

Speaking of orgasmic, Ken's new maca bars are infused with the recommended daily dose of Peruvian maca, which he tells me is known for its energy-producing and aphrodisiac qualities. There are also divine truffles.

Other products are the hugely popular garlic chutney, a pure minced garlic and minced garlic with paprika; pickled- and hot-pickled garlic; three- and four-year-aged garlic; and garlic salad dressing and marinade. Ken also sells fresh and dried garlic, seed, greens and braids. You'll find this charming gentleman and his garlic products all over the island, including at the Nanaimo and Duncan farmers' markets. In season, you can always find him at the Gabriola "Agi Hall" Farmers' Market on Saturdays and the Silva Bay market on Sundays, and at the Saltspring Island Garlic Festival in August. Ken and Llie have opened a gelato store on Willow Street in Chemainus that offers 180 different flavours on a rotating basis as well as homemade cookies and "all our great garlic products." If you have the chance, go directly to the source; Llie's gardens and the irresistible chocolate studio are open year-round. And don't forget to pay your respects to the animals.

Gabriola Agricultural Association Farmers' Market

Tannie Meyer, one of the founders of the Gabriola Agricultural Association Farmers' Market, is showing me around her farm. We're meeting here because it's January and the market is closed for the season, not least to give the busy vendors a break.

The Gabriola market is one of the area's largest, with 85 regular and up to 20 "casual" stalls. Tannie says the casual vendors are those who take their chances on market day, bringing whatever is abundant in their gardens that week. "After winter," Tannie says, "the market is a big social event. It's like coming home again."

> "We want the kids to be able to pick food directly from the garden and eat it without any concerns."
> —Tannie Meyer, G. A. A. Farmers' Market

Vendors include Ken Stefanson and Llie Brotherton of Gabriola Gourmet Garlic with their wonderful garlic products and Llie's beautiful baskets; Ike MacKay of Berry Point Fruit and Honey, who brings apples, pears, cherries and honey; Jocelyne Boulanger and Michael Bean of Auld Alliance Farm, who are well known for their herbs and attractively bottled vinegars; Helen Cox and Dale Ferguson of Early Dawn Farm with cucumbers, flowers, peppers, strawberries and more; and Jacinthe and Peter Eastick of Freedom Farm, who come with eggs, greens, chickens and pheasants. There is also a full-service kitchen for snacks and lunch.

Tannie's "6 Meyer Farm" is well represented at the market. Tannie, her husband, Jeff, and her three young children have a regular stall where they sell potatoes and their popular "Meyer corn." The whole family is up before the sun on market day to harvest the produce and then have a big breakfast before heading down to the Agi Hall. Tannie tells me they have always grown organically because "we want the kids to be able to pick food directly from the garden and eat it without any concerns."

Heavenly Flowers and the Good Earth Market Garden

There was a good rain the night before I went to visit Rosheen Holland. "Bring your gumboots," she advised me. I parked on the road and tramped down a muddy path into the woods. Her home appeared in a clearing, smoke wafting from the chimney. Rosheen was at the door, inviting me in for freshly brewed green tea.

I'd heard great things about the vegetables and flowers grown by Rosheen and her husband, Bob Shields. They had worked in the landscape-maintenance business in Vancouver for 12 years, then thought it would be better to have their own land and grow for themselves. The original idea was to grow ornamentals and trees, but they found their land was best suited to annuals. Actually, they have two pieces of land on Gabriola. The small parcel on the island's warm, south end is ideal for "starting a lot of our babies." The plants are then moved to the couple's mid-island property, which sits on a flood plain. There, they flourish in the rich soil.

Rosheen and Bob began selling their wares from the Gabriola Farmers' Market when it started eight years ago. Their produce and flowers were instant successes, but as the market grew from a handful of stalls to over 100, they found it more difficult to serve their loyal local customers. Rosheen says that the huge crowds at the market meant "people were struggling to find us, and then actually get to us." So they decided to operate exclusively from their farmgate and by special order.

The special orders are often for Rosheen's extraordinary floral arrangements. She's popular with brides, who visit her flower gardens ("a riot of colour in summer") a week before their weddings, usually with their mothers, to choose the blooms for their big day. Rosheen displays her arrangements at the farmgate, each thoughtfully wrapped in water-filled bubblepacks. Rosheen tells me her flowers are so hardy that they can last up to two weeks.

Rosheen and Bob grow an impressive range of vegetables, many larger than life, like the giant onions Rosheen pulls out of her cold storage to show me. She attributes their quality to the fact that they are organically grown. The couple is always feeding the soil with good things like seaweed, which they get from the east side of the island. "Our soil is 80 percent humus, which acts like a giant bag of peat moss on the plants and makes things grow big

Rosheen Holland of Gabriola's Heavenly Flowers and the Good Earth Market Garden shows off a bouquet of her famous flowers at the Gabriola Agricultural Association Farmers' Market.

and healthy." Rosheen feels they have a responsibility to produce high-quality produce. "After all," she tells me, "our customers are our neighbours."

Before I leave, we have a wonderful conversation about cooking for oneself versus eating in restaurants. Rosheen loves cooking from the bounty in her garden. She believes "a meal doesn't go anywhere without the best ingredients, and organic ingredients make a meal exceptional." Taught by her mother to understand "what good food is and what it tastes like," she, like me, finds it a challenge to eat out unless the food quality is exceptional.

I leave Rosheen's cozy cottage in the woods and run into Bob cutting firewood. Even though Rosheen has impressed on me that farming "is not as romantic as people think," for the moment I am enchanted by the appearance of their rural idyll.

LANTZVILLE/ NANOOSE BAY

The Book Worm Café

There are certain cafés one simply must know about, that serve the kind of food Oscar Wilde might say "causes happiness." For a peripatetic foodie like me, there is nothing more gratifying than knowing where to find wholesome, delicious and creative food just off the beaten track. The Book Worm Café is such a spot, and I am indebted to Barbara Ebell of Nanoose Edibles for pointing me in its direction.

The café is owned by sisters Vicky Adamson and Chris Thomas, who grew up in Nanaimo. Vicky is an art teacher who helps out in the café when she can; Chris is the chef. Chris spent 15 years in Prince Rupert, where she also cooked in a café. Moving to Nanoose five years ago, she began looking for a place of her own.

Owner and chef Chris Thomas of The Book Worm Café sets up a stand at the Harvest Bounty Festival.

Poached Salmon Salad with Blueberry Salsa

CHRIS THOMAS, THE BOOK WORM CAFÉ

Serves 4. A great luncheon salad, whose flavour is matched by its beautiful combination of colours.

2 lb	fillet salmon, poached in wine, water and fresh herbs	910 g
6 c	mixed salad greens	1.4 L
1	red pepper, julienned	1
4 tbsp	creamy lemon and chive dressing	60 ml
1 c	blueberry salsa	240 ml

Dressing:

Combine in food processor or blender:

1	egg	1
2 1/2 tbsp	lemon juice	37.5 ml
1 tbsp	Dijon mustard	15 ml
	salt and pepper, to taste	

With motor running, slowly add:

1 1/2 c	olive oil	360 ml

Stir in:

1/4 c	finely chopped chives	60 ml
	zest from 1 lemon	

Blueberry Salsa:

Mix together and let sit one hour:

1 c	fresh blueberries, coarsely chopped	240 ml
1/2 c	finely diced onion	120 ml
4 tbsp	chopped cilantro	60 ml
1 tbsp	fresh lime juice	15 ml
1/2	jalapeño chile, finely diced (or more, to taste)	1/2
1 tsp	sugar	5 ml
1/2 tsp	salt	2.5 ml

To compose the salads, make a bed of greens on each of four plates, drizzle each with 1 tbsp (15 ml) of the dressing, top each with 1/4 of the salmon left in big chunks, and spoon over 1/4 of the blueberry salsa.

The Book Worm Café had sold used books and served food, but only from a hot plate. Chris and Vicky put in a new kitchen and introduced the neighbourhood to some very good cooking — what Chris calls "casual, West Coast contemporary." She makes everything from scratch except the bagels.

She relies on local suppliers and enjoys changing her menu with the seasons, running with what's available. Nanoose Edibles is the vegetable and fruit source. They provided such lovely strawberries last summer that the café served strawberry shortcake every day. A farmer supplies the eggs, another the chicken and turkey, and local fishers bring in sockeye salmon and shrimp. Chris serves organic, fair-trade Karma Coffee from nearby Errington.

Morning coffee is incredibly popular at The Book Worm Café, and Chris' customers have her trained to make them a different type of muffin every day. One group of retired gentlemen meets there every morning at ten o'clock, and Chris says the conversation is fascinating. I'm reminded of my father's Kaffee Klatsch that also meets at 10 o'clock precisely, behind Oak Bay's tweed curtain, to discuss their portfolios and other weighty matters.

On one side of the café, Chris exhibits local artists' work. As with the food suppliers, she is committed to providing a venue to local artists. She also holds music evenings on Fridays to showcase local talent.

I dropped in on a June afternoon and enjoyed the café's Thai Noodle Salad with Nanoose Edibles' greens and asparagus, then left with the only portable piece of pie I've encountered. The café's pie-shaped O'Henry Bar is a sinfully solid creation of chocolate, peanut butter and Rice Crispies that's perfect for road trippers like myself. Next time, I'm looking forward to trying Chris' famous lemon meringue pie.

Harvest Bounty Festival

Like Feast of Fields on the island's south end in September, the Harvest Bounty Festival is well worth the price of admission. It's coordinated by the Harvest Bounty Festival Society and held at Nanoose Edibles in late August. Also like Feast of Fields, it's a good idea to call well ahead for tickets for this fabulous celebration of local agriculture, food, drink and the culinary arts. Actually, the first year I attended it, the festival was held at Dave and Marnie Evans' 350-acre farm in Qualicum Beach, and I was first in the gate.

Getting there early proved to be beneficial that Sunday, because many of the churches were still in session, and I had beaten the crowds. It gave me the opportunity I most enjoy:

meeting one-on-one with the growers and chefs, and enjoying their exquisite food offerings in a relaxed way.

I found myself grazing first for food and wine, then gravitating to a bench or picnic table where I could enjoy not only the food, but also the other people. I managed to eat and drink my way around the whole exhibition! The Harvest Bounty Festival has a homey, small-community feel even though the exhibitors come from all over the island.

I met up with Mary Ann Hyndman Smith and Edgar Smith of Natural Pastures Cheese and Christie Eng of Shady Creek Ice Cream, who called me over to "try this tuile with roasted banana ice cream" as it was "just right" to eat — and it was delicious. Sandy and Eric McLean of McLean's Specialty Foods joined me for a sample of the 2001 pinot gris from Ruth Luxton at the Glenterra Vineyards table.

Barbara Ebell of Nanoose Edibles reports that "as part of our strategy to have this event inform and educate the public about the availability and high quality of locally produced food, future festivals will include students and instructors from the culinary programs in some of the regional high schools."

Nanoose Edibles

It's 9:00 A.M. on a clear Monday morning in Nanoose Bay. I've ferried across earlier this morning from Vesuvius on Saltspring Island, excited to see Barbara and Lorne Ebell's popular Nanoose Edibles farm. Such is the quality of their produce that chefs like Andrew Springett of The Wickaninnish Inn actually have orders couriered to them.

I've been asked to join a culinary arts class from Malaspina College that is touring the farm with instructor Gordon Cower (formerly of Sooke Harbour House). They're a lively bunch of 20-somethings whose enthusiasm for the whole growing process is infectious.

Our hostess, the indomitable Barbara Ebell, is a former manager of women's programs for B.C.'s Ministry of Agriculture. Lorne holds a Ph.D. in agriculture and has worked for the provincial and federal governments. The couple retired a few years ago, realized longevity ran on both sides of their family, and worked out what they were going to do for the next 40 years. They turned to their 23-acre property in Nanoose, thought they would plant a few apple trees and some raspberries, and are now going full-tilt with a variety of herbs,

20 kinds of nutritional greens and other veggies, flowers and fruit, a box program and a large farmstand.

Located as they are, in a non-farming community, Barbara says it hasn't always been easy, but they are determined to make a go of organic farming. It's the lowest-lying property in the area, located on an old estuary, with some clay and some gravel base. When they took over the land, the soil was seriously degraded. They've spent a lot of time raising its nutritional level through cover-crop plantings that just get tilled in, and reverse rototilling. They have their own water supply, with a drip-irrigation system operating from six zones on the property. The drip system is used when the wind blows to ensure that water goes where it should and is not wasted.

Nanoose Edibles was certified organic in 1997. When Barbara is asked to explain the road to organic certification to the Malaspina students, she cites a lowly onion. The certification body (in her case, BCARA) requires detailed records on when it was seeded, transplanted and harvested. The way the food is grown and handled must be recorded every step of the way. It's a process that is both laborious and costly, but ultimately gives the consumers complete confidence in what they're buying.

Barbara learned her growing techniques through her association with the Pacific Northwest branch of the North American Direct Farm Marketing

Nanoose Edibles' owner Barbara Ebell rings up a sale for Malaspina College's culinary arts instructor Gordon Cower.

Farmer's Lunch

Barbara says she loves this quick and easy shake when she's working in the fields: "With all the bending over, I don't want a heavy meal in my stomach."

In a blender, combine to taste:

V-8 juice
nutritional greens
cayenne pepper

Association. At one of their meetings in Portland, Oregon, she happened to be sitting next to the owner of Nicky's Greens, a California business focussed on growing nutritional greens. Nicky befriended Barbara and took the time to explain how her business worked. It was a fortuitous meeting.

Barbara says her first taste of "bitter" herbs was at the Herald Street Caffé in Victoria where she ate a delicious salad of greens with quail eggs. To her, "bitter is one of the great tastes of the culinary arts," but she says most people want their greens devoid of bitterness. It's certainly a taste worth acquiring, as the nutritional values are impressive.

Fresh is important to Barbara, who notes that green vegetables lose their nutritional value at a rate of 10 percent per day. She says: "Eating only a lettuce salad probably puts you in a negative nutrition mode." And, of course, eating fresh and local

"We're still hunters and gatherers, still working with the basic tools."

— Barbara Ebell, Nanoose Edibles

is also good for the economy. Local organic chard is ultimately less expensive because there's no waste. So the moral is, the closer you can get to the grower and the sooner you can eat that just-picked produce, the better.

As a member of the BC Agritourism Alliance, Nanoose Edibles is marketing the farm to Vancouver Island visitors "as a place to stop and enjoy as well as buy local products." The glorious farmstand is open year-round, proffering the farm's own produce as well as that of other food producers in the region. New in 2005 is an organic flower boutique for flower lovers with a conscience about toxic sprays among us!

PARKSVILLE

Little Qualicum Cheeseworks

My parents join me on a drive through Qualicum Beach to the 68-acre dairy farm where Clarke and Nancy Gourlay tend a small mixed herd of Ayrshire, Holstein, Canadienne and Brown Swiss cows and make wonderful fresh and ripened cheese. We are greeted by Tiger, a lovely ginger cat, and Nancy Gourlay, who cheerfully shows us around the cheese factory. Nancy says they pride themselves on making cheese from their own "best-quality milk." Their cows are "fed only sweet grass and grains." No pesticides, fermented feeds, growth hormones or antibiotics are used on the farm, and the Gourlays are active supporters of sustainable agricultural practices and the humane treatment of animals.

From their small operation come French-style *fromage frais*, which the Gourlays recommend "served with raspberries for an awesome breakfast treat"; raclette, the raw-milk cheese that transforms boiled potatoes into a melting treat; feta, in its own whey or in a sun-dried tomato, garlic and rosemary marinade; San Pareil, a seasonal soft cheese with a "mixed" rind; and other treats like my mother's favourite, Caerphilly.

One of their most popular creations are the fresh cheese curds that are produced on Thursdays after 3:00 P.M. (locals have this recorded on their BlackBerrys!). They are delicious eaten on their own, but are best known as the indispensable ingredient in *poutine*, the Quebecois concoction of French fries topped with fresh cheese curds and gravy. (If you've never tried *poutine*, go directly to Pirate Chips in Nanaimo, where owner Angela Negrin uses Little Qualicum Cheeseworks' squeaky-fresh curds and a dynamite vegan gravy that make this rustic dish sing.)

Black Forest Par Frais

NANCY GOURLAY, LITTLE QUALICUM CHEESEWORKS

Serves 3. When I asked for a recipe, Nancy demurred: "I'm afraid I'm not a chef and hardly ever have time to do anything other than just eat cheese or melt it over whatever's handy." But she did have a great idea for "instant cheesecake" that never fails to please the dessert mavens in my household.

1 8 oz	tub natural *fromage frais* (keep the tub)	1	260 g
1/4 c	sugar		57 g
3 tbsp	cocoa powder		45 ml
3 tbsp	kirsch (or more to taste!)		45 ml
1/4 tsp	real vanilla extract		1.25 ml
	good quality granola		

Let the *fromage frais* warm up slightly for easier mixing. Mix everything except the granola together thoroughly. Spread 2 tbsp of granola on the bottom of the tub. Press the "chocolate cheese" back into the tub. Chill. When ready to serve run a knife around the edge and turn the mini "cheesecake" out onto a plate. Cut and serve with a dollop of cherry pie filling or canned cherries.

Clarke and Nancy worked for the Humanitarian Aid Organization in Switzerland, Lebanon, Kosovo and Afghanistan before returning to Vancouver Island with their three sons in 1999. They bought the farm that had been owned by dairy farmer Jim Lowry in the late 1800s, and have retained his sweet old cabin on the site. They were inspired by the wonderful cheese they ate in Switzerland "to set out to learn and practise the ancient and noble art of cheesemaking." It seems that their cheesemaking benefits from the "cool, moist climate in the shadow of Mount Arrowsmith," which has proven to be ideal for the ripening of washed-rind cheese.

QUALICUM BEACH

Creekmore Coffee

I once had the pleasure of sharing a stall at Victoria's Banana Belt Fine Foods' customer appreciation day with two wonderful fellas, Richard Lewin of Golda's Fine Foods and David Creekmore of Creekmore Coffee. Suffice it to say, I learned a few things about promotion from both of them. And I sure developed a taste for BuzzRight coffee, a dark-roasted, full-bodied blend that is one of Creekmore's most popular.

David and Elaine Creekmore have always been "coffee hounds," but their careers took them in other directions. David was a furniture maker and then a salesman for the largest beverage company in Alaska; Elaine was a children's librarian. Elaine says: "David and I are very different. If you had told me 10 years ago that we'd be working together, I wouldn't have believed you, but we love it."

It turns out their differences have made them a great team. David is very gregarious, so he's responsible for the marketing, promotion and delivery of their coffee. Elaine enjoys the roasting process and has become so expert that she almost never refers to her daily logbook when roasting a batch of green beans.

Together, they are very proud of their Little Red Primo drum roaster, and treat me to an exclusive demonstration. They are rigorous about roasting in small batches to ensure the quality and consistency of the coffee they sell. Elaine turns on the machine and waits for the burners to reach a certain temperature. She is a petite woman, but has no difficulty shouldering 40 pounds of green coffee beans and pouring them into the roaster.

Each type of coffee requires a different starting temperature. Today, Elaine is roasting Peruvian beans, and she is able to tell by sight (the colour of the beans as they roast is visible through a glass window) and sound (at around 400°F, the beans start to pop like popcorn). There is also a "tryer," a small spout that extracts a few beans from the batch as it's roasting. Depending on what she sees in the sample, Elaine may adjust the temperature up or down.

Michael, Elaine and David Creekmore operate Creekmore Coffee in Qualicum.

After the beans are roasted, Elaine releases them into the cooling tray where a continuous agitator with steel brushes kicks off the chaff. The chaff goes directly into a collecting vessel and is then put on the Creekmores' compost pile. It takes at least seven minutes to cool the beans, and then they are weighed. What started out at 40 pounds has been reduced to 33.5, as beans lose between 12 and 25 percent moisture in the roasting process.

Elaine records every batch in her logbook, taking note of how the different coffee beans from different countries react. David points to their many sources of organic coffee: bags of beans from Peru, Indonesia, Sumatra and Colombia are stacked around the room. Their decaffeinated coffee is made from beans from the well-known Mexican Isman co-operative.

David says that with coffee, "freshness is everything," and that's why he does his own distribution. This is a real family affair with their son, Michael, a science student at the University of Victoria, active in the business during school vacations.

Fore & Aft Foods

Years ago, I used to enjoy breakfasts at a little café on the dock at Brentwood Bay, just north of Victoria. In addition to serving meals, the café sold wonderful jams and condiments.

Wandering around the What's Cooking? cookshop in Qualicum Beach, I came across jars of the divine Fore & Aft antipasto, a taste from my past. The labels showed that the company was now in Qualicum Beach.

Medallions of Pork Tenderloin with a Ginger Grapefruit Sauce

BEVERLEY CHILD, FORE & AFT FOODS

Serves 4. Chris Tyrrell tested this dish on dinner-party guests, and declared the result "beautiful, tender, juicy, moist — perfect." He cooked the pork for 20 minutes, then let it rest for 10 minutes before slicing. Says Chris: "This sauce is to die for!" Fore & Aft makes a good grapefruit marmalade.

2	whole pork tenderloins	2
Marinade:		
1 3/4 c	grapefruit marmalade	420 ml
4 tbsp	soy sauce	60 ml
4 tbsp	medium sherry	60 ml
1 tbsp	sesame oil	15 ml
2 tbsp	finely chopped garlic	30 ml
2 tbsp	finely chopped fresh ginger	30 ml
1/2 c	water or white wine	120 ml
1	can good quality consommé	1
1 1/2 - 2 c	crème fraîche	360 - 480 ml

Mix ingredients together and pour over pork. Marinate for a minimum of three hours, but preferably overnight. Remove pork from marinade and set aside. Add consommé to marinade and bring to boil. Simmer to reduce by half. At this point, add the crème fraîche and continue to simmer. While sauce is thickening, sear to brown the two tenderloins in 1 1/2 tbsp (22.5 ml) olive oil. Transfer pork to roasting pan and bake 20 to 30 minutes at 350°F. Slice pork into medallions and drizzle sauce over meat. Serve with fresh greens and rice, and garnish with fresh grapefruit.

With no address or phone number to follow up, I had to do a bit of serious foodie sleuthing before I knocked on a door that was opened by Beverley Child, co-owner of the company. "When we left Brentwood Bay, we ran the teahouse at Filberg Lodge in Comox for five years, then started our own catering company." Actually, she and her husband and business partner, Patrick Brownrigg, had never stopped making their condiments. Beverley recommends grinding 2 tbsp Balsamic Jelly, 2 tbsp chopped garlic and enough pistachio nuts with mortar and pestle until it forms a thick paste. Use this lively paste to dress a pork or chicken roast during the last 20 to 30 minutes of oven time.

Wine jellies, jams, vinegars, chutneys and that great antipasto are all available from their commercial kitchen, at Muffet and Louisa's and Slater's First Class Meats in Victoria and at What's Cooking? in Qualicum Beach. A very popular new product is Balsamic Jelly, which is good with sharp cheese, baked Brie or cold meats, as well as with roast lamb and oysters. The couple sources a lot of their ingredients locally, and most of the fruit is organic. Trained at Dubrulle in Vancouver, Beverley says she is delighted to be doing what she does and seems pleased to be rediscovered by one of her old customers.

La Boulange Organic Breads

If you expect to find an elderly French gentleman behind La Boulange breads, you would at least be half right. Roger Floch had been a baker in Bordeaux before bringing the spirit of levain breads to Cumberland, British Columbia.

John Taraynor was a carpenter who happened to be working on a building project in Qualicum Beach with a fellow who knew Roger. At that time, Roger had his house on the market and was looking to sell his bakery and return to France. John was reminiscing about his epiphany over a sourdough bun in Zurich (when he ate that bun, he realized he'd never eaten good bread before). There was no doubt that John, looking for a change of careers, was in the right place at the right time. He and his wife, Jean Wilson, bought the business from Roger, who stayed nearly two years to train them. When he returned to France, the couple hired two locals, Ron Postl and Jamie Barter, neither of whom were bakers, and their success has pleasantly delighted them all. Ron formerly owned a local gift shop specializing in environmentally friendly products, and Jamie is a musician.

The mixing machine takes pride of place at La Boulange Organic Breads.

Jamie says they're passionate about what they do, that "the weird thing is, it's about the bread. I'd be bored if I was making donuts, but this is a fascinating journey through 48 hours." They all seem to have inherited a certain fanaticism from Roger, who was obsessed with the microbiotic requirements of making the bread, and they turn out very impressive loaves: seven-grain flax, seven-grain raisin and nut, kamut/spelt multi-grain (my husband's favourite), 100 percent rye, rye with whole-wheat flours, kamut, spelt, French and a new rice bread. There also are organic raisin squares that practically make a full meal.

The bakery is now located on John and Jean's six-acre property in Qualicum Beach, in what was once the horse barn. The property was formerly owned by Jean's parents; when they wanted a smaller place in town, the two couples agreed to exchange houses!

I arrive just as their baking shift is over, and Jean and the boys are having a cup of tea. We sit around in the bakery, surrounded by loaves of bread on the cooling racks, chatting about the importance of levain, the wild culture that's made from the flour itself. Roger used to tell them that, from a nutritional point of view, "Yeast is the enemy," so they are very rigorous about using their secret-recipe levain.

As we chat, local folk drop by to pick up their bread. Ron, a Vermont transplant, goes off with a loaf of multi-grain, telling me: "This is real, artisan bread. I moved here to be closer to La Boulange." A woman who had picked up La Boulange kamut bread in Vancouver sent Jean an email when she got home: "Where's your outlet in Manhattan?"

La Boulange makes about 2,000 loaves of bread a week for outlets in Vancouver and the Lower Mainland, Victoria, Campbell River and on Saltspring, Hornby and Gabriola islands. Their Cinelli gas-fired, rotating-tray oven bakes up to 160 loaves at a time. It really is a 48-hour process to make each loaf, and John says they're taking expansion very slowly. Eventually, he would like to install a wood-fired oven to make some rustic loaves.

Qualicum Beach Farmers' Market

One Saturday morning in September, my parents and I visited the Qualicum Beach Farmers' Market with one thing on our minds: apples. In particular, Mother was after Cox's Orange Pippins, and she was soon rewarded at the East Cider Orchard table (East Cider Orchard is actually on Denman Island, but Kris Chand, president of the Qualicum market, tells me they often welcome vendors selling "things we don't have locally in order to widen our offerings").

Kris and his wife, Maria, operate Blue Heron Farm in Parksville, a 12-acre property with five to six acres in certified organic cultivation. Their story is an interesting one, in that Kris was a business consultant to Fortune 500 companies and Maria managed a chocolate shop in Vancouver's tony Kerrisdale neighbourhood when they decided to spring from the rat race. Kris's family had farmed in India. He had spent his summers working in the Port Alberni mill while attending university, so moving to Vancouver Island to start a farm was "like coming home."

Kris laughs as he describes his former colleagues' reaction when they see him farming ("eyes roll"), but he and Maria have never been happier. He is quick to give Maria "all the credit" for the actual farming side of the operation; he organizes the distribution of their 40 to 45 crops to Granville Market's Zara Pasta Specialties, Heaven on Earth health-food store in Qualicum Beach, Cormie's Farm Market on the Island Highway near Parksville and through the Qualicum Beach Farmers' Market (where they sell nearly 75 percent of their produce).

While garlic is their largest crop, Kris tells me they "can't grow enough of things like fava beans, Tuscan onions, garlic scallions and mixed lettuce — people want variety and the specialty vegetables." This year, the Wickaninnish Inn's chef dropped by the farm, and The Pointe Restaurant is now a customer, receiving the Chands' just-picked squash, garlic, beets and leeks by daily courier.

I first met Kris when he chaired the Harvest Bounty Festival at Nanoose Edibles. He was a founding director of the Qualicum market and served as its vice-president for four years. What he likes about the market is that "it's exclusively a food market. All of our vendors are directly associated with food production."

While Mother focussed on apples and my father chatted to an old colleague from Victoria, I visited with Marilyn Mant and Tami Treit of RainBarrel

Farm, Beverley Child of Fore & Aft Foods, Barbara Ebell of Nanoose Edibles and Clarke Gourlay of Little Qualicum Cheeseworks. This is a lively, food-focussed market that gives customers a great taste of the variety and quality of food in the Oceanside area.

RainBarrel Farm

Mother and daughter Marilyn Mant and Tami Treit pick dahlias for four or five hours every Friday, in order to have enough bouquets for the Qualicum Farmers' Market on Saturday mornings. Whether they have 70 or 100 bouquets on their stall, they are quickly bought up.

Also on Fridays, they prepare beautiful baskets of fruits and vegetables from the farm for their brown-box customers. The baskets are so artistic that I was stopped in my tracks when I saw them at the Harvest Bounty Festival. They also supply the local Thrifty Foods and Quality Foods with their lettuce mix and other veggies.

When I visit Marilyn and her husband, Henry, on their 35-acre farm on the outskirts of Qualicum Beach, I can see that their exquisite produce comes from a long history of hard work. Henry's parents arrived in the Qualicum area from England in 1913 with very little money. Over the years, they slowly bought land, five acres at a time, until they had 150 acres.

Today, the Mants raise miniature horses, Muscovy ducks and hundreds of plants: 300 broccoli, 200 cabbage, 200 cauliflower and endless corn, beets, tomatoes, English cucumbers, zucchini, peppers, raspberries, strawberries and grapes. There are 700 dahlia plants, which Marilyn is getting ready to dig out for storage until next season.

The Mants have always farmed organically, but when Thrifty Foods said they'd buy a significant amount of produce if the Mants were officially certified, they went through the process. The soil and their farming practices were so exemplary that the certification process took less than a year. Like many farmers I've met, Marilyn would rather not have the cost and amount of paperwork that certification involves, but she is adamant that her family eat organics. "I've got a grandchild," she tells me, "so I'm not going to grow food with tons of junk on it."

Marilyn and Henry live in a most interesting home — their former hayloft. As we enter the house, Marilyn points to where the cows used to be milked. Local potter Larry Aguilar has recently moved into another house on the property and set up a studio for public visits.

Grapevine on the Bay at Genoa Bay supports local food producers and offers a spectacular view.

Rows of kiwi plants form part of this spectacular view from Kiwi Cove Lodge, near Ladysmith. Luckily, deer and birds have no interest in this fruit, and rabbits are deterred by chicken wire on the vine bottoms.

Chef John Grove is bringing back some of the classics at Page Point Inn, Ladysmith.

Rows upon rows of nutritional greens at Nanoose Edibles — certified organic in 1997.

Sandy and Eric McLean tell it like it is at McLean's Specialty Foods in Nanaimo: "If we don't have it, you don't need it."

Secret-recipe levain loaves baking at La Boulange Organic Breads, Qualicum Beach.

Grilled lamb sirloin with green peppercorn demi-glace at Martine's Bistro in Comox.

Sieffert's is a favourite weekly stop of Chef Marcus Aartsen of Martine's Bistro.

Master cheesemaker Paul Sutter and assistant Haiden Smith at Natural Pastures Cheese Company in Courtenay.

Head chef Debra Fontaine among the garden delights at Hollyhock retreat centre on Cortes Island.

The gardens at Hollyhock have been looked after for over 20 years by head gardener Nori Fletcher, using the biodynamic/French intensive (BFI) method.

Clayoquot Organics, near Tofino, supplies top local restaurants with produce. The gardens are run by Melanie MacLeod.

Meet Puddle Jumper, the new buck at Westerly Wynds Farm near Ucluelet.

Artie and Lisa Ahier at their Sobo Global Cuisine catering cart in Tofino.

A beautiful banquet table at The Wickaninnish Inn, between Ucluelet and Tofino.

Chef Andrew Springett pleases all the senses at The Pointe Restaurant in The Wickaninnish Inn near Tofino.

Situated on a rocky point surrounded by water on three sides, The Wickaninnish Inn offers direct access to spectacular Chesterman Beach.

DENMAN ISLAND

Bien Tostado Custom Coffee Roasting

Over and over again, delicious food and drink surface where one might least expect them. I'd enjoyed Bien Tostado coffee beans in Denman Island Chocolate's rich espresso chocolate bar in Victoria, and then in a cappuccino at the Cowppuccino Café on Denman Island while waiting for a ferry to Hornby Island. When I finally had some time to spend on Denman, I was determined to find the roaster of this wonderful organic java.

Elaine Head's story began in Colorado where she met her future husband, Colombian-born Steven Carballeira. Steve's grandfather was a coffee broker in New York, who introduced the lad to good coffee at an early age. When his grandfather passed away, Steve inherited his old German coffee roaster.

By this time, the couple had married. Steve missed living by the ocean, and Elaine wanted to live in Canada, so they headed out to find "home." They chose Denman Island and began playing around with that coffee roaster. Says Elaine: "We had no intention of going into business, but one thing led to another."

Now, two years later, they are roasting over 6,000 pounds of organic Colombian coffee annually. Steve calls their business "a nano-roastery," in deference to the larger, but hardly huge, micro-roasteries. Elaine says they had three goals when they started out: they wanted to roast wonderful-tasting coffee; they wanted to roast only organic beans; and they wanted to have personal contact with their customers, whether restaurants or individuals.

Elaine had been turned on to organics when her daughter developed sensitivities to food additives. She claims her child's health improved 100 percent through eating organic food, and she is now delighted that her grandchildren are being raised in the same way. She is concerned about the health of people who are growing crops with pesticides, and is determined not to handle any coffee beans that haven't been grown pesticide-free.

She tells me that they "don't want to be Nabob"; they want to stay small and high quality. Elaine keeps a record of every coffee that her customers buy, along with their comments and suggestions.

Coffee Pie

Serves 8. The filling is like pudding — rich and creamy. This pie will satisfy any coffee maven's craving.

1/4 c	flour	60 ml
1/8 tsp	salt	0.6 ml
2/3 c	sugar	160 ml
1 c	very strong coffee	240 ml
1 c	milk	240 ml
2	egg yolks	2
2 tbsp	butter	30 ml
1	plain or nut pie shell, baked	1
2 c	whipped cream	480 ml
1	square semi-sweet chocolate	1

In a heavy saucepan whisk together the flour, salt and sugar; add coffee and milk and mix well. Cook over low heat until thickened, stirring constantly. Quickly stir one cup of hot mixture into beaten egg yolks and return mixture to saucepan to continue cooking. Stir while cooking one minute longer. Add butter and cool. Pour into pie shell and cool completely. When the pie is cool, cover with whipped cream and grate chocolate over top.

Bien Tostado roasts only seven certified organic Arabica Latin American coffees; Mesa comes from beans grown on a plantation on a Colombian mesa (an old, flat-topped mountain). All are mountain- and shade-grown. Two of the coffees are exported directly by small grower co-ops, which enable the growers to negotiate their own prices.

Elaine ships coffee throughout North America. They supply one customer's Caribbean-based yachts, and many individuals order regularly from New York, Colorado and California. British Columbia restaurants as far as the Queen Charlotte Islands brew their beans, and a Fanny Bay kayak-adventure company takes Bien Tostado along on its 10-day paddling and gourmet-food excursions around the islands.

Steve continues to work as a hydro-geologist, doing mainly environmental work. Elaine, who is now a lifetime away from her career as a construction manager for university and college laboratories, has never been happier, roasting small-batch fresh coffee on their 10-acre apple and plum orchard near Chickadee Lake.

Cowppuccino Café

The Cowppuccino Café came into view at exactly the right time for an organic Bien Tostado java before I boarded the ferry to Hornby Island. It's a little caravan with a deck, situated in Gravelly Bay. The café attracts the ferry crowd, cyclists and many locals who make a regular stop for coffee, freshly baked muffins and brownies and lunch items like tacos made with veggies from the nearby farms.

Owner Evelyn Martins grew up on a ranch in California's Salinas Valley, and tells me she became a property owner on Denman Island 17 years ago "because of a ghost!" She had been visiting Expo '86, and came over to Vancouver Island to get away from the crowds. While staying at the Qualicum College Inn, she lost her car keys and was forced to spend an extra day there. She blames the inn's famous ghost for the loss of the keys, but thanks it for allowing her to tarry longer and discover the Gulf Islands. When she came to Denman, she bought a 67-acre waterfront farm close to the ferry terminal.

Evelyn and her daughter-in-law opened the Cowppuccino Café four years ago because "you couldn't even get a glass of water while waiting for the ferry," and it has been a popular seasonal meeting spot ever since. She has plans to open an eco-retreat at Driftwood Farms in the next year or so. A cancer survivor, she wants to "share what I've learned about nutrition, spiritual healing and alternative medicine" with people who could benefit.

Denman Island Chocolate

Ruth and Daniel Terry WWOOFed their way around Europe and the interior of British Columbia, got turned on to organics, and finally settled on Denman Island. Like many Gulf Islanders, Daniel worked a variety of jobs, including recycling-depot manager, firefighter and carpenter.

Ruth holds a master's degree in English from Cambridge University. Four years ago, she made vegan truffles (no cream or butter) for the island's annual Christmas craft fair, and people went crazy for them. Having sourced high-quality organic chocolate from Belgium, hazelnuts and raspberries from the Fraser Valley's In Season Farms, fair-traded Nicaraguan coffee and pure orange and mint essences from England, Daniel began to develop the ultimate organic chocolate bar. He is a self-taught chocolatier and marketer, who clearly thrives on the business side of things. As Ruth, who continues to make truffles for special orders, says: "He likes selling chocolate and I like giving it away."

Their goal is to become a complete "bean-to-bar" chocolate factory, but for now, they're working feverishly to produce 1,350 bars a day, many for seriously addicted customers like myself.

The Denman Island Chocolate factory is not open to the public, but its chocolate bars are available at over 200 retailers on Vancouver Island.

Denman Island Farmers' Market

Anne de Cosson of East Cider Orchard is a big promoter of the Denman Island Farmers' Market. She recently wrote to tell me that "our tiny market grew in stature this summer and we hope to keep growing." I was keen to mention it in this second edition as many Vancouver Island growers tell me that folks now arrive at their local farmers' markets with *An Edible Journey* in hand.

The Denman market is held on Saturday mornings at the Old School Centre to coincide with the on-site recycling depot's hours of operation. It reminds me of Saturdays on Galiano Island, when I would regularly drop off the week's recyclables before visiting their seasonal market in the community centre on Sturdies Bay Road. On the islands, it's important to remember that the markets aren't just about shopping for fruit and veggies; they're also essential social meeting places for islanders, many of whom live in some degree of isolation during the week.

Anne says: "The original Old School was built in the early 1900s and was used continuously until the 1980s when it had the distinction of being one of the oldest two-room schoolhouses still in operation." A new school building replaced it in 1989, and the old one now houses the market, the recycling depot, a women's centre and a meeting room.

At the market, you'll find East Cider Orchard, Windy Marsh Farm and the Denman Island Fruit and Nut Farm represented, and you can expect an "increase in size and variety" every year. Anne says: "We plan on more baked goodies, Denman specialty produce and products, crafts, music and kids' stuff."

East Cider Orchard

The sun is just beginning to dip in the sky as Anne de Cosson and I sit on her back patio, watching a promenade of peacocks through the orchard (seriously!) and sipping apple cider from the second pressing of her Gravenstein apples. Anne was happy to take a break from painting an upstairs bedroom to chat with a curious urbanite.

She and her husband, Larry Berg, had worked at Capilano College in Vancouver, travelled through India and then had the chance to house-sit for friends on Denman Island. Anne had been raised on her father's homegrown vegetables, and she was always aware of the marked contrast between garden-fresh and store-bought.

The couple lost no time finding a property on this very peaceful island. They bought their orchard in 1979 when it was nothing but a fallen-down house and 25 apple trees. They got together with two other families and formed a co-operative called Apple Lane Orchards. The co-op seemed like a good idea then, but over time, the families found differences in their growing philosophies, and the de Cosson/Berg contingent struck out on their own at East Cider Orchard.

It was always important to Anne to grow organically, so theirs is a fully certified operation, and all the juice, or soft cider as they call it, is pasteurized. Anne says they never know how much money the orchard will generate, as organic farming is much more dependent on weather and other forces of

Crabapple Jelly

ANNE DE COSSON, EAST CIDER ORCHARD

I bought a big bag of crabapples from the Cobble Hill Farmers' Market and enjoyed making Anne's jelly. It's the perfect accompaniment to pork and poultry.

Place about 6 lbs (2.75 kg) of whole, washed crabapples (Anne likes the Dolgo crabs) in a large kettle and cover with water. Boil until the apples explode and the water turns pink. Remove to a jelly bag, and let the juice drip out. Measure 5 cups (1.2 L) of the juice and combine it with 4 cups (1 L) of sugar in a large saucepan. Boil the mixture for about 10 minutes or until it reaches the jam stage (220°F). Pour it into sterilized rubber-ringed jars and let them sit until the jelly is set.

nature than conventional farming. They have 1,000 trees from which they make between 300 and 900 gallons of cider per year.

They take the apples by the truckload to Bill LePage, of The Cider Press in Courtenay. Bill presses it into four- and two-litre jugs, and then it's sold at Vancouver's Granville Island and East Vancouver markets and at the Courtenay Farmers' Market.

At harvest time, the whole family pitches in, together with 8 to 10 WWOOFers. As Anne says: "The world comes to work in our orchard, so it's been a really interesting experience for our family. We've had lots of workers from the Czech Republic when it opened up."

Jacquie's Ices

In 1970 Jacquie Barnett and her then-husband, having built a boat in their Chicago backyard, set out for three and a half years at sea. "We were anti-war protestors," she tells me. They had a friend on Denman Island and sailed on up. Thirty-three years later, Jacquie has a thriving ice-cream business on the island.

She started with cattle, but "it gets very hot on my side [the west side] of the island. It's hot until ten o'clock at night," so she was looking for a cooler occupation. She spotted a 1957 white Dodge truck in Courtenay one day and thought it would make an excellent ice-cream truck. Fifty dollars later, the truck was hers. "It overheated all the time, so I would put ice cubes on the carburetor." Jacquie started making ice cream for local fairs, driving it around in the Dodge. Sometimes she had leftover stock on her hands, so Jacquie's Ices at the ferry to Hornby Island was established 20 years ago. It's a cute trailer with big photos of Einstein enjoying an ice cream cone just like you and me.

Jacquie picks the wild plums and rhubarb from her property and adds them, along with chocolate, vanilla and other gourmet ingredients, to ice cream. She makes her own giant waffle cones, and "people just love them." She says she loves to watch tourists recharge on the island. People buy her ice cream, then sit on a rock and look out to sea. "It's a great form of meditation," she tells me, and I agree as I devour a rhubarb-chocolate double scoop (no worries: I'll work it off writing!).

Windy Marsh Farm

The contrast between the strip malls of any modern city and the back roads of any Gulf Island is startling. The malls offer a parade of predictable fast-food magnets — different city, but same fatty smorgasbord. Rural roads produce erratic offerings — a farmstand around the bend that only sells beans and flowers, and then nothing for 10 kilometres. Ah, but the unpredictability of snacking from the back-road farmstands is the whole point. It's an adventure, and every trip is a clean canvas for the intrepid hunter-gatherer.

On a late summer afternoon, my husband and I were touring the back roads of Denman Island, enjoying the scenery, but feeling peckish. Up ahead, we glimpsed a farmstand. Beans and flowers? Well, yes and no. The Windy Marsh farmstand, a labour of love by Bob and Velda Parsons, has a range of produce to convert any hot-blooded, fast-food junkie. We dive right into a basket of sun-warmed raspberries.

The Parsons grow 100 percent organically, and Velda says they strive for variety: big, cream-coloured vegetable marrows, dill weed for a nickel a stem, shiny fresh snow peas, just-picked red raspberries, parsley, kale, beet thinnings, zucchini, artichokes, peppers, cucumbers, tomatoes, fat shelling peas, potatoes and lettuce. Their chickens produce enough eggs for, as the sign says: "one dozen per family, please."

She and Bob, a boat builder, bought the farm 12 years ago. They had been living on a float home in Genoa Bay, but says Velda: "It was in danger of sinking from the number of plants we had growing on it — especially tropical plants." A New Zealander, Bob has always grown tropicals and today coaxes papayas and bananas in his greenhouse.

Velda told me they looked around the Gulf Islands, and settled on the 10-acre Denman Island property because it was located next to a marsh, and "water is essential for growing veg." It's proven time and again to have been a wise choice. They bought the property with "every cent we had," cleared three acres, and have learned to grow what suits the soil.

Velda says they grow organically because it is "morally correct," but, like many local producers who sell to people who know them, they feel no need to certify. They grow primarily for their farmgate, and sell any surplus at the in-season Saturday morning farmers' market held next to the elementary school.

Hornby Island

The Flower Lady

Anna MacKay's beautiful smile radiates out from behind bunches of red, yellow and fuchsia gerberas in French florists' vases. I could be on South Granville, but wait — these flowers actually have fragrance. Anna and I chat as she nibbles on her lunch of pakoras from another vendor's stand.

Anna MacKay's radiant smile and gorgeous posies light up her stall at the Hornby Island Farmers' Market.

She tells me there were 300 residents on the island when she moved here 30 years ago from Ontario, looking for an alternative lifestyle. She has raised three children on the island, and the population has grown along with them — to about 1,200 permanent residents.

Like many growers, she is concerned that "people don't remember what good food tastes like." She and several others started the market 12 years ago so they wouldn't have to sell at the farmgate. She enjoys being in direct contact with the buyers, and thinks "the most positive thing that could happen [in our food-distribution system] would be to cut out the middle man, cut out the transportation." Like many others, she is concerned about the food miles, and advocates eating only what we grow locally.

Hornby Island Co-op

No visit to Hornby is complete without a stop at the co-op, the island's heartbeat, where shopping for groceries and supplies plays second fiddle to picking up your mail, checking out the bulletin board and meeting up with friends. It's the most social grocery store I know.

Produce manager Sue Horner, a former sign-language interpreter from Vancouver, is unpacking organic veggies, and stops to tell me where they all come from. The store buys a lot through Vancouver's Wildwest and Thrifty Foods' wholesale distributor, but when a resident arrives at the back door with a bag of plums, they're also set out for sale. The result is an impressive range of organic fruit and vegetables and a good selection of dry goods. Bread is baked fresh daily by the island's Cardboard House Bakery.

This is the best place to pick up picnic supplies before heading out for the day to Tribune Bay or Ford Cove.

Hornby Island Farmers' Market

Every market has its own special flavour. To me, the Hornby Island Farmers' Market is a vibrant statement of how things could be if the world didn't encroach. Certainly, it has that latter-day hippie look and feel, but once you've met the vendors and sampled their wares, you will appreciate the quality of food grown with great understanding and lovingly prepared. The local musicians and an exotic belly dancer add an air of festivity.

Savoie Farm

Chatting with Andrea and David at the Savoie farmstand in the market led me to one of the most magical flower and vegetable gardens on the west coast. "You'll find Elaine at the farm today because she's setting up for to-night's art exhibit," said David. I will always remember my journey to the farm at the end of Carmichael Road, how the sea seemed to rise up and meet me when I stopped the car.

I found Elaine Savoie in her house on the property, cleaning up for 150 guests who were coming that evening for her annual art exhibition. The house originally had no electricity or running water, and she has only recently installed a phone. Her paintings are a unique style of chicken iconography, which has been well received by the artistic community and, not surprisingly, questioned by the religious sector. She welcomes me like an old friend, and doesn't hesitate to take me out to see the gardens and meet her sister and gardening partner, Mary.

We cross a nondescript field before I stop in my tracks at the first sight of their garden. I cannot believe that, just six years ago, this was also a field. Today there are vast plantings of veggies and herbs: squashes, basil, thyme, blueberries, hot peppers, onions, asparagus, strawberries and more, mostly grown in raised beds to keep the roots out of the water. There are rows upon rows of cutting flowers like dahlias, gladioli, bachelor's button

(Mary's favourite) and statice. On one section, local basket maker Alistair Hesseltine grows willow for his craft. To complete the picture, there are a dozen Hereford cows just nonchalantly wandering about. Mary and I walk over to the property's big pond, from which they run a drip-irrigation system. When the pond gets low, they cut the watering to every second day.

The farm was started in the 1920s by the girls' grandfather, Leo Savoie, who came from France with his Métis wife, looking for paradise. He certainly found it: 80 waterfront acres on the north side of the island. Their father continued the tradition of growing his family's food. When he passed away, the land was divided into two 40-acre parcels. The girls, with their brother, Remi, hold title to both sections, and their closest neighbour is a cousin who operates a cattle ranch.

Elaine paints and tends the vegetable beds. Mary lives close by. She is the custodian at the local school, but her passion is the flowers. In summer, bunches of her fresh and dried flowers are sold at the market and also from a stand across from the Cardboard House Bakery. In the cooler months, Mary and her mother make dried flower sachets.

Mary tells me she started growing organic because she wanted to buy organic strawberries at a reasonable price. The farm offers fair prices, particularly on bulk orders over five pounds.

The Sushi Lady

Tania Hale has always gravitated to the island lifestyle. She spent years on Cortes before moving in the early 1990s to Hornby, where she says there is "freedom, but still an economy." She wanted to be part of the market, which she views as a wonderful creative outlet. She loves meeting the shoppers and catching up with fellow vendors every Wednesday and Saturday.

On market days, she rises early to pick herbs and veggies from her own organic garden. Then it's into the kitchen where she loves "making a big mess." The results of that mess are little jewel boxes of exquisite sushi, so beautiful that I looked at mine for several hours before eating it.

Tania makes different kinds of sushi every week, but she always has a vegetarian option. She decided on sushi because "it's fun to make," and she always has a good response. With a glass of her cool lemonade, this west coast foodie experience rates very high on my list.

Tania also produces a useful map of the island that can be purchased at the co-op.

North Island

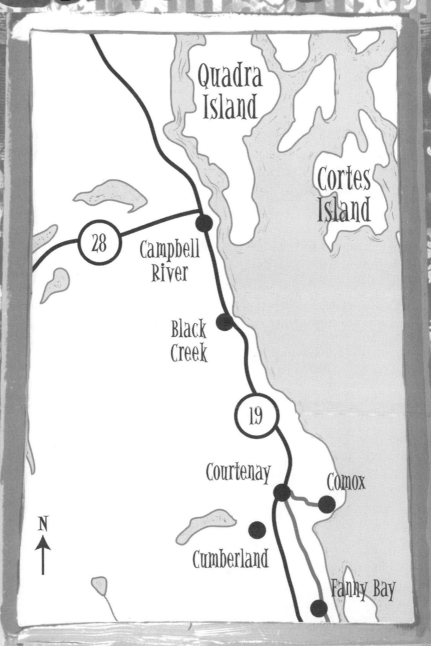

Quadra Island

Cortes Island

28

Campbell River

Black Creek

19

Courtenay

Comox

Cumberland

Fanny Bay

N

o an urbanite like myself, the North Island means the Comox Valley. Of course Vancouver Island extends farther north, but let's just say that will be another book. Immersing oneself in the valley itself and northern islands of Quadra and Cortes provides a wealth of foodie experiences, from the best doughnuts on the planet to a cheese factory that could be in the Swiss Alps to a Gulf Island farmstay that I wish every city family could experience.

In fact, in the last couple of years this area has become a significant culinary destination. Read on, and also refer to *EAT* magazine's regular updates on its farms and feasts.

BUCKLEY BAY

Fanny Bay Oysters Seafood Shop

Debbie Prowse has managed the Fanny Bay Oysters Seafood Shop since it opened ten years ago. She tells me the popular store was the brainchild of Glen and Sharon Haddon, who "had a vision for a full-service seafood place, where previously, people just sold what they caught from wherever they were." The couple's parent company, Fanny Bay Oysters Ltd., has operated a processing, packaging and distribution plant in nearby Fanny Bay for 20 years. Besides supplying the shop, they export to Europe, Asia, the United States and across Canada.

Breaded Oysters

FANNY BAY OYSTERS SEAFOOD SHOP

Serves 4. Often the simplest preparations are the tastiest.

16 oz	shucked Fanny Bay oysters	454 g
3/4 c	white flour	170 g
1	egg	1
2 tbsp	lemon juice, whisked together with egg	30 ml
2 c	finely crushed cracker crumbs	454 g
1/4 c	butter	57 g
1/4 c	cooking oil	59 ml

In a pot on your stove, cover oysters with water and gently boil for 3 to 5 minutes. Drain, cool and proceed. In separate bowls, dredge the oysters in the flour, shaking off the excess. Then dip the oysters into the egg mixture and roll them in the cracker crumbs. In a large non-stick frying pan over medium heat, melt the butter with the oil. Cook the coated oysters until they are a nice rich brown, then turn them over to finish. Serve hot.

The store sells vast quantities of fresh and individually quick frozen (IQF) shucked Pacific oysters and live banquet (shucked, on the half shell) and IQF Manila clams. The Fanny Bay oysters, the *Crassostrae gigas,* are "firm oysters — very salty, very sweet, with a cucumber flavour and a thick, fluted shell that is easy to open." A couple of years ago, the shop put out an oyster cookbook after running a competition among their loyal customers. The oyster recipe here is from that book. Anne Harty, who works in the shop, told me: "The difference with this recipe is that the oysters are boiled first, which plumps and firms them and smoothes out the after-bite."

Depending on the season, you'll find fresh or frozen skate, snapper, ling cod, sole, tuna, ahi tuna, halibut, halibut cheeks, swimming scallops, clams, mussels and salmon. Debbie says that while they "focus on shellfish," she is "able to pick the best of other fish and fish products from within the region." There are great takeaway-and-go-sit-on-the-beach finds like rice noodle wraps from Gold Phoenix Asian Foods in Courtenay and Yama Sushi from Black Creek, which are delivered to the shop daily. There is cold- and hot-smoked salmon from Hornby Island Seafood and house-made chowders, fish pâtés and smoked oysters.

When I visited the shop, there were a couple of 20-something lads from Vancouver stocking up on fresh oysters for the weekend. As Anne loaded up a large plastic bag of ice with the banquet-style crustaceans, they told her it was their "first time." So she added a tub of spicy cocktail sauce and we all told them to enjoy themselves.

CUMBERLAND

Cumberland Village Bakery

Since I last visited Cumberland, John Auchterlonie had retired and the bakery that bore his family's name for 80 years sat vacant for many months. With no warm, sticky, yeasted doughnuts coming out of the oven in the early mornings, there was no question that depression and sugar withdrawal had settled over this quaint little town. Then along came David Murray and Megan

Sommers, two townsfolk who worked as tree planters but had the Dubrulle's baking program behind them. They realized they were "taking over a business with a large reputation," but have proven themselves up to the task.

Happily, David and Megan inherited the original doughnut recipe from Mr. Auchterlonie, but the new Cumberland Village Bakery is about a lot more

David Murray took time to chat with me after his morning rush.

than doughnuts. "We want this place to have a real community feel," says David, as we chat on the whimsical twig bench produced by local furniture-maker Michael Chesters. And community feel it does have. Local residents stream in for the 10 types of bread from artisan sourdough rye to roasted garlic and feta; for the raspberry and blueberry cream cheese Danish (it's a good thing that I have to drive three hours to buy these or I'd be eating them every day!); the almond croissants with ground almond filling; the green onion and cheddar and black olive and feta bread rolls; and of course those quintessential doughnuts.

I arrived one drizzly morning as the next batch of doughnuts was proofing. It had been two years since I'd eaten one and I couldn't wait! David says the secret is hard to define. Sure, they're handmade in small batches (just 15 at a time) and they're hand-dipped in sugar, but "it's a pretty standard recipe." It used to be that folks queued to buy them, because when they were gone, which was usually by 9:00 A.M., they were gone. Today, David and Megan make sure that doughnuts are coming out of the oven all day long to keep the sugar hounds happy.

David tells me that he and Megan have "lots of ideas and inspiration," and will gradually introduce more artisan breads and pastries. They still want to satisfy the local market with classics like the sandwich loaves and butter dinner rolls, but have also introduced organic grains and vegan specialties to tantalize taste buds. Also on offer are their house-made soups, meat pies, sausage rolls and local cheeses — great news for those of us whose edible journeys take us to this sweet little town.

Hazelmere Farms

When Lijen and Sherlene Hua emigrated from Taiwan three and a half years ago, they took their time finding the perfect farm and the perfect crop. They had never farmed — he was a civil engineer and she had worked for a consumer co-op back home — but they knew they "wanted to be close to nature and do something we really believe in."

They finally came upon 63 acres near Cumberland, where they are creating a certified organic, self-sustaining farm. They raise chickens, ducks and sheep and are growing Oriental vegetables including burdock and cucumbers, as well as garlic. Their number-one crop is wasabi, which I first sampled at the Harvest Bounty Festival in September. Sherlene encourages me to visit in the spring when her acre of wasabi "looks its most lovely." It is a mass of little white flowers, which, along with the entire plant, are edible. The leaves and flowers are slightly spicy and make lively additions to salad.

Wasabi takes at least two years to harvest, so Sherlene and Lijen are only just coming into their first big marketing year. They already sell their wasabi to several local restaurants and Edible Island grocery in Courtenay and will be expanding their distribution to other locations on the island.

COURTENAY/ BLACK CREEK

Edible Island Whole Foods Market

Another inviting organic grocery store is Edible Island, a shop that makes me want to become a resident of Courtenay. Begun 22 years ago by

three entrepreneurial local women, Sue Tupper, Sue Clark and Jackie Somerville, it draws appreciative customers from all over the Comox Valley. It's also the perfect stop for your picnic supplies when you're touring in that area. I picked up some La Boulange bread, Natural Pastures fresh curds and organic cherry tomatoes for a picnic.

The owners came from diverse working backgrounds: the recording industry, graphic arts and private- and public-sector accounting. Jackie says they share "a passion for healthy, clean food and a concern for the environmental impact of mass production." Their shelves are lined with between 50 and 75 percent organic foodstuffs, and they "choose organically grown and non-GMO certified products whenever possible."

Hot Chocolates

I had the good fortune to visit Hot Chocolates mere hours before Valentine's Day when the store was a press of Cupidean fervour as people happily queued to buy sweets for their sweethearts. Passing through the doorway, I was hit with an explosion of red wrapping, chocolates stacked high and intoxicating aromas. Naturally, I swooned. Shop manager Arlene Wallace and long-time employee Ruth Vanderlinden, whose Swiss heritage rightfully makes her "the shop's chocolate critic," were quick to revive me with a steaming mug of the secret-recipe hot chocolate and two bonbons: a classic truffle and an organic Australian orange slice dipped in dark chocolate. A regular customer, entering the shop and eyeing my indulgences, nodded approvingly.

Hot Chocolates is one of those small, family-run establishments whose success we can somehow all feel pleased about (must be the theobromine and phenylethylamine in chocolate that imparts those benevolent feelings). It was started nearly 20 years ago by Deanna Gagnon and her daughter, Sherry Marshall-Bruce, and is now run by Sherry and her husband, Jorden Marshall. It has grown to 32 employees, but still manages to retain its original philosophy of handmaking small batches of chocolates and truffles using no preservatives.

Once I'd revived, Arlene gave me a requisite hairnet and invited me to view the "factory," a large and spotlessly clean room next door to the shop where all the chocolate-making, packaging and shipping takes place. I was reminded of a tour earlier this year of the famous Peyrano chocolate factory in Turin, and realized, even though I now understand "how they get the caramel in the bar," that there is still a mysterious aspect to chocolate that will always make these behind-the-scenes tours exciting for me.

My love affair with Hot Chocolates continued a couple of days later when I "coerced" my husband into sampling a few more sweets that I'd brought back from my edible journey: a raspberry heart filled with buttercream and raspberry confit; the Berry Quartet taste expolosion, a milk chocolate truffle made with four different berries, coated in dark chocolate and dusted with dried berry powder; a *fleur de sel* caramel that reminded us of the French patisseries; and the Asian-inspired Ko Chang, a chocolate-dipped truffle of coconut milk, lemongrass and kaffir lime that had us wishing we could buy such hedonistic pleasures closer to home. An extensive line of sugar-free chocolates is also available. My diabetic father proclaimed the chocolate-dipped ginger and orange creams "delish."

Sweet indulgences are not limited to *Theobroma cacao* here. In summer, there are 24 house-made gelati flavours to choose from, all made with special Italian equipment and containing "as many fresh local organic fruits, berries and herbs as we can get ahold of." I sampled blood orange, strawberry made with quark and probably the best maple walnut ice cream ever. Hot Chocolates is the place to treat yourself to an authentic milkshake, tea, organic El Café Negro coffee or one of those superb hot chocolate beverages (Arlene did allow it's made with the shop's dark chocolate, but her "recipe" stopped there!).

As I reluctantly went to leave, an American woman, buying chocolates for her Courtenay hosts, anxiously asked, "Do you deliver to the States?" and seemed to relax instantly when told: "All the time." Cupid must be thinking, like Puck, "what fools [for love and chocolate] these mortals be!"

Natural Pastures Cheese Company

Third-generation Comox Valley dairy farmer Edgar Smith was the former president of the local co-operative creamery, the oldest association of its kind in British Columbia. When the co-op was sold to a conglomerate, he was concerned. He wanted to ensure that the industry continued to be viable in his community and, most importantly, that it employed local people. He decided to make cheese.

With help from his wife, Mary Ann Hyndman Smith, and their partner, Rick Adams, Edgar founded the Natural Pastures Cheese Company just a year ago. They brought in a Swiss-trained cheese master, Paul Sutter, whose artisan cheeses have already gained national acclaim. Their Comox Camembert, Boerenkaas and Cumin Seed Verdelait were awarded gold medals at the prestigious Canadian Cheese Grand Prix.

I visited Edgar and Mary Ann, wanting to know the secret behind their seemingly overnight success. It was no surprise to discover that the secret was passion for their product, good planning and plain hard work. They are also devoted to their local market. Edgar says demand for their cheeses far outweighs supply at the moment, but they are committed to filling local orders first. Mary Ann, who takes their cheese to the Courtenay Farmers' Market, says she is touched by people with tears in their eyes who thank her for bringing them "a taste of their childhood."

No product is more likely to generate those tears than their fresh cheese curds, which fly off the grocers' shelves. Handmade curds are noshed straight from the packet, but many people use them to make the popular Quebecois dish, poutine. The curds are sprinkled over a plate of piping-hot french fries (organic potatoes, please!), then smothered with hot gravy.

Mary Ann was a caterer in Vancouver before marrying Edgar and moving to the valley. She brings a discriminating palate to the company, and tells me she is inspired by different ingredients and how they come together to create west coast fusion flavours. She works with Paul to develop the company's original cheese recipes. Case in point is the Wasabi Banzai. As I taste it with Mary Ann, she

explains why I'm enjoying it so much: "First, you are hit by the wasabi, then the fresh garlic, and finally the rounded, curvaceous flavour of the ginger." Whatever the design, the outcome is addictive, and I'm not surprised that this is another cheese she can't keep on the shelves.

Once I'm appropriately attired in a white "spacesuit" and gumboots, Edgar takes me on a fascinating tour of the cheese factory. The simple story is that the milk comes directly to the back door from their own 1930s, heritage dairy farm in Comox. It is immediately pasteurized. One side of the factory is dedicated to producing semi-hard cheese; the other to soft.

We first enter the semi-hard production area, where the pasteurized milk is placed in a 4,000-litre vat. The curds are separated from the whey, pressed into moulds and placed in a brine solution for two days. They are then cured in the aging room at an average temperature of 11°C for a period appropriate to their type (from six to eight weeks, or up to 10 months). After the aging process, some of the cheeses are also waxed.

Pasta Primavera with Garlic and Chive Verdelait

MARY ANN HYNDMAN SMITH, NATURAL PASTURES CHEESE COMPANY

Serves 4. This recipe makes the ultimate family dinner, served with a healthy salad and freshly baked baguette.

8 oz	rotini, twists, spirals or penne	225 g
1 tbsp	olive oil	15 ml
2	cloves garlic, minced	2
1/8 tsp	red pepper sauce (such as Tabasco)	0.6 ml
2	small zucchini, sliced	2
2	small yellow squash, sliced	2
1 c	thinly sliced carrot	240 ml
1	medium red onion, cut into eighths	1
1/4 c	chicken broth	60 ml
1/4 c	lightly packed fresh basil leaves, chopped	60 ml
1/2 c	oil-packed sun-dried tomatoes, chopped	120 ml
1 c	grated Natural Pastures Garlic and Chive Verdelait Cheese	240 ml
1/4 c	chopped fresh parsley	60 ml

Prepare pasta according to package directions; drain. In a medium skillet, heat oil and garlic. Stir in pepper sauce, add zucchini, squash, carrots and onion and stir-fry until tender crisp, about five minutes. Add chicken broth and simmer one minute. In a large serving bowl, toss together pasta, vegetables, basil and sun-dried tomatoes. Garnish with the grated cheese and parsley.

Across the way, the soft cheeses are made in smaller batches. They take less time to make and age, but need more attention. The cheeses are formed, left to drain, then turned over and drained again. When dry enough, they are placed in a brine bath for just 30 minutes before being set out to age for up to two weeks at 15° to 16°C. It is at this stage that the trademark white moulds develop on the outside of the cheeses. In the final stage, the Bries and Camemberts cure at 6°C. Natural Pastures buys a special paper from France to wrap the soft cheeses in. Edgar says the paper quality is critical: one layer has microscopic holes that allow the cheese to breathe and the other provides hygienic protection.

Edgar is committed to mastering his craft. He tells me how deeply satisfying it is to see the milk come directly from his cows, "a still-living biological system that produces the wonderful taste of the cheese." For him, the cheese-making "completes the whole cycle of the farmer in touch with the craftsman and the consumer."

Before I leave, he proffers a sample of Sky Blue Cheddar, another successful example of contrasting flavours created by Mary Ann and made by Edgar and Paul. I savour the combined creaminess of the blue Stilton and the solidness of the white cheddar, and realize how much the couple's commitment to make the highest quality handcrafted cheese is reflected in their products. When, several weeks later, I serve only Natural Pastures cheeses o n my cheese tray, friends think I've been around the world to please their palates. Natural Pastures won several awards at Toronto's Royal Agricultural Winter Fair in 2004.

On Line Farms

Price Lang was a househusband in Royston before his life took an interesting turn. Having raised "two great kids," he remarried, moved to Abbotsford, and established On Line Farms. "This was long before the whole online Internet thing," he explains. "Our farm was located on Zero Avenue, which basically is the line between Canada and the US border. We really were 'on line'!"

Price's wife, Marjan de Jong, draws on her Dutch dairy-farming background and had previously worked with Susan Davidson of Vancouver's renowned Glorious Garnishes. She is a natural grower. Price, on the other hand, had no previous farming experience, but they managed to hit the gourmet vegetable market at the right time, and, in 1988, their farm was the largest of its kind in the province.

So, how did On Line Farms end up moving to the Comox Valley? Price says they had concerns about the poor air and water quality in Abbotsford, so they drove around the valley looking for property. They chose 24 acres in Black Creek, just north of Courtenay. They grow veggies on five acres and pasture other people's cows on the rest of their land.

When they moved the farming operation from Vancouver, they wisely started small. The local restaurants were big supporters, particularly the fishing resorts. Price says it was fun hearing from the chefs that Bob Hope, Eric Clapton, Bill Gates, George Bush and many other visiting sport fishermen were dining on their gourmet vegetables.

Owners Marjan de Jong and Price Lang at their On Line Farms market.

I find Price taking a well-deserved break on his front porch. There are bunches of horsetail drying overhead that he will later make into a tea to spray on the greenhouse crops to prevent fungus. Living and working on the farm, he says he has learned to schedule breaks like these. He and Marjan have always believed that "you are what you eat." He says they choose organics personally because "it's the best and the healthiest food, the natural extension by our generation to get cleaner and more conscious, to find the ways and means to lead a healthier life."

He shows me the farm's Flowform, which they made themselves under licence through a biodynamic farm in Duncan. It's an intriguing sculptured series of vessels based on the principle that water rejuvenates itself through its own natural movements. The Flowform is fed by their own well. De Jong adds a concoction of camomile, oak bark, dandelion and other organic composts and they spray the water on their plants to promote larger and healthier produce. Price encourages me to stop and listen to the water flow, its steady rhythm sounding like a heartbeat.

Biodynamics is the next logical stage for On Line Farms, which is already certified Demeter, the highest international level of organic certification. The Demeter standards determine the methods for plant production, including such things as compost and preparation usage and the outlawing of genetically modified material.

On Line Farms' vegetables are for sale at their own farmstand, at Courtenay's Saturday farmers' market and through Thrifty Foods' wholesale distributor.

What is Biodynamic Farming?

It grew out of anthroposophy, the spiritual science articulated by Rudolf Steiner, an Austrian-born philosopher, in 1924. He had been approached by a group of European farmers trying to solve the problem of soil decline. His holistic approach to agriculture "notes the interrelationship of all kingdoms — mineral, plant, animal and human — and their intricate correspondence to the rhythms and activities of the larger cosmos."* Biodynamic farming follows Steiner's ideals of self-contained farms, community-supported agriculture, quality over quantity, treating the soil as a live element and close observation of nature.

*from *What is Biodynamics?* by Sherry Wildfeuer at www.biodynamics.com

Seaview Game Farm

It's just starting to sprinkle as I pull in to the 175-acre Seaview Game Farm, but rain doesn't dampen spirits here. The horse-drawn wagons keep taking visitors around this stunning acreage, stopping to visit the 400 fallow deer and petting-zoo residents. Inside the food store, Seaview's general manager and well-known chef, Michel Rabu, is answering questions about the many products on offer: various cuts of venison, lamb and chicken; a seasonal variety of herbs and veggies grown on the property; and his own special-recipe herb and berry vinegars and vinaigrettes. There are some intriguing spice mixtures including one with juniper berries that he is recommending to a man for cooking venison.

I tour the extensive vegetable garden with Dan, who has been gardening for 16 years, mainly on Cortes Island. He tells me that they are determined to protect people from pesticides, so they use only fish compost and their own chicken manure. The produce is used by the food store and sold at the seasonal Courtenay Farmers' Market. In the tomato greenhouse, we come across the farm's owner, Paul Pflager, quietly picking fruit. He takes one look

Sautéed Venison

Michel Rabu, Seaview Game Farm

 My husband, Clive, gets the credit for obtaining this recipe. Understandably tired of having me overcook his venison, he asked Chef Rabu for a foolproof preparation. Michel obliged, as we sat with him overlooking the vegetable gardens.

First, get your frying pan hot and add a tablespoon (15 ml) of olive oil. Sauté some finely chopped shallots and a few sliced mushrooms. Michel says he would choose chanterelles when they're in season, but morels, oyster or portobello work well. Sauté the vegetables until brown.

Add a couple of venison steaks or tenderloins to the pan. Sauté just two minutes each side — the worst thing is to overcook venison. Sprinkle with crushed black pepper and remove to warming oven.

Deglaze the pan with about 2 tbsp (30 ml) Madeira (Michel's preference), port, Cinzano or sherry, letting it reduce by about one-third (takes 4 to 5 minutes). Add 2 tbsp (30 ml) heavy cream and stir until the sauce is a rich, brown colour. Add 1 tsp (5 ml) butter to emulsify. Plate the venison and pour the sauce over.

at my open-toed sandals and, with a twinkle in his eye, warns me that no pesticides means more snakes and spiders.

I sit down with Michel to commiserate about how people are eating these days. Michel grew up on the family farm in Brittany. He was a top hairdresser when he first came to Canada, but after a trip to Vancouver Island with his father, he opened Gourmet by the Sea restaurant in Campbell River. "My father and I couldn't believe this place: oysters on the beach, watercress and chanterelles growing wild." After running the restaurant for 25 years, he sold it to his son, Daniel, who continues to operate it.

Paul proposed to his future wife in Michel's restaurant. Every time he came in after that, he kept asking Michel to "come and run his farm." Michel said only when he retired from the restaurant would he consider that, and the rest is history. Michel feels he has come full-circle now that he is back working on a farm.

He loves being part of this whole agricultural-tourism concept because he can educate people about what food should taste like. He's "fed up with what looks good but tastes terrible," so he ensures that the food store only stocks what's in season — there are no forced crops sold here.

We agree that it's discouraging to stand in a grocery store lineup and watch people spend more than they need to because they're buying so much processed food. Michel is now teaching weekend cooking classes for small groups in which he shows that it is actually cheaper to cook from scratch with organic ingredients. The cooking classes include Seaview accommodations.

Tita's Mexican Restaurant

I ran into Martin Metz in Portuguese Joe's where he was buying fish for his wife, Lisa's, 40th-birthday dinner, which he was preparing at home that evening. While I was sorry they wouldn't be on the line that night at their downtown Courtenay restaurant, Tita's, I was pleased to at least have a reservation at this popular spot that Lisa calls her "giant art project."

Named for Tita, the exuberant heroine in the novel *Like Water for Chocolate*, who "is born and raised in the kitchen and finds an outlet through cooking to express her powerful emotions," this deep yellow hacienda exudes South American *alegría de vivir*. Even before stepping into the cosy dining rooms (there are two), I linger in the remarkable organic gardens that surround them. An article about Tita's gardens in *Gardens West* magazine (June 2002) shows the proliferation that I can only imagine when I visit in January. Food crops including squash, purple cabbages, quince, fig, everbearing strawberries, calendulas, thyme, filigree-leaf fennel, jalapeño and Anaheim peppers, sunflowers, red amaranth and quinoa were carefully planted by Lisa so she and her cooks "wouldn't need to reach more than two feet in any direction" to access their ingredients. This garden is the palette of South American artwork, the hues that speak to hot climates and long, warm nights drinking tequila and dancing to mariachi bands. But perhaps I digress.

What's for supper? Heather Standish, the restaurant's manager, has "worked and eaten here almost every day for the past five years," and is exceptionally knowledgeable about Mexican food and its flavours (which in Mexican cuisine go deep, way deep, and tend to surprise one's palate from beginning to end). She settles me at the bar and suggests a starter of ceviche tostada made with snapper that has been cold-"cooked" in fresh-squeezed lime juice and tossed with the house pico de gallo salsa. It reminds me of those killer tacos made by Lisa Ahier at Sobo in Tofino and really awakens my taste buds, which have been focussed on North American cuisine for several days.

Another taco is topped with black beans (cooked without oil), pasilla chile and a mixture of local wild mushrooms seasoned with roasted garlic, feta cheese, red onions and cilantro. The combination is earthy and satisfying. I order guacamole and more taco chips and sample some of the sauces that are all made from scratch. Heather and I compare notes. Her favourite is the Olvera, created by Lisa in honour of Olvera Street in Los Angeles where "every second establishment serves it." It is a smooth and spicy sauce of avocados, tomatillos and roasted jalapeño that comes on cool and then packs a fiery punch; mine is the *mole de chabacano* made of apricots, onions and mulato and pasilla chilies, which usually envelops broiled wild boar chops from Twin Peaks Farm, but which I enjoy with chicken. Another couple of noteworthy sauces are the *mole rojo*, a classic mole with plantains and tomato, and *mole con pollo*, of chilies, onions, spices, nuts and chocolate, in which pasture-raised chicken thighs from Tanadice Farm are gently simmered.

Other Courtenay suppliers to Tita's menu include Natural Pastures Cheese Company, which custom-makes its Queso Fresco cheese, Greg of Eatmore Sprouts ("he's a chef turned gardener and I'm a gardener turned chef," says Lisa, "so we have a great relationship"), and Glen Elwin Farm, which supplies the lamb.

Tita's beverage selection acknowledges the North American love affair with Corona beer, sangria, margaritas, et al, but recommends pairing a good wine with the "rich and lively flavours" of their entrées — a pinot grigio from Cowichan Bay's Vigneti Zanata, perhaps, or one of the menu's organic offerings: Côtes du Ventoux syrah or the Colli Euganei Merlot, which I enjoyed straight through to *zpostres*. And speaking of dessert, leave room for the signature ancho chocolate ganache that's enlivened with the tastes of raisin and chile or the classic Mexican flan, which Lisa decorates in summer with strawberries from her garden.

The journey of Martin and Lisa began 20 years ago in Vancouver and took them to the Yukon (where Lisa had a bakery/café) and Berlin before they decided they "wanted to live somewhere in the Canadian wilderness." They settled for 12 years on Maurelle, a fairly large but sparsely populated island (says Lisa: "When we left, the population fell to 15") near Quadra. It was there that Lisa "really honed my gardening and cooking skills." Growing their own food, raising their own meat, they were largely self-sufficient. The Metzes raised their family on Maurelle and found the quality of life so good that the move to Courtenay and shopping in grocery stores again were challenging: "At first," says Lisa, "we didn't know what to eat."

COMOX

Martine's Bistro

Christine Cameron tells me that, years ago, she was "always the girl sitting at the bar waiting for the chef to get off work." That chef was her husband, Marcus Aartsen, and it didn't take her long to decide to join him in the restaurant business. They owned Beecher Street Café in Crescent Beach, White Rock, before looking for a quieter lifestyle on Vancouver Island. Attracted to Comox's "charm and closeness to nature, to the farms, sea and mountains," they bought the former Pythian Sisters' Hall and transformed it into one of the most appealing dining rooms I know.

Named Martine's (a composite of their names), it is warm and welcoming — and that's even before one is formally greeted. I loved the well-integrated Patrizia Didiomente stone sculptures and her colourful canvasses on the walls, the antique wagon-wheel light fixtures, the expansive patio with colourful tubs of peppers and herbs, the sea view and, as the room begins to fill with diners, the sense of merriment all around me.

When dining alone, I often head to the bar, which usually offers three advantages: interaction with staff, great view of the room, and the opportunity to chat with other solo diners in a casual way. At Martine's Bistro, the bar has that appealing, solid, urban kind of feel that I've also enjoyed at Victoria's Cafe Brio and Brasserie L'École. I don't need to tell foodies that where one sits can be every bit as important as what one eats.

So, happily ensconced at the bar, what's to eat at Martine's? Chef de Cuisine Marcus tells me he "likes doing the traditional dishes in a fresh way." He's originally from Holland, so there are some Indonesian influences on the menu like *nasi goreng* as well as brew balls, Dutch-style meatballs. While the couple makes a point of buying from their special haunts on the mainland for items like fresh Kaffir lime leaves, taro root and saffron, they draw deeply on the fresh, local, seasonal ingredients of the Comox Valley.

Marcus shops weekly at Seiffert's Farm in Comox and, in season, he and his chef, Mike Eagles, are known faces at the Courtenay Farmers' Market. Christine tells me she loves growing the restaurant's peppers and herbs and often buys "things like beautiful purple radicchio" from Courtenay's Edible Island Whole Foods Market.

Having been on the road most of the day, I'm keen to try the fare here. Eating alone is a bit of a disadvantage, in terms of being able to sample a menu widely, so I ask Christine to join me for appetizers. She makes a pot of South African Roibos tea, and we order calamari prepared in a very light tempura batter with tsatziki; oven-baked goat cheese heaped with roasted garlic and served with nice thin crostini smeared in fresh basil pesto; garlic prawns with a piquant jalapeño aioli and some mixed green salad with kalamata olives and feta cheese that have been marinated in balsamic vinegar. "*Eten smakelijk*," Christine says to me, and Marcus smiles. When she returns to the busy dining room, I enjoy grilled sirloin of lamb with a green peppercorn demi-glace, garlic mashed potatoes and green beans. This is fresh, delicious comfort food, perfectly executed, and I eat heartily.

In addition to the busy lunch and dinner schedule, Martine's Bistro sometimes presents wine-and-food-pairing nights, alternating local food and wine themes with those of other countries. Christine says she really enjoys "pushing the envelope" on menu and special event design, and these evenings have always been sell-outs. Christine or a wine rep speaks to the wines, and the chef in charge of each course introduces it to the diners.

Regrettably, I'm full and must pass up dessert, but I do enjoy one last cup of Roibos for the road and one last glance around this place for truly *mooi eetkamer* (good eating).

Portuguese Joe's Fish Market

The late José Domingues Veloso of Portugal courted his wife, Nilda of northern Spain, after swimming across the River Mino to see her. After she married him, he came on his own to Canada to see if they could spend their lives here. He first went to Nova Scotia, then Kitimat, where he worked building bunkhouses for the miners. Eventually he made his way to Vancouver Island, where he found that the Comox Valley reminded him of home. He put down roots and sent for Nilda.

José worked for Crown Zellerbach in the valley and bought a 25-acre farm. He always fished, and it was that passion that led him to open the now-legendary Portuguese Joe's. He and Nilda and their children lived above the shop on Comox Road, which I visited with great expectations.

It was exactly the no-fuss, no-muss place I'd imagined, with a beautiful array of fresh and frozen wild seafood and a well-worn counter with a box of plastic bags, twist ties and a massive stack of newspaper sheets. Sons Eddy and Cecil were serving customers hand-over-hand. A long queue of customers raised their eyebrows and smiled in unison as Eddy measured two pounds of prawns by sight, then threw them on scales that confirmed his measure to the ounce. Having been raised in the business, these guys know their fish.

Cecil is bagging peeled shrimp that his other brother, Lito, had caught that day. "Lito," he tells me, "is the spitting image of our father." He and Eddy debate whether Lito was actually born in the taxi right in front of the shop or in the taxi heading to the hospital. With Nilda away for the weekend, this debate can't be resolved, but suffice it to say that "Lito is the serious fisher," the Veloso most closely tied to the product they sell.

This has been a family operation since the early 1960s (the exact date becomes another point of debate between Eddy and Cecil). There are two other employees, a Vietnamese couple whom the Velosos helped when they first arrived in Comox. They've assisted with the cutting and filleting for 15 years.

Cecil stops for a chat over the counter, and tells me about the early days, the huge support of the military personnel based in Comox. He shows me a wall of military crests and a photo of his father that hangs above an old adding machine. He decries the fast society that "doesn't stop like you and I are doing now, to have a chat, to shop locally. It's cultural; it's about having a relationship." I agree with the loss and realize this is one man I don't have to preach to about the Slow Food philosophy, the way I tend to do in the city.

The gentleman standing beside me, a customer for 25 years, orders up some shrimp and herring and Cecil is back in action. I nibble away on a piece of house-candied salmon and think of that invigorating, life-changing (even Byronesque!) swim across the River Mino.

QUADRA ISLAND

Topcliff Farm

Linda Lessard is puréeing vast quantities of cooked apples when I visit her. Her partner and children are away for the weekend, and she is gleefully preparing hundreds of jars of strawberry and raspberry jam and applesauce for the upcoming Christmas market. She's in full production mode with three large cauldrons of confection bubbling away, jam jars sterilizing and row upon row of filled, ruby-coloured jars cooling on her table.

Her foodstuffs are fully organic. When the local market had no organic lemons for the applesauce, she substituted limes that were. She uses no sugar, just the lovely Prima apples from her orchard and the lime juice, and the taste is sensational — tangy and refreshing. The jams are sweetened with natural Links honey from Quadra Island or organic apple juice. Berries in the jams are left whole, just the way I like them and hard to find in the sea of "fruit spreads" at most grocers.

Linda has come to operating an organic farm on a Gulf Island honestly. A teacher, she left Quebec 24 years ago looking for the rural life. She taught for a while in Campbell River, a 10-minute ferry ride from Quadra Island. Eventually, she and John, a silviculturist, bought their 10-acre haven on Quadra and they began organic growing in earnest six years ago.

Linda's focus is fruit: Totem strawberries, raspberries, blueberries, gooseberries and red and white currants are laid out in elegant formation on three-quarters of an acre. I think the Sun King himself would have had no better fruit gardens at Versailles. He certainly would have had no better scarecrows than the ones, fashioned by Linda's two children, that guard her large, sweet strawberries. In the one-acre orchard, there are half a dozen types of apples, plums, cherries, pears and hazelnuts, and she can step out of her kitchen door to the small culinary and medicinal-herb garden.

A vegetarian for over 20 years, Linda feels organic is the only way to go. Her children have known nothing else, and she is proud that, when they shop with her, they hold up items and ask, "Mum, is this organic?" before putting it in the cart.

Linda learned to cook at home in Quebec, then put her skills to the test at a tree-planting camp on Vancouver Island. Today, she is popular on Quadra for her dairy- and gluten-free baking that she sells at theatre and concert concessions. Locals and visitors can shop at her farmgate in season. She has many repeat visitors, including a couple from Texas who drops by every year for her strawberries. In December, Linda opens the farm on Saturdays so folks can "come for an apple cider while shopping for gifts or for the table or both."

CORTES ISLAND

Cortes Café

If you're lucky enough to be visiting Cortes Island on market day, or indeed, on any postal delivery day, then you'll want to eat at the Cortes Café. Established in a cosy back room of Manson's Hall, full of local art and artsy people, the café dishes up delicious fare.

I stopped shopping in the market to enjoy the last piece of their homemade carrot cake and a good cup of coffee and soak up some of the local colour and chat around me. It was a warm haven on that cold winter's day, and I loved listening in on the market-related conversations: "I bought some lovely Ribston Pippins from Bill Wheeler," "Does L. J. have her Brie en croûte today?" and: "What do you say we grab an ice cream before we go?"

Cortes Island Farmers' Market

The Cortes market runs year-round. Its offerings change with the seasons, with a little island eclecticism thrown in. In summer, there's lots of fresh produce, but don't be surprised to be in a lineup for the organic ice cream in winter.

John Gordon is a photographer whose lovely images of island flora and fauna sell from his gallery at Smelt Bay. He and his wife, Ruby, decided they should offer something in addition to the photographs and settled on ice cream. It's proven to be a big hit, especially the organic berry flavours (made from their home-grown strawberries, raspberries, loganberries, blackberries, even tayberries).

Lisa Jo Osland caught my eye with her mane of red hair and celadon silk jacket. Her stall was laden with goodies, and she was surrounded by children, four of whom turned out to be her own. Her story put the whole island lifestyle into perspective for me. A caterer in the film industry, she and her family were living the urban life in North Vancouver before they moved to Cortes for one reason: Linnaea School, the famed environment-oriented private school for children that operates from a 350-acre farm. L. J. caters the school's hot organic lunch program, in addition to her private catering and weekly market offerings. I only wish her lunch program could be instituted at all schools, in place of the un-healthy "pizza or hotdog days."

I meet a customer of hers, Bud, who says L. J. has "really made a job for herself" on the island. In addition to her catering, she will begin teaching an Asian fusion workshop at Hollyhock in the fall.

L. J. presents her goodies as "more fooling around from L. J.'s kitchen," and on the day I visit, the selection is awesome: Giant Raviolis (for poaching and napping with a favourite sauce); pastry-covered Salacious Brie ("for when your sweetie's coming over"); Garlic Cream (a "pasta positive" sauce that's also delicious on garlic bread); homemade fettuccini and bocconcini. As I'm on the road, I buy the bocconcini to nibble on. This generous helping of tiny mozzarellas marinating in fresh herbs and olive oil is sealed in an airtight bag and lasts me four road-trip days without refrigeration.

 Brigid Weiler proffers a range of botanical body products. She is a cook who has worked in the island's tree-planting camps and also at Hollyhock. I buy a copy of her wonderful book (*Recipes from Garden, Sea and Bush*, Winnipeg: Rasmussen Company, co-written with Jill Milton), which is full of instructions for great back-to-the-land fare. Brigid leads mushroom-foraging walks on Saturday morn-ings in season.

Also on offer the day I visit the market are a huge selection of apples from Bill Wheeler and Mary Clare Preston's Inner Coast Nursery, incredible baking such as baguettes and cookies, and Wild Harvest smoked salmon from Andrea and Gary Block. The craft stalls are equally impressive with reasonably priced homeknit sweaters, slippers made from handspun sheep's wool and jewellery fashioned from elk antlers and feathers.

Hollyhock

The first time I visited Hollyhock and stood on its beach, looking out to sea, I felt I was standing on the edge of Planet Earth. The property has a special, indescribable quality that one has to experience to understand. And, of course, that quality and the array of New Age, experiential learning programs have kept people coming from all over the world for 20 years.

The next time I visited was to interview head chef Debra Fontaine for this book. It was in late November, when Hollyhock is essentially closed. There was a small group of writers using the lodge for a retreat; it was otherwise quiet, but still magical. Debra invited me to sit by the fire with her, and we talked about

Wilderness surrounds Hollyhock, enhancing one's sense of sight, smell, touch and taste.

her responsibility to feed up to 140 people every day, many of whom are on special diets or suffer from food allergies.

The week before, she had cooked the last dinner of the season for workshop participants: local salmon, sautéed local prawns with pesto made from Hollyhock basil, mushroom risotto with asiago, baked squash and chocolate mousse. She spent five hours stirring the huge pot of risotto, and loved every minute of it. "I choose what I am the most passionate about, what gives me the most joy," she tells me.

Debra first came to Cortes Island at three weeks of age when her father began appraising logging camps on the island. Then the family started holidaying there. When Debra was 29, she felt the pull of Cortes and left her busy life in Vancouver where she worked as an architectural draftsperson.

After some catering stints and private cheffing on the island (which she still does in the off-season), she began cooking at Hollyhock. Working with a brigade of 22 to 25 people, she says each meal "is like doing a big party." She approaches cooking like an artist approaching a canvas, telling her cooks she wants "healthy, fresh food with great taste that also catches the eye. I'm looking for lots of textures — soft and chewy and crunchy — and colours; and a balance of heat." It's important, she says, to think about food both visually and texturally, and to be mindful of "how it is going to sit in the stomach."

Thai Baked Tofu with Red Curry Sauce

DEBRA FONTAINE, HOLLYHOCK

Serves 8. "This dish is good served with jasmine rice and black Thai rice. If you make both rices, you can arrange them on a serving platter in a yin-yang symbol, which looks beautiful. Serve with a stirfry of pea pods and red peppers." — *Debra Fontaine*

Baked Tofu:

2	packages firm tofu, cut into 16 equal pieces	2

Mix together with a whisk:

1/4 c	tamari	60 ml
1/4 c	vegetable oil	60 ml
1/4 c	lemon juice	60 ml
1/4 c	garlic purée	60 ml
1/4 c	ginger purée	60 ml
1/2 c	peanut butter	120 ml
1/3 c	brown sugar	80 ml
	(omit the sugar if there is sugar in the peanut butter)	
1	jalapeño pepper seeded and finely chopped	1
1 c	sliced shiitake mushrooms	120 ml

Coat the tofu with the above ingredients and put in a well-oiled casserole pan, cover and bake at 350°F for 1 hour. Stir every 20 minutes. Uncover for the last 20 minutes. While the tofu is baking make a red curry sauce to pour over it.

Red Curry Sauce:

1/4 c	red curry paste	60 ml
1 14 fl oz can	coconut milk	414 ml
1 tbsp	sugar	15 ml
3	lime leaves OR	3
1 tsp	lime zest	5 ml

Sauté the curry paste in a little vegetable oil to release the flavour. Add the coconut milk, sugar and lime zest and cook on a very low heat. Do not allow to boil. When the tofu dish is plated pour curry sauce over.

Hollyhock subscribed to a vegetarian-only kitchen until 11 years ago, when fish was introduced. Debra says she is open to free-range poultry. She cooked a big turkey dinner at Thanksgiving that was hugely popular. She wondered if the vegetarian model hadn't gone a bit too far when a guest asked: "Did you debone the tofu?"

Debra loves the veggies and herbs she cooks which travel only a few feet from Hollyhock's gardens to its kitchen. The growers provide daily lists for the cooks of what will be available from the garden the next morning. All produce is picked before the sun heats the plants. Menu planning follows what the earth provides, not what has been driven for three days up the I-5 from California.

Head gardener Nori Fletcher has worked the Hollyhock gardens for over 20 years using the biodynamic/French intensive (BFI) method she learned at the Farallones Institute in California. Her assistant, Myann Reid, is a graduate of Linnaea Farm's ecological gardening program. Their training and passion are reflected in their incomparable kitchen garden.

Debra took the culinary program at Dubrulle in Vancouver four years ago and cooked at The Waterfront Hotel there, but she soon retreated to the ultimate retreat, Hollyhock. This, she tells me, is her home and she loves it. In the spring, she teaches a hands-on, deliciously passionate cooking workshop. "In prawn season, we take participants out on the boat, we pick our veggies from the garden, we dig for clams." Next spring, I hope to be one of those clam diggers.

Reef Point Farm

When Queen Elizabeth II and Prince Philip stayed with their relatives, the Markgräf Max and Markgräfin Valerie von Baden, on the Twin Islands, just off Cortes, Ginnie Ellingsen was called over to cook for six weeks. Such is Ginnie's modesty that I wouldn't have known that had Debra Fontaine of Hollyhock, on learning I was spending the night at Reef Point Farm, not sent me off with a wink and a suggestion: "Ask her about cooking for the Queen."

Not only did Ginnie tell me about that singular experience, but she kindly shared her photographs of the very relaxed sovereign enjoying her holiday. Of course, what was cooked and what was eaten by Her Majesty could not be revealed, but the story certainly gave me a window into the interesting world of Ginnie and her husband, Bruce.

Bruce's great-grandfather was the first white settler on Cortes — Michael Manson, for whom Manson's Landing is named. The property he and Ginnie live on, a 96-acre west-facing waterfront paradise, has been in the family since

The bed-and-breakfast at Reef Point Farm on Cortes Island.

1938. I had a stimulating morning walk with the couple through their apple, cherry, filbert and walnut orchard and vegetable gardens, and down to the beach. Ginnie planned to harvest seaweed for the gardens later that day, and wanted to check on the tide.

While their rambunctious dog swam out to annoy the seals, we stood at Sacred Point on their property and looked across to Mitlenatch Island, which had been owned by the Manson family prior to its becoming a provincial park. Bruce tells me that Michael Manson and his brother, John, used to row their sheep out to graze on Mitlenatch for the summer. "John's wife, Margaret, used to love staying out there. The lack of trees and its openness reminded her of the Shetland Islands where they came from. During the tough times of the Dirty Thirties, they stopped grazing the sheep there because of the poaching that went on."

We walked to the beach on one of the remaining horse-logging roads. Horses were used to drag logs to the water to be floated off to buyers in the late 1880s when Japanese settlers logged the island. Bruce has worked in the forest industry, and now runs his own sawmill on the island with one of his four sons.

Breakfast Scones

GINNIE ELLINGSEN, REEF POINT FARM

Makes 8 large scones. As a Brit, I take pride in the scones I make for teatime. Ginnie's recipe has replaced my own as the most delicious. I fantasize that these were actually served to Queen Elizabeth when Ginnie cooked for her on the Twin Islands, but I will never really know.

2 c	unbleached flour	480 ml
1/4 c	wheat germ	60 ml
2 1/2 tsp	baking powder	12.5 ml
2 tbsp	brown sugar	30 ml
1/2 tsp	salt	2.5 ml
1/3 c	butter	80 ml
1/2 c	currants or raisins	60 ml
2	eggs	2
1/3 c	buttermilk	80 ml

Combine flour, wheat germ, baking powder, sugar and salt. Cut in butter with pastry blender or two knives until flour mixture resembles fine bread crumbs. Add currants or raisins. Beat eggs and milk together and add all at once to flour mixture. Knead a few strokes until dough holds together. Divide in two pieces and pat each into rounds, then cut each into quarters. Place quarters on ungreased baking sheet and bake at 425°F for 15 minutes or until golden brown. Take care not to overbake!

As a board member of the Cortes Eco-forestry Society, Bruce is committed to selective logging and logging in situ, meaning that he takes his own Mobile Dimension sawmill into the woods "on a light-duty road system, to cut logs from roadside piles or bunks." He built his own house from timber taken from the property. Bruce is also helping with the divestiture of some 4,000 acres of Weyerhauser-owned lands on Cortes.

I loved my cozy room at Reef Point Farm, and was honoured to have dinner en famille with the Ellingsens. Ginnie's interest in serving only locally produced foods (much from her own garden) shone through in her cooking, and I enjoyed a lovely beef daube (made with beef from the island's Linnaea Farm), mashed potatoes, Ginnie's French beans and pickled beets. There was a local birthday girl at the table that night so Ginnie had made a first-rate and not overly sweet chocolate cake, which she served with her own canned peaches. As it stormed outside, the rain sheeting down on the kitchen's tin roof, we were a very contented and convivial party inside.

Reef Point Farm has connections to the famed ReBar restaurant in Victoria: son David was a prominent fixture there before pursuing his photography career full-time in Vancouver, and Lizzie, the restaurant's longest-serving and seriously fun server, is a good friend of the Ellingsen family.

The morning I reluctantly left, I opted for the lighter version of breakfast: a fresh fruit salad, Ginnie's currant scones and steaming coffee. Everything was presented on good English china and everything was scrumptious. Reef Point Farm is a place to immerse oneself in peace and tranquillity as well as to eat and sleep like a queen.

The Tak

Every Gulf Island seems to have a particular casual restaurant where a cross-section of the locals hang out. None of them are about decor; all focus on good, hearty food at reasonable prices. There's Jan's Café on Hornby, Pistou Grill on Pender, Barb's Buns on Saltspring, The General Store on Saturna, and The Lovin' Oven on Quadra. On Cortes, it's The Tak, so naturally I headed there first.

Their lentil-walnut burger turned out to be a real treat: a piping hot, fat patty served on a toasted kaiser with lettuce, tomato, mayo and Dijon mustard. It was just the fuel I needed on a rainy day before hitting the famous Friday market across at the community hall. The Tak's owner, Scott Mercs, was on the line that day, so I met him later to chat about his restaurant and the food culture on Cortes.

He's owned the place for four years, having previously managed the island's Floathouse Restaurant, and cooked in Squamish and Whistler. He says Cortes is "an incredible food community," but it's more about people growing their own than active retailing.

There is a seasonal brown-box program run by the island's largest organic farm at Blue Jay Lake. In the winter months, the Cortes Connection truck picks up a load of organic food from ProOrganics in Vancouver, and it is divided up among a committed group of local residents. Scott hopes that venture will eventually develop into a permanent co-op market to increase islanders' accessibility to organic food.

Cortes has its share of natural living pioneers including Dr. Andrew Weil, who is a homeowner here and has often led workshops at Hollyhock, and Russell

Lentil Walnut Burgers

SCOTT MERCS, THE TAK

Makes 12 to 18 burgers, depending on desired size. I'm fussy about vegetarian burgers because they are often boring. The almond burgers at Victoria's ReBar restaurant and these lentil-walnut beauties are first-rate.

3	medium onions, diced	3
2	large carrots, grated	2
2 tbsp	cumin seeds	30 ml
1 tbsp	turmeric	15 ml
2 1/2 tbsp	coriander	37.5 ml
4 tbsp	basil	60 ml
4 tbsp	dill	60 ml
1 tbsp	pepper	15 ml
1 tbsp	curry powder	15 ml
1 tsp	cumin powder	5 ml
4 c	lentils	960 ml
5 c	walnuts	1.2 L
2	potatoes, cooked and mashed	2
2 c	breadcrumbs	480 ml
2 tbsp	salt	30 ml

Cook the lentils until soft, then drain well for one hour. Roast walnuts in oven until lightly browned. Sauté onions, carrots and cumin seeds until soft. Add all the other herbs and spices and sauté gently for five more minutes. Mix all ingredients in a food processor. The mixture should hold together when formed into a patty. If too dry, add some water. If too moist, add more breadcrumbs. Sauté the patties and serve immediately on a whole-grain bun, with lettuce, sliced tomatoes, mayo and mustard.

Precious, who founded Caper's organic grocery in Vancouver, and originally ran a food store on Cortes.

Scott feels his restaurant "fills an important function" in such a small community as Cortes, where, in the winter months, some people feel a sense of isolation. There is always a friendly welcome and a hot cup of coffee when they open the door.

West Coast

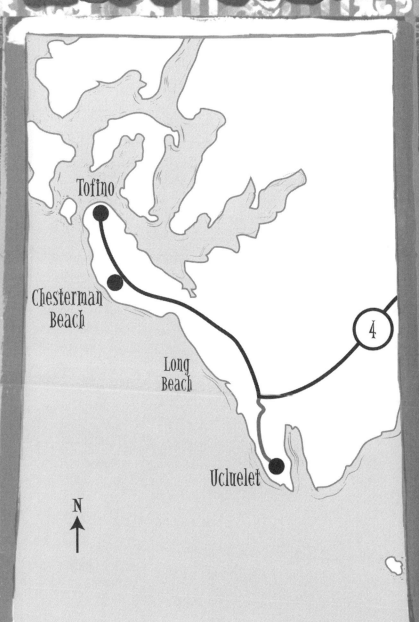

Tofino

Chesterman
Beach

Long
Beach

Ucluelet

4

N

n this trip, I'm in the company of two New York food writers and a producer from the American Food Network. We have been following the famous Relais & Châteaux Gourmet Trail™ from Rob Feenie's lauded Lumière restaurant in Vancouver to The Aerie on the Malahat to Hastings House on Saltspring Island. Our final destination is The Wickaninnish Inn on Tofino's Chesterman Beach. It's been a delicious journey, with lots of good food and drink and excellent company at every stop.

We're heading north on the Trans-Canada Highway, the sun miraculously breaking through the clouds as we gaze across to the Sunshine Coast on the mainland. At Parksville, we turn left and begin to cross over to the wild west coast of Vancouver Island.

Coombs is the traditional stop to stock our picnic hamper. No kidding, there are goats on the roof at Coombs General Store, a novelty worth seeing. And inside, the selection of food amazes: Lavazza coffee, Italian pastas, Cadbury's chocolate, fruit, vegetables, cheese, breads, and no one leaves without a big ice cream cone — 25 flavours. There are also many small craft and souvenir kiosks surrounding the store.

In 1949 Tofino mayor Tom Gibson had persuaded a young doctor, Howard McDiarmid, to start his medical practice here when there were only 300 people in the little fishing village of Tofino. Over the years, McDiarmid bought the land where he and his family would eventually build The Wickaninnish Inn.

Beginning in the 1970s, an active green community developed from both local people and American pacifists. Clayoquot Sound is probably best known for the massive logging protest in the summer of 1993, when 12,000 people set up a peace camp near the Kennedy River Bridge.

UCLUELET/TOFINO

Chocolate Tofino

I'm always impressed when people follow their passion. Gordon Austin graduated as a Red Seal chef from Malaspina University-College in 1996 and went to work at Château Whistler. He completed his journeyman papers in the pastry department of The Wickaninnish Inn under the tutelage of Matthias Conradi, and eventually took over the department when Conradi left.

He began to notice the big demand from guests "for all things chocolate." When Bernard Callebaut gave a workshop at the Wickaninnish, Gordon "really picked his brains about the specialization and the entrepreneurial side of chocolate-making." With help in the costing and bookkeeping department from his wife, Leah (she runs the spa at The Wickaninnish Inn), Gordon opened his own chocolate shop near The Beaches grocery.

Stepping inside, one is immediately oohing and ahhing at the aroma from a big pot of bittersweet chocolate that is bubbling away. The display cases hold many promises of ecstasy, so choosing is difficult. I sample the shop's popular Clayoquot blackberry and white chocolate bonbon. Gordon often picks the berries himself and makes them into a compound that he "freezes to ensure a supply of flavour year-round." The marzipan truffle is a wicked combination of marzipan with a layer of honey ganache dipped in bittersweet chocolate. The chocolate-dipped organic orange peel is a personal favourite.

Gelato is very big here in summer, either on its own in a cone or made into decadent sundaes. The product is made as close to the Italian version as possible, with "concentrated flavours of fruit, chocolate or vanilla." The shop always tries to have a non-dairy option on hand: the tofu latte flavour is a big hit. Chocolate Tofino also produces elaborate wedding and birthday cakes, often wrapping the whole in chocolate *couverture*.

Gordon says: "Making people happy through the use of classical ingredients and fresh ingredients is my thing." He aims to expand his production area this summer so that he can sell chocolate to other places and "make more people happy."

Clayoquot Organics

When Melanie MacLeod began farming 22 years ago, she first had to "beat back the rainforest." Japanese settlers had done intensive growing in the area in the 1940s, but farming on the wild west coast has never been easy. Melanie comes from a long line of Lower Mainland farmers, so she's been able to put her considerable knowledge to work on an acre of land close to Tofino and managed to carve out a thriving organic vegetable business that supplies the top local restaurants. She grows in raised beds and greenhouses, and plans to expand to meet her customers' increasing demands.

Trish Muehlebach and Jenny Cohen, gardeners at Tofino's Clayoquot Organics.

Living in so remote an area, with little produce locally grown, residents are even more keenly aware of the food miles associated with importing fruit and vegetables. Melanie has filled a void in local food production, and happily, it is now difficult to eat out in Tofino without encountering her beautiful produce.

Festival of Oysters and the Sea

Like Feast of Fields on the south island and Harvest Bounty Festival on the mid-island, Tofino's oyster festival is a benchmark local event that I highly recommend. It's a celebration of the fruits of the local oyster fishers, and literally thousands of oysters are consumed (one year, I understand, 4,000 oysters were slurped in four hours at the Oyster Gala!).

Held in mid-November, the festival offers boat tours to the oyster fields (see my private tour with Oyster Jim Martin); seminars with marine biologists on "where oysters live, what they eat and, perhaps most interestingly, the legends of what they can do for you when you eat them"; an oyster brunch and a stupendous oyster gala, where oysters are presented every which way by all the prominent local chefs.

Tofino, and particularly Lemmens Inlet in Clayoquot Sound, where most of the deep-water oyster tenures are situated, produces around 50,000 gallons of bivalves annually. The District of Tofino has marked the industry's significance by declaring November "Oyster Month in Tofino." Many of the luxury hotels offer special rates for the festival weekend, but getting tickets to the oyster festival can be challenging. It's best to book everything ahead if your edible journeys will be taking you to Tofino in November.

I'm a bit shy around bivalves, so I asked around at the oyster gala before selecting three fine specimens to sample. Artie and Lisa Ahier of Sobo had sandwiched a locally smoked oyster, wasabi cheese from Natural Pastures Cheese Company, some Thai-style green papaya sauce and pea shoots between two homemade organic potato chips that packed a powerful punch. Long Beach Lodge's Rob Wheaton had smoked oysters in chai tea, then served them on the half-shell with a champagne ginger vinaigrette and wasabi tobiko on a pea-shoot salad. The recipient of the 2004 juried award and my personal fave was the Asian oyster baked in spinach, onion and miso broth by Tough City Sushi's chef Jojo Villaresis.

In Tin Wis Resort's "Oyster Palace," decorated in blue paper jellyfish and filled to capacity with an eager foodie crowd, the chefs performed admirably. When everyone was finally sated with oysters and a great deal of local wine had been consumed, the dance floor was cleared and The Continentals, a local jazz ensemble, sparked hours of dancing.

P.S. Another reason to take a west coast edible journey in November is the colourful parade of pumpkins that runs for several kilometres starting at Cathedral Grove. At Halloween, locals traditionally line the side of the highway with hundreds of carved pumpkins. It's one of those unique organic events, which somehow reminds us that there is a place in all our lives for whimsy, especially on a grey fall day. En route to the oyster festival I drove my husband crazy for at least half an hour with frequent "oh look, there's another stand of pumpkins."

The Goat Lady

Years ago, the Wickaninnish Inn's Nanoose Organic Greens and Ucluelet Goats' Cheese Salad with Sun-dried Blueberry and Sesame Vinaigrette led me to Jane Hunt. It was another once-in-a-lifetime foodie adventure, and I'll never forget her. Former Wickaninnish chef Jim Garraway had given me Jane's phone

Jane Hunt with a few of her 27 goats at Westerly Wynds Farm, Ucluelet.

number with the instruction that, as this was a radiophone, I would need to say "over." Piece of cake. Jane and I had many successful conversations before I headed into the wild hills behind Ucluelet to meet her at Westerly Wynds Farm.

Jane graduated from the first veterinary class at Guelph University in 1964, and set up a clinic in Victoria's Vic West neighbourhood. Her husband, Don, says it got a bit crazy some nights when animals were being brought in from accidents. Twenty years later, seeking a more peaceful life, they bought 15 acres in the hills outside Ucluelet from a logging syndicate, and embarked on a journey toward self-sufficiency.

My trip to the farm is both breathtaking and poignant. Much of the area has been logged, and when I spot a black bear cub foraging for food in the middle of a clearcut, my heart stops. Jane's instructions are very specific, and once I've made two rights, a left and a very sharp right, the farm and a frisky welcoming committee of 27 goats are before me.

The goats are Saanen, brought from Alberta. The youngest, Summer, is six weeks old the day I visit. The eldest, Clinton, is a fearless buck who has a little smooch through the fence with every doe that passes by. Poor Clinton doesn't know yet that a new buck has arrived on the farm. Jane and Don drove to Abbotsford "in a raging snowstorm" to bring back Puddle Jumper, who is settling in nicely in his own pen. There are many other residents: peacocks, ducks, guinea fowl, pheasants, turkeys, chickens, French Angora rabbits, Great Pyrenees dogs, Shetland sheep, alpacas and 13 cats.

One can only marvel at the extraordinary tableau vivant created by the many creatures, organic gardens, the house and a dozen outbuildings ranging from a barn to a water tower. And even though everything seems to be in motion, there is a peace and stillness to the place that makes me see why the Hunts chose to settle here. There is also a stunning view of Barkley Sound from the top of the cliffs. Jane says every kid has taken a plunge over the cliffs, and she's managed to coax each one up with a rope.

Jane started making the goat cheese nine years ago and "selling it to hippie friends." It was soon coveted by locals, including Rodney Butters, The Wickaninnish Inn's trail-blazing chef. Rodney often visited Jane with his cat, and the sublime chèvre started to appear on the inn's dinner menu.

Out of a very small fromagerie in the back of her house, Jane pasteurizes 50 to 60 litres of goats milk and produces 35 pounds of cheese a week. She always has chèvre and feta on hand for her regular customers, and, in the summertime, makes butter and ice cream, which the local children love, from the leftover milk.

I leave with chèvre, feta and a bar of the nourishing goat's-milk soap, impressed as always by the passionate people behind these small cottage operations, and thrilled to have met the woman whose cheese now sings on the plates at the Boat Basin restaurant in Ucluelet.

Oyster Jim

It's 7:00 A.M. on a clear spring morning as Jim Martin slips his skiff into the still water of Grice Bay. We're heading for his famed oyster beds, scattered throughout the islands of Clayoquot Sound.

To understand the oysters, one first needs to understand their shepherd. Oyster Jim is a seriously rugged guy, a former boiler-maker who emigrated from Colorado to the sleepy little fishing village of Ucluelet in 1985. He is a gentle giant, a man with great capacity for invention and work study, who is as eloquent describing his patented holistic exercise program as expressing his delight at the little acts of kindness from the boys in his Scout troop. It's no overstatement to call him a legend in these parts. Whenever I mention his name, folks praise his local accomplishments and unwavering community spirit.

He recently brought a great dream to fruition when he and a battery of volunteers blazed and marked out the 2.5 km Wild Pacific Trail. Skirting the coastline around Ucluelet, it provides hikers with stunning vantage points of the ocean and islands below. I think of Jim each time I hike that trail, grateful for his determination to preserve the area's unique rugged beauty.

I'd heard about Oyster Jim long before our breakfast cruise. His large, succulent oysters are featured on the menu at The Wickaninnish Inn, where my fellow diners always rave about their meatiness and sublime flavour. One of the chef's recent takes on these amazing oysters was Three Oyster Jim's Clayoquot Sound Roasting Oysters with Basil Goat's Cheese Crust, Garlic and Pancetta, and Horseradish Root Ketchup.

It doesn't get much better than this: breakfast served by Oyster Jim Martin.

I was determined to try my first Oyster Jim oyster with the man himself. Charles McDiarmid told me some of the best meals he's ever had were sitting on a log with Jim — a pile of oysters, a shucker and a few squeezes of lemon juice. It sounded like a hunter-gatherer's dream date.

Charles had explained to me: "A lot of places grow oysters on inflated drums that go up and down with the tide, but Jim grows his on the shore. The tide goes in and out. They take longer, but they turn out plumper, juicier, larger." As my experiences with oysters had more often than not been chewy, I was ready for something sensational.

Jim tells me to put away my notebook and pen just before he lets out the throttle, and we are skimming the water through Fortune Passage en route to Kershaw and Wood islands. This is indeed a fortunate passage, for we are not long out when a school of porpoises crosses the bow. Jim says they're used to his boat now, so our presence doesn't disturb their herring feast. Within seconds, Jim has spotted a black bear searching the shore for rock crabs, and he shuts off the motor so we can take a closer look. He has been keeping an eye on the bear for two years, and thinks it was orphaned early on.

Before my tour of the oyster beds, we head over to Wood Island, where Jim lights a small fire on the beach and fuels my anticipation of the feast to come. We scramble back over barnacled rocks, and I gladly accept a piggyback ride through shallow water to the skiff.

The cultivation process is simple. Jim starts the oysters at home from larvae and small barnacle chips. They next go into nursery trays that are laid out on the beach. The temperature in these waters is perfect for growing shellfish. As the oysters grow, Jim spreads them along the beach, separating out the single units from the clusters. At this stage, the oysters are susceptible to attack by rock crabs, so Jim has devised a special collapsing crab fence. It does a good job of keeping the crabs at bay, but collapses as necessary to allow spawning salmon through.

Once the oysters reach three inches in length, they are transported to trays that get stacked under water. There are up to 95 stacks at any given time, each containing 1,200 oysters. We cruise over the stacks, en route to the oysters' final resting beach, and Jim harvests a dozen specimens. He delights in the beautiful shell formations, and promises me a delicious breakfast.

Back on Wood Island, with the fire smouldering nicely, Jim roasts his prize oysters. He grows them specifically to be cooked in the shell, and within 10 minutes, they're ready to shuck. Jim hands me what proves to be the biggest, juiciest, most flavourful oyster I have ever eaten. He shows me where to start, and how to spoon the flesh out. I'm sitting on a log with the oyster guru of Clayoquot Sound, enjoying the unsurpassed calm of early morning and thinking life can't get much better than this. Pass the seafood sauce, eh?

Raincoast Café

With memories of some extraordinary rice cakes served with a roasted cashew and ginger sauce, I arrive back at the Raincoast Café to chat with owners Lisa Henderson and Larry Nicolay. It's mid-afternoon, one of the rare quiet times in their day. The restaurant is open for dinner only, so the prep work is mostly done and the flowers are arranged. Larry is taking time to check the evening's reservations, and Lisa draws me over to a corner table.

The couple first came to Tofino from Vancouver 13 years ago. They'd spent a summer looking around, and found themselves managing the Alleyway Café, a charming little place tucked in behind shops in the centre of town. Their time at the Alleyway was enjoyable, but, as Lisa says: "It didn't feel like ours."

When the opportunity to be part of a brand-new building came up, they jumped at it. Larry's brother, who had previously designed restaurants in Vancouver, including Global and Crush, was their designer, and other family members pitched in too. The result is a small but functional prep room, and an open kitchen along one wall of the cleanly executed dining room. There are interesting flower arrangements, but generally the design is understated — a perfect foil for the food.

Lisa was a secretary who moonlighted in the front of house of various Vancouver restaurants. She is a self-trained chef, with no pre-conceived notions about what she should or should not be cooking.

Wild Rice Cakes with Roasted Cashew and Ginger Sauce

LISA HENDERSON, RAINCOAST CAFÉ

Serves 6. I once had a conversation with Satva Hall of Monsoon Coast Exotic World Spices about the huge range of interpretations of "vegetarian" on restaurant menus. We agreed that finding something exceptional is rare. These tasty rice cakes are exceptional.

4	medium russet potatoes	4
1 c	wild rice	240 ml

Boil potatoes in their skins until tender all the way through. Put aside. Meanwhile, boil wild rice with plenty of water until the rice pops and the inner whites are exposed (this is crucial to an edible rice cake). Strain and let cool. Peel and grate cooled potatoes and place in medium bowl. Add wild rice. Then add:

1 tbsp	salt	15 ml
2 tsp	pepper	10 ml
1 tbsp	cumin	15 ml
	good pinch of dried and crushed rosemary	
1/3 c	fresh basil, finely chopped	80 ml
4	green onions, thinly sliced	4

Mix together. Adjust flavours, if necessary. Form into 12 balls and then shape into patties. Shape sides so the patties look like little hockey pucks. Layer with wax paper between patties.

Roasted Cashew and Ginger Sauce:

In a blender combine:

3/4 c	roasted cashews	180 ml
1 tbsp	fresh ginger	15 ml
2 tbsp	soy sauce	30 ml
	vegetable stock or water to desired consistency	

Arrange seasonal vegetables on plate. Ladle the cashew sauce beside the vegetables and arrange two rice cakes in a stacked manner on top of sauce. The rice cakes can be served as a vegetarian main dish or as a starch for chicken or fish dishes.

Lisa Henderson and Larry Nicolay are the delightful owners of Tofino's Raincoast Café.

She and Larry agree that their goal is always "to challenge ourselves and other people."

They are inclined to Asian flavours, and allow me to label their style as "modern, with Asian influences," but really, anything goes. Lisa's Thai fish bowl includes local and exotic fish and shellfish, rice noodles, passion fruit, coriander and jalapeño with coconut cream. Fresh Sooke trout is stuffed with Dungeness crab and cilantro lime cream cheese and served with yam mash. Cowichan Bay Farm's chicken is matched with shiitake mushrooms, balsamic shallot cream and herb-roasted new potatoes. Lisa was excited about a dish served the previous night in which she had wrapped halibut in skunk cabbage leaves.

She says she is inspired by what comes in the door from her local suppliers: Clayoquot Organics, Trilogy Fish Company and the neighbouring fishers, shellfish growers and mushroom, fiddlehead and edible-flower pickers. Wines are mostly from British Columbia, with several organic choices; the coffee is Nicaraguan organic, and the teas are Tazo. As members of the Endangered Fish Alliance (a coalition of concerned chefs searching for sustainable options), Lisa says they "are diligent about serving only non-endangered, local and sustainable fish and shellfish."

Dinner is served seven nights a week. Reservations are highly recommended, but people have been known to straggle in close to closing time, and Lisa makes sure they're fed. The restaurant seats 24 plus two high stools right in front of the kitchen (great for nosy foodies like me), and it regularly turns over three or four times a night. With recommendations from *USA Today*, *Travel and Leisure*, Frommer's and *Best Places in the Northwest* and, recently, a recipe in *Bon Appétit*, Raincoast Café is indelibly inked on the culinary map.

Shelter Restaurant

Since I last travelled to Tofino to write the first edition of *An Edible Journey*, the restaurateur Jay Gildenhuys has opened Shelter. Jay had been a fixture on the Victoria restaurant scene since 1995, when he opened the charming Cho Cho's in Oak Bay, a small coffee shop that I frequented with my father and niece. He later launched Suze, a funky fusion place with a reputation all its own, and the non-stop Lucky Bar.

He told me he had been coming to Tofino for years, always admiring the building that housed The Crab Bar, a restaurant started by John Fraser of Trilogy Fish. One night, Jay was "working on the floor at Suze in Victoria," and suddenly decided to call the owner of that building to see if it was for sale. Coincidentally (or not, if you believe there are no coincidences in life) "the guy was coming to Victoria the next day and suggested a meeting." In short order, Jay sold Suze, bought the building of his dreams in Tofino and established the warm and cozy Shelter. As a necessary adjunct to any professional life in the food industry in Tofino, he also quickly learned to surf.

Early on, Jeff Keenliside (formerly of Victoria's Cafe Brio) was in the kitchen, but when Jeff moved on, Jay cajoled Jesse Blake into taking the helm. Jesse had taken a break from cooking to do a stint at salmon and trout guiding, but he soon accepted Jay's invitation. He comes to the culinary world with a background in health food. His father, food and travel writer Joseph Blake, owned Oak Bay's Earth Household natural-foods store for 15 years. Jesse told me that he and his two brothers would sit at the dinner table and chant: "Meat, meat, meat!" After graduating from the Camosun College culinary program, he took his cheffing skills to Tofino's Schooner Restaurant, The Loft and Long Beach Lodge, where he worked with Lisa Ahier. Her "Tex-Mex, totally cool style of cooking" had a big impact on his traditional repertoire.

Warm Chèvre Salad

JESSE BLAKE, SHELTER RESTAURANT

This recipe enables you to prepare a salad like a chef ("a little bit of this, a little bit of that") while ensuring that the vinaigrette is exactly right.

Vinaigrette:

Part A
one part honey
one part apple cider vinegar
fresh thyme, leaves only
fresh parsley

Part B
three parts olive oil
salt and pepper to taste

Combine Part A in a food processor. Leave the machine running and add Part B. Add some diced, double-smoked bacon that has been cooked off, caramelized onion and roasted garlic cloves to a hot pan and quickly sauté. Add some braising greens like chard, kale or spinach and vinaigrette to taste. Remove the pan from the heat and cover until the greens wilt slightly. Mix greens and dressing well, plate and crumble some soft, unripened chèvre on top.

Jesse is sourcing wild fish "straight off the boat" as well as through Trilogy Fish. Produce, which had been coming from Clayoquot Organics until it closed, is supplied by the irreplaceable Nanoose Edibles.

My husband and I were given a table next to the fire downstairs (upstairs, there is a large dining room with water views and there is a wildly popular, heated deck for spring to early fall feasting). The first good sign was the presence of other restaurateurs: Ron Gauld of Tough City Sushi was having dinner at the bar, and John and Donna Fraser of Trilogy Fish were sitting close by. We were warmly greeted by Marco Lilliu, the restaurant's manager. He's a local boy who is spending his winters finishing up a political science degree at the University of British Columbia. He owned his own lounge in Tofino for a while, but is now delighted to be part of "the dynamic team" at Shelter.

Marco is responsible for the restaurant's wine list and those great seafaring martinis with names like Dead Calm, South Easterly and Gale Warning.

Shelter is a fish-lover's Mecca. Crispy prawn spring rolls with a sweet and spicy chili dipping sauce were excellent, as were the clam linguini with thyme (from the restaurant's own herb garden), roasted garlic cream and Parmegiano Reggiano and the prosciutto-wrapped halibut fillet with prawn risotto, roasted red pepper tomato sauce and organic spaghetti squash. We were full, but I couldn't resist the frozen vanilla parfait with a pistachio and orange caramel crust and a nice tipple of Vigneti Zanatta's Glenora Fantasia Brut to finish the meal in style.

If you're looking for shelter from the surf or from whatever you're doing on the wild west coast of Vancouver Island, beat a path to the door of Jay Gildenhuys' locally entrenched restaurant. From fruity martinis on the patio in summer to house fries with smoked paprika mayonnaise on winter movie nights in the great room upstairs, Shelter is the ultimate in culinary comfort.

Sobo in the Garden

In a classic case of "I'll have what she's having," I order a large cup of thick white noodles in miso broth with chunks of tofu and salmon, topped with sliced wild green onions that a young Native girl harvested just that morning. It is a simple, nourishing "best food" experience for which I thank Sushil Saini, Victoria food writer and teacher, who happened to be in the lineup ahead of me at Sobo. Her recommendation of anything is good enough for me.

The noodles were prepared by chef Lisa Ahier, formerly of Tofino's Long Beach Lodge Resort, who, with her husband, Artie, has launched "the purple people eater," a smart-looking steel catering truck, painted royal purple, that has attracted a loyal local clientele since it opened in April 2003. Says Lisa: "We've discovered that, with local support behind us, we could do whatever we want." Customers include cooks and wait staff from all the major restaurants in this beach community — always a good sign that the food is first rate.

When Lisa worked in big hotel kitchens, she often said to her friends: "If I only had a little taco stand ..." Here it is now, in all its glory, with a fabulous selection of seafood, noodle and salad dishes that represent the best kinds of healthy, fresh, fast food.

The "little taco stand" was moved to its present location only recently, when Lisa and Artie also took over the former Pamploma Café in Tofino's Botanical Gardens. Lunch is still served from the catering truck (don't ever take that away from us!), but customers can now choose to sit at the original picnic tables and benches next to the truck, at covered patio tables and inside the restaurant itself where there are lovely views of the garden. When the truck closes at 5:00 P.M., a dinner menu is offered in the restaurant complemented by local beers and wines. The new location "gives our customers a lot more of Sobo!" says Lisa.

The lineups had become too long, and Lisa and Artie realized they weren't meeting their demand with just the truck. The new arrangement still has that casual feel, and the larger prep kitchen in the restaurant enables Lisa to "get my creativity out, particularly for our regulars who eat here every day. I'm able to make more daily specials, more curries, more seafood stews and molés." As a mom, Lisa says she is "so inspired by the little ones, the children who are really digging good food," and she is pleased to be "firing up the next generation to get into what our grandparents had — pure foods, quality ingredients grown close to home."

Sobo, which stands for "sophisticated bohemian," is a name that Lisa coined and thousands identify with. When she appears on television, she "gets calls from all over" to find out how people can get to her fresh, seasonal food based on Vancouver Island ingredients. Those who can't make it for dinner because they're in California, for example, will be pleased to hear about the couple's recently released *Sophisticated Bohemian Cookbook* (Sobo in the Garden, 2005). I don't have my hands on it yet, but I do have my fingers crossed that Lisa's killer fish taco recipe will be included.

Trilogy Fish Company

When I arrive at the Trilogy Fish Company, owner John Fraser is about to leave for North Sea Products, one of the few remaining plants that buys from the local commercial fishers. John buys all his fish locally, and he normally buys directly, too, but with the summer visitors already pouring through the door, he's run a bit low today. I seize the opportunity to ride with him, and we head down to the docks.

A couple of First Nations men are unloading a catch of sockeye salmon from their boat. John goes off to claim his order, and I chat with Rocky, one of the fishers. He says he loves to fish, loves to be out on the ocean. Fishers have been hurting badly from the recently depleted salmon stocks, but he feels the fish are starting to come back.

John returns with an iced haul of four- to seven-pound salmon, and loads them into the truck. When we return to Trilogy, his wife Donna is there to help

John's Favourite Salmon

DONNA FRASER, TRILOGY FISH COMPANY

Serves 4 to 6. A perfect preparation for the buffet table — delicious served hot or cold.

1	2 1/2 lb (1 1/4 kg) side of salmon (preferably chinook)	1
1/4 c	butter, softened	60 ml
3-5	cloves (to taste) fresh garlic, chopped	3-5
1 heaping tbsp	Demerara-style sugar	15 ml
1 heaping tbsp	dry mustard	15 ml

Preheat oven to 350°F. Place salmon fillet skin side down on a foil-lined cookie sheet. Mix all ingredients together, then spread evenly over the fillet. Bake for 20 to 25 minutes.

NOTE: To test for doneness, press your thumb down on the thickest part of the fillet. The flesh will part on the grain when done. Remove fish from the oven and serve with rice and your favourite vegetables or salad.

carry them in. John gives my city shoes a horrified look, and passes me some Wellington boots and a hat. After I wade through a pan of clean water and wash my hands, he takes me into the processing area.

One of his employees, Drew, is filleting salmon, taking a lot of pride in his work. We first enter the cold-smoke room, where the curing temperature is set at 5°C. John grows his own alder at home and chips it to fuel the cold smoker. He never lets his cold-smoked fish get over 10°C, because "the cooler you keep it, the better it tastes." In the hot-smoke room, he also uses chipped alder. The process takes about six hours. The finished product is immediately put into a 4°C blast cooler for two hours, then vacuum-packed before being transferred to the shop cooler out front.

John fished these waters for 30 years, mainly for crab. He used to love crabbing because "you could get around the inlets and see everything." When he turned to fish smoking, he thought he would be able to fish for six months, and smoke for six months, but the business has boomed and basically, he's needed on shore. For now, he's fine with that arrangement, as he and Donna still get out for a little sport fishing.

I know of no more immaculate, well-stocked fish shop than that run by Donna at the front end of the Trilogy Fish Company. The iced displays of hot-smoked, cold-smoked, candied and fresh-off-the-boat salmon as well as halibut, tuna and cooked crab are impressive. The range of condiments and spices will inspire even the most reluctant cook. I was delighted to find fleur de sel, a wide variety of olives, tapenade, seafood sauces, vinegars, oils, salad dressings and all the fixings for sushi.

Donna originally came to Tofino to work as an X-ray technician. Like many here, she liked it so much that she did a variety of things to ensure she would be able to stay. A stint with a forest company and running her own art gallery came before the fish company. Now, she and John are building their dream home overlooking the inlet, and even though she swears she'll "never work another summer," she obviously enjoys her sun-drenched, happy shop.

It's June, and the summer visitors are wafting in. Donna and her sister are busy serving customers looking for something local and tasty for dinner. Out back, John is taking care of sport fishers who need their catches cleaned and vacuum-packed. Between customers, we compare food notes. Donna says she's looking for a new line of salad dressings, so I tell her about the wonderful golden sesame dressing from Occasional Occasions that I discovered at Nanoose Edibles, and she gives me one of the better tips I've had when she sends me off to meet "a superb organic chef," Lisa Ahier of Sobo. The Trilogy

The little fish store that could: Trilogy Fish Company in "downtown" Tofino.

Fish Company now serves delicious crab and shrimp sandwiches in the style of a "lobster dog," and a daily chowder that goes fast (especially the halibut-and-smoked-salmon version!).

The Wickaninnish Inn

I am seriously luxuriating in a south-facing double bathtub, looking out as far as the eye can see towards Hawaii. From somewhere out there come the airy notes of Vivaldi, and I pop my head out of the bubbles to see a lone flautist on the rocks below. A siren calling unsuspecting guests to venture forth into dangerous seas? No, merely a little pre-dinner music, Wickaninnish style.

The Wickaninnish Inn is a west-coast wonder, situated on the rugged and startlingly beautiful promontory that juts out between North Chesterman and Mackenzie beaches. Managing Director Charles McDiarmid describes the inn's style as "rustic elegance." Certainly, one feels immersed in nature, yet no first-class amenity is spared. Any traveller, gourmet or otherwise, would be hard-pressed to find better.

I'm dining this evening with a party of six women. Let's see if the chef can make us all happy!

The decor of bar and dining room is very powerful, very sympathetic to its natural surroundings. The first things one notices are the vast windows, and the sensation that there is no real boundary between room and beach, table and ocean. The overhead cedar beams and pillars have been adzed by local carvers the late Henry Nolla and his son. The adze, originally used by First Nations, has been used here to create a pebbled texture that seems to bring the outside in. Henry was also responsible for carving the impressive front doors and many other features throughout the inn. Today, Nolla's legacy lives on through the carvers who operate from his little hut on Chesterman Beach.

The bar has a modern feel that, happily, has not sacrificed comfort for looks. Big, inviting chairs and couches in different-sized groupings make the perfect stop before or after dinner. When someone in my party orders a Scotch, it comes in one of Charles' father's heavy crystal gentleman's glasses. Even my New York City companions are impressed with the bartender's ability to pour every au courant cocktail they request.

A couple of steps down from the bar is The Pointe Restaurant, a semi-circular room set around a blazing open fire. The carpet has a rippled effect like the sea it seems to meet. Deep orange-coloured sconces on the walls become more noticeable as the sun sets. Eventually, the dining room is lit only by the sconces and candles set in rocks on the old-growth fir tables, and is it my imagination, or has someone opened a window? How could we now be hearing the surf? Actually, another magic wand has been waved behind the scenes: microphones strategically placed outside are allowing the crashing waves to be heard beneath the classical music. Such a brilliant score.

Our very beautiful waitress, Tara, sets the tone with a detailed discussion of the menus. Since it is April, the inn is still celebrating the Pacific Rim Whale Festival, so there's a special menu devoted to the fruits of the area: gooseneck barnacles, salmon, Dungeness crab, quail, asparagus. The whale festival celebrates the migration of the gray whale from late February to early March, or, this year, until mid-April. The resident whales stay until the fall. I've been in the dining room when a whale is spotted breaching close to shore, and discovered that the natural entertainment can, in fact, match the cooking here.

There is always a distinctive seafood menu, based on the local catch. These are enormously prolific waters, with high plankton content. Clams, crabs, scallops, mussels and oysters abound. The federal government regulates the fishery, opening and closing it as stocks allow. In recent years, there has been pressure on the salmon and halibut stocks, and the fishers have to catch their quotas or lose their licences. Sometimes an octopus is caught in a crab trap, and sometimes there are sea urchins on the menu.

The chef works with a kitchen brigade of 15. There are three to four cooks on the line at any one time, and 600 brilliant plates a night come out of the kitchen. The restaurant now seats 85, but plans call for a bit more seating and a re-engineered kitchen. Dining at The Pointe is a relaxed and friendly experience, yet service is 100 percent proper, with all dishes for each course arriving at the same time, borne by the requisite number of servers. The wait staff are not only nice, but highly knowledgeable, and not just about the food, but about the area and all aspects of the inn. I know Charles McDiarmid is a graduate of Cornell's hotel management school, and my impression is that everyone else is too!

This evening, our menu begins with the sexy Spiced Oyster Shooter (a big hit with the girls). The Carpaccio of Rock Scallops with Roast Grape Tomatoes, Tomato Oil, Smoked Salmon and Chervil Salad is so fresh and flavourful that many in our party order it two nights in a row. A silky Roasted Dungeness Crab and Brandy Bisque with Crab and Leek Dumpling follows; Lemon and Mint Sorbet is presented in an ice bowl with a feather of Lavender Fern from the forest; Pan-Seared Steelhead is served with Octopus and Wild Mushroom in Puff Pastry with Snow Peas, Corn and Vanilla Emulsion. The seafood menu closes, as it opens, with something sensual: Caramelized Honey Parfait with Fresh Raspberries and a Peach Schnapps Sauce.

Seared Pacific Halibut and Steamed Vancouver Island Mussels with Saffron and Fresh Herb Spaetzle, Greens and Smoked Heirloom Tomato Broth

MICHAEL BEBAULT, THE WICKANINNISH INN

Serves 4. The Pointe Restaurant brings the sea to your table, and this is a great example from the kitchen's repertoire.

Halibut:

4	portions fresh line-caught halibut (6 oz/170 g each)	4

Spaetzle:

2	large eggs	2
1/2 c	milk	120 ml
1/3 lb	flour	150 g
	pinch salt	
	pinch freshly ground pepper	
0.017 oz	saffron	1/2 g
1 c	water	240 ml
2 tbsp	fresh chopped parsley, cilantro, thyme and basil	30 ml
1 tbsp	unsalted butter	15 ml

Broth:

4	medium heirloom tomatoes	4
1	shallot, peeled and finely diced	1
1	clove garlic, peeled and minced	1
1 tbsp	white wine	15 ml
1 c	vegetable stock	240 ml
	apple wood smoking chips	
12	fresh Vancouver Island mussels (3 per person)	12

Greens:

4	small clusters mixed greens	4

Spaetzle: Cook the saffron in one cup of water until it becomes a vibrant yellow liquid and has reduced by three-quarters. Remove from heat and cool. Whisk the eggs in a bowl. Add the milk, salt, pepper and saffron liquid. Add the flour while whisking until a thick batter is reached. If it is too thin, you may have to add a little more flour. Incorporate the herbs and allow the batter to rest for one hour before cooking to relax the gluten. Over a large pot of boiling water, place a colander and press the batter through the holes. When the dumplings rise to the surface, allow to simmer for one or two minutes, then remove and cool quickly in ice water and drain well.

Broth: In a smoker, smoke the tomatoes long enough so that they take on a rich smokey flavour (approximately 10 minutes in heavy smoke). Sweat the shallot and garlic for two or three minutes and deglaze with the white wine. Add the tomatoes and vegetable stock and bring to the boil. Allow to simmer for 15 to 18 minutes. Remove from heat and pass through a fine chinois or sieve and keep warm. **To serve,** steam the mussels in the tomato broth until they open. Sear both sides of the halibut in a small amount of oil and place in a 350°F oven for approximately four minutes or until cooked but still tender and moist. Sauté the spaetzle in butter until hot. Place the spaetzle in a large soup plate and put a small cluster of the greens on top. Place one portion of halibut on top of the greens and three mussels in each dish. Pour the smoked tomato broth over top of the halibut. Garnish the halibut with a teaspoon of beluga (or other) caviar.

The Pointe's à la carte menu is actually a well-thought-out prix fixe, allowing guests to choose three, four or five courses. This fall, the choices fell under the evocative headings of autumn beginnings and late harvest continuation. I went straight to Wild Roasted Mushroom and Amaretto Purée with Toasted Walnut and Blue Cheese Strudel, and blissfully continued with the Seared Pheasant Breast with Braised Rutabaga, Cranberry Compote with Apple Cider Reduction and Aged Balsamic Syrup.

Vancouver Island's wild west coast area is not exactly a farming community, but here and there some exceptional food is being raised and produced — the best of which is regularly featured on The Wickaninnish Inn's menus. Charles McDiarmid generously introduced me to some of the remarkable local food producers, whose stories you've just read.

A New Conductor: Chef de Cuisine Andrew Springett

Having long regarded the Wickaninnish Inn's Pointe Restaurant as "a finely tuned orchestra," I was curious to meet its new conductor, Chef de Cuisine Andrew Springett, and taste his culinary arrangements. My opportunity came in January during the area's exciting storm-watching season and just before Springett took a quick trip to New York to visit some of his mates.

Meeting with a chef before dinner service can only heighten one's expectations for the meal ahead, and my early afternoon coffee and chat with Springett was no exception. His credentials are stellar: he has worked in such restaurants as Toronto's Fairmont Royal York and North 44 and Vancouver's Diva at The

Chef Andrew Springett is the new "conductor" of The Pointe Restaurant.

Met and the Four Seasons, with such elite chefs as Michael Noble, Rodney Butters, Kerry Sear and Bruno Marti, and participated in high-level culinary competitions including *Bocuse d'Or* and the World Culinary Olympics. He's also had some inspiring "off-road" cooking stints — at the famous Daniel's in New York ("they knocked me about a bit," he laughs, "but I learned a lot") and at the exclusive $1,500-per-guest-per-day West Coast Fishing Club in Port Louis, Queen Charlotte Islands, which gave him "a whole new respect for seafood. I was able to work with cheeks from 150-pound halibut and wings from 40-pound skates."

During a seven-month break from formal cheffing, he cooked in a seafood place in Nairobi, Kenya, learned to make samosa dough from a woman there and had "the best meal of my life on Mykonos at

a restaurant where you walk right into the kitchen and point at what you want to eat." On that extended edible journey, he enjoyed cooking whatever he found at the markets (he mentioned a goat's head and, like Anthony Bourdain, thrives on "trying everything once").

This is a chef who knew what he was going to do for a living when he was in Grade 9. He credits his home economics teacher, John Haen at North Surrey Secondary, with planting the culinary seed, as well as his older sister with whom he cooked and took cooking classes "as a hobby."

When he was invited to take the conductor's baton at the Wickaninnish a year ago, Springett brought with him his experience in "some magical kitchens, respect for the product and the ability to develop close relationships with growers." He started having "cook's and producers' meetings" when he was in Vancouver in order to "source the freshest, sexiest ingredients in the soil and sea." He's developing those close relationships with Vancouver Island farms like Nanoose Edibles and Qualicum Beach's Blue Heron Farm as well as Tofino's Medicine Farms and First Nations' foragers. Chanterelles, chicken-of-the-woods and coral mushrooms, and cynamocha berries are examples of the seasonal produce that arrives at his kitchen door. "You just can't buy that quality through the food-distribution companies," says Springett.

He says that Tofino reminds him a lot of the Queen Charlottes in that "it's a cook's playground where the seasons dictate the menu." Springett sources cold-smoked salmon from Rick Burns of the *Pacific Provider* and hot-smoked salmon from the area's Salmon Masters. Both are beautifully presented at dinner later in his signature salmon-tasting starter. Cowichan Bay Farm's pasture-raised chicken is also on the menu here, as are the local Pacific beach oysters.

Springett says the real challenge of running a five-star restaurant in a remote location is getting staff "with the right level of experience." He's solved that one by reintroducing a chef's apprenticeship program in conjunction with Vancouver Community, Camosun and Malaspina colleges. The Pointe Restaurant takes one pastry and two hot-kitchen apprentices at a time in order "to maintain a strong brigade in the kitchen and create a bit of magic here."

That magic was certainly evident at dinner, where I was able to sample a wide range of Springett's cooking from the daily tasting menu. Tasting menus have generally given way to à la carte presentations, but the Wick has wisely maintained a daily tasting selection for those of us who like to graze. As my dining companion also chose the tasting menu, I was able to taste 10 dishes at one sitting. (While that may seem excessive, I'm the woman who, in only an hour, tasted and judged 35 pies at the Metchosin Day Pie Contest. Some metabolisms know no bounds.)

From a delicate, lemony, smoked salmon and foie gras parfait, its richness well paired with Vigneti Zanatta's Glenora Fantasia sparkling wine, to a deeply satisfying maple-roasted Blue Heron Farm's squash soup with apple crème fraiche and toasted almonds that resonated with the Provençal rosé-style 2002 Pinot

Gris from Alderlea Vineyards and a glazed Cowhican Bay Farm duck breast served with confit of duck leg, mashed potato and blood orange sauce in tandem with a glass of pinot noir from Alderlea, Springett's cooking soared from sublime to sublimer.

I had challenged sommelier Chris Mustard, a graduate of Dubrulle's in Vancouver and formerly of The Aerie Resort, with pairing only regional wines to my meal and was really impressed with his choices. While he did have to veer into the Okanagan for a couple of picks, he was able to represent Vancouver Island's Alderlea, Vigneti Zanatta and Venturi Schulze, and Saturna Island vineyards in his selections. A highly knowledgeable and unpretentious sommelier, Mustard gives the profession a good name, particularly to those of us on steep oenophilic learning curves. I'd say he is well on his way to meeting Charles McDiarmid's goal: "to ensure The Pointe Restaurant has the undisputed best wine list in British Columbia."

Dogwood Lounge

The Wickaninnish now offers two styles of accommodation: the original building or Wickaninnish at the Pointe, and the newly built Wickaninnish on the Beach. I made a point of staying in the latter, which has the same "rustic elegance" as the Wick at the Pointe, but with a more casual feel. Amenities include an exercise room for rainy days; a library and Internet lounge, where there's a nice selection of books and magazines and big comfy chairs to flop into; and the beach-level Dogwood Lounge, where coffee and sweet treats are available all day long.

The lounge has a unique coffee bar fashioned from the trunk (with its roots still intact) of a yellow cedar that toppled over in a storm. The trunk has been levelled off on one side to create a unique countertop. When I dropped in after an invigorating walk on Chesterman Beach, server Michael had just put on a fresh pot of coffee and taken delivery of a pear and frangipane tart from the inn's

The Wickaninnish Inn General Manager Charles McDiarmid.

pastry chef. With a copy of *The Globe and Mail* in hand, I was all set to curl up by the fire and enjoy some tranquillity.

Michael told me the lounge is "a great place to watch the sun rise over the trees on the beach." It's also the place to buy souvenirs for your friends back home — house-made "aphrodisiac chocolates" anyone?

Breakfast

I write this for my fellow peripatetic breakfast hounds, those whose day is made by finding a sensational breakfast, and who are lost without it! Others may care little or not at all that The Wickaninnish Inn gets breakfast right every morning.

To begin, you will be greeted by one of several seriously healthy-looking waitresses, who has inevitably surfed before starting her shift. She proffers the daily juice special, which today is a combination of freshly squeezed apple, melon and blackberry. Its beautiful amber colour and exotic flavour awaken the senses, and encourage one to take in the view.

Ah, so this is Chesterman Beach in the morning, a mile and a half of sand immaculately cleansed by the evening's rain, the sun illuminating a blue sky and calm ocean. The low tide has already invited strollers, joggers and surfers to venture forth, and two eagles, residents of a tree on the inn's north side, are soaring and seeking their own repast. All is quiet across at the Leonard Island Lighthouse, one of the last remaining manned lighthouses on the west coast. What's not to love, starting the day with this spectacular, peaceful, yet ever-changing vista and a promising breakfast menu at hand?

You can have breakfast any way you want it. Sometimes, I have a lovely bowl of oatmeal, served up with juicy raisins, steamed milk and crystals of deep brown sugar. At other times, I go for the Eggs Benedict with Ucluelet Goats' Cheese and Organic Spinach served on a homemade English muffin and accompanied by really good pan-fries. It is unspeakably rich and satisfying. My husband appreciates the man-sized British cooked breakfast that is made to his specifications: scrambled eggs; roast potatoes; smoked salmon; stone-ground toast and homemade preserves, all of which he chases with a skinny cappuccino.

As we tuck in, one of the eagles steals our attention by sweeping seaward for its own breakfast. A man sets up his tripod on the rocks. The elderly couple next to us finishes their breakfast. He walks around to pull out her chair, and they head out for a leisurely stroll along the beach. We are in no hurry, either. We finish our own breakfast in the lounge, sunk deep into armchairs with coffees and newspapers at hand, yet still glued to the view.

Photo Credits

(Credits for photos in the colour sections are identified by a "C" before the page number)

Adrian Dorst: C16 (bottom)
Aerie Resort: C4
Alderlea Vineyards: 131
Andrei Fedorov: 61, 64, 65, 67, 70, 71, 178, C2, C3 (top)
Blue Grouse Vineyards: 134
Brasserie L'Ecole: 4, 6
Chateau Wolff: 145, 146
Christopher Letard: 158
Creekmore Coffee: 221
Elizabeth Levinson: 29, 51, 75, 103, 107, 111, 117, 138, 162, 163, 187, 212, 216, 234, 248, 270, 272, 274, 277, 283, 288, C1, C3 (middle and bottom), C5 (bottom), C6 (bottom), C7 (top), C9 (top), C10 (top), C11 (top), C12 (top and middle), C14, C15 (top)
Engeler Farm: C8 (top)
Fairburn Farm: C7 (bottom), C8 (bottom)
Gabriola Gourmet Garlic: 208
Gary Hynes: 24
Gordon Browne: C13 (bottom)
Greg Osoba: C13 (top)
Hastings House: 77, 80, C6 (top and middle)
Hollyhock: 259
House Piccolo: 83
Kiwi Cove Lodge: C9 (bottom)
La Boulange Organic Breads: 224, C11 (bottom)
Maclean's Specialty Foods: 202
Monsoon Exotic World Spices: 93
Natural Pastures Cheese Company: C12 (bottom)
Retta Moorman: 8, 11, 20, 24, 28, 30, 31, 39, 48
Rob Malnychuk: C15 (bottom)
Rosheen Holland: 211
Reef Point Farm: 262
Steeples: 150, C5 (top)
TouchWood Editions: 133, 136, 149, 189, 190, 198, 200, 204, 206, 245, C10 (bottom)
Vinoteca Restaurant: 142
Wave Hill Farm: 91
Wickaninnish Inn: 290, C16 (top)
Wild Fire Bakery: 37

Contacts

SOUTH ISLAND
Victoria
Brasserie L'École
restaurant • dinner only
1715 Government Street
Victoria, V8W 1Z4
Tel: (250) 475-6260
www.lecole.ca
eat@lecole.ca
Sean Brennan, chef/owner
Marc Morrison, sommelier/owner

Cafe Brio
restaurant • dinner year-round, lunch in summer
944 Fort Street
Victoria, V8V 3K2
Tel: (250) 383-0009
www.cafe-brio.com
reservations@cafe-brio.com
Sylvia Marcolini and Greg Hays, owners
Chris Dignan, chef

Caffé Fantastico
coffee shop
965 Kings Road
Victoria, V8I 1W/
Tel: (250) 385-BEAN (2326)
www.caffefantastico.com
ryan@caffefantastico.com
Ryan and Kristy Taylor

Cucina
restaurant/caterer • lunch Tuesday – Saturday • dinner and special events by appointment
Loft 10
532-1/2 Fisgard Street
Victoria, V8W 1R4
Tel: (250) 360-1348
Mirjana

Feys & Hobbs Catered Arts
catering, party and event planning, wholesale and retail food sales
1 - 845 Viewfield Road
Victoria, V9A 4V2
Tel: (250) 380-0390
Toll free: 1-877-500-5267
www.feysandhobbs.com
inquiries@feysandhobbs.com
David Feys, owner and chef

Fourways Meat Market
butcher
3500 Quadra Street
Victoria, V8X 1G9
Tel: (250) 382-2431
Fax: (250) 382-2437
Dave Robinson

Hernande'z
restaurant • open from 5 p.m. for pre-ordered burrito dinner on Fridays and prix fixe dinner on Saturdays by reservation only
749 View Street
Toro
lunch kiosk • open Monday to Friday, 11 a.m. to 3 p.m.
743 View Street (pedestrian entrance to the View Street Parkade)
Victoria, V8W 1J9
Tel: (250) 884-6566
Jerson Hernandez and Tamara Koltermann, owners

Italian Bakery
bakery, grocery and café
3197 Quadra Street
Victoria, V8X 1E9
Tel: (250) 388-4557
Alberto Pozzolo and Janet Cochrane

Mirage Coffee
1122 Blanshard Street
Victoria, V8W 2H6
Tel: (250) 384-4980
Percy Bojanich, owner

Moss Street Market
farmers' market Saturdays, 10 a.m. to 2 p.m., May to late October plus special Christmas market
corner of Moss Street and Fairfield Road (Sir James Douglas School)
Tel: (250) 361-1747
Marinie Smith

Ottavio Italian Bakery & Delicatessen
bakery, delicatessen and coffee bar
2278 Oak Bay Avenue
Victoria, V8R 1G7
Tel/Fax: (250) 592-4080
Monica Pozzolo and Andrew Moyer

The Personal Chef
caterer • by appointment
1330 Mt. Newton Cross Road
Saanichton, V8M 1S1
Tel: (250) 544-1/80
Fax: (250) 544-1185
jennycameron@pacificcoast.net
Jenny Cameron

Planet Organic
organic grocery
3995 Quadra Street
Victoria, V8X 1J8
Tel: (250) 727-9888
www.planetorganic.ca
Diane Shaskin and Mark Craft

Pure Vanilla Bakery and Café
bakery and café
105-2590 Cadboro Bay Road
Victoria, V8R 5J2
Tel: (250) 592-2896
Audrey Alsterburg

Share Organics
home delivery • call or email to arrange
1885 St. Ann Street
Victoria, V8R 5V9
Tel: (250) 595-6729
Fax: (250) 595-6721
www.shareorganics.bc.ca
susan@shareorganics.bc.ca
Susan Tychie

Spinnakers Brewpub
brewery, pub and restaurant
308 Catherine Street
Victoria, V9A 3S8
Tel: (250) 384-2739
www.spinnakers.com
Paul Hadfield

Travel with Taste Tours
culinary tours • call to reserve
#1 – 356 Simcoe Street
Victoria, V8V 1L1
Tel: (250) 385-1527
www.travelwithtaste.com
info@travelwithtaste.com
Kathy McAree

Wild Fire Bakery
bakery
1517 Quadra Street
Victoria, V8W 2L3
Tel: (250) 381-3473
Cliff Leir and Erica Heyerman

Zambri's
restaurant • lunch and dinner
#110-911 Yates Street
Victoria, V8V 4X3
Tel: (250) 360-1171
Fax: (250) 413-3231
www.zambris.com
zambris@shaw.ca
Jo and Peter Zambri

Saanich/Brentwood Bay
Arbutus Grille & Wine Bar at
Brentwood Bay Lodge
849 Verdier Avenue
Brentwood Bay, V8M 1C5
Tel: (250) 544-2079
Toll free: 1-888-544-2079
Dining reservations: (250) 544-5100
www.brentwoodbaylodge.com
Matthew Opferkuch, General
Manager
Alain Léger, Executive Chef

Marley Farm Winery
1831D Mount Newton X Road
Saanichton, V8M 1L1
Tel: (250) 652-8667
www.marleyfarm.ca
info@marleyfarm.ca
Michael and Beverly Marley, owners

Shady Creek Ice Cream Company
producer not open to public • product sold through Vancouver Island retailers
7268 Veyaness Road
Saanichton, V8M 1M2
Tel: (250) 652-8256
eng@islandnet.com
Christie Eng

Southern Vancouver Island
Foraging Trail
Tartan Public Relations
Victoria
Tel: (250) 592-3838
Deirdre Campbell

Metchosin
Happy Valley Lavender and Herb
Farm
farm • open in season • call ahead for hours • annual Lavender Festival
3505 Happy Valley Road
Victoria, V9C 2Y2
Tel/Fax: (250) 474-5767
www.happyvalleylavender.com
lynda@happyvalleylavender.com
Lynda Dowling

Metchosin Farmers' Market
farmers' market Sundays, 11 a.m. to 2 p.m., mid-May to mid-October
Municipal Grounds, Happy Valley
Road
Metchosin
Tel: (250) 474-3156
Bob Mitchell

Sooke
Cooper's Cove Guesthouse and
Angelo's Cooking School
5301 Sooke Road
Sooke, V0S 1N0
Tel: (250) 642-5727
Toll free: 1-877-642-5727
www.cooperscove.com
info@cooperscove.com
Angelo Prosperi-Porta and Ina
Haegemann, owners

Little Vienna Bakery
6-6726 West Coast Road
Sooke, V0S 1N0
Tel: (250) 642-6833
www.littlevienna.com
Andreas and Michelle Ruttkiewicz,
owners

Markus' Wharfside Restaurant
*open for dinner year-round Tuesday to
Saturday, Tuesday to Sunday in July and
Aug • lunches may be booked in advance
for parties of six or more*
1831 Maple Avenue
Sooke, V0S 1N0
Tel: (250) 642-3596
www.markuswharfsiderestaurant.com
markuswharfside@hotmail.com
Markus and Tatum Wieland,
owners

Ragley Farm
*farmgate • open Saturday year-round,
also Sunday in season*
5717 East Sooke Road
Sooke, V0S 1N0
Tel: (250) 642-7349
Fax: (250) 642-1946
ragley@telus.net
Josephino Hill

The Seaweed Lady
*producer • product available through
Vancouver Island retailers • tours by
appointment*
Outer Coast Seaweeds
2018 Penang Road
Sooke, V0S 1N0
Tel: (250) 642-5328
www.outercoastseaweeds.com
outercoastseaweeds@shaw.ca
Diane Bernard

Sooke Harbour House
restaurant and inn
1528 Whiffen Spit Road
Sooke, V0S 1N0
Tel: (250) 642-3421
Fax: (250) 642-6988
www.sookeharbourhouse.com
info@sookeharbourhouse.com
Sinclair and Frédérique Philip, owners
Edward Tuson, chef

Tugwell Creek Honey Farm
*farmgate • open Wednesday to Sunday,
11 a.m. to 4 p.m., April to August • tours
by appointment*
8750 West Coast Road
Sooke, V0S 1N0
Tel: (250) 642-1956
www.tugwellcreekfarm.com
dana-l@shaw.ca
Robert Liptrot and Dana Le Comte

Saltspring Island
The Bread Lady
*bakery • not open to the public • bread
sales at Market-in-the-Park (see listing)*
251 Forest Ridge Road
Saltspring Island
V8K 1W4
Tel: (250) 653-4809
pvanhorn@saltspring.com
Heather Campbell

Bright Farm
*not open to the public • produce available
at Market-in-the-Park (see listing) and the
Organic Market (see listing)*
176 Tripp Road
Saltspring Island, V8K 1K5
Tel: (250) 537-4319
ceagle@saltspring.com
Charlie Eagle, Judy Horvath and
Bree Eagle

Hastings House
*restaurant and inn • closed late
November through mid-March*
160 Upper Ganges Road
Saltspring Island, V8K 2S2
Tel: (250) 537-2362
800-661-9255 Canada and USA
Fax: (250) 537-5333
hasthouse@saltspring.com
www.hastingshouse.com
Shirley McLaughlin, manager
Marcel Kauer, executive chef

House Piccolo
restaurant • dinner only
108 Hereford Avenue
Saltspring Island, V8K 2V9
Tel: (250) 537-1844
www.housepiccolo.com
piccolo@saltspring.com
Piccolo Lyytikainen, owner/chef

Jana's Bake Shop
*bakery and coffee bar • open after Labour
Day, Mondays to Fridays, 7 a.m. to 4 p.m.;
Saturdays 8 a.m. to 2 p.m.; after the May
long weekend, daily, 7 a.m. to 4 p.m.*
324 Lower Ganges Road
Ganges, Saltspring Island
V8K 2V3
Tel: (250) 537-0029
islandtoisland@canada.com
Jana Roerick and Marcus Dowrich,
owners

Madrona Valley Farm
*farm and bed & breakfast • produce
available at Market-in-the-Park (see
listing)*
171 Chu-An Drive
Saltspring Island, V8K 1H9
Tel: (250) 537-1989
www.madronavalleyfarm.com
info@madronavalleyfarm.com
Michael and Jeanne-Marie
Ableman

Market-in-the-Park
farmers' market Saturdays, 8:30 a.m. to 3:30 p.m., first Saturday in April to last Saturday in October
Centennial Park, downtown
Ganges, Saltspring Island
Tel: (250) 537-4448
www.saltspringmarket.com
CRD Parks and Recreation

Monsoon Coast Exotic World Spices
producer • not open to the public • product available at Market-in-the-Park (see listing) and through Vancouver Island retailers
280 Robinson Road
Saltspring Island, V8K 1P7
Tel: (250) 537-9447
Fax: (250) 537-1311
www.monsooncoast.com
Satva and Chintan Hall

Moonstruck Organic Cheese
dairy and cheese company • not open to the public
1306 Beddis Road
Saltspring Island, V8K 2C9
Tel/fax: (250) 537-4987
www.moonstruckcheese.com
grace@saltspring.com
Julia and Susan Grace, owners

Morningside Organic Bakery and Café
108 Morningside Road
Saltspring Island, V8K 1X1
Tel: (250) 653-4414
Alan Golding and Manon Darrette

Salt Spring Flour Mill
producer • not open to the public • product available at Market-in-the-Park (see listing)
169 Dogwood Lane
Saltspring Island, V8K 1A4
Tel: (250) 537-4282
dogwoodlane@saltspring.com
Pat Reichert

Salt Spring Vineyards
vineyards, winery and bed-and-breakfast • July to early September, daily, 12 noon to 5 p.m.; early September to early May, Saturdays only, 12 noon to 5 p.m.
151 Lee Road
Saltspring Island, V8K 2A5
Tel: (250) 653-9463
www.saltspringvineyards.com
vineyards@saltspring.com
Bill and Janice Hartley, owners

Saltspring Island Cheese Company
producer • not open to the public • product available at Market-in-the-Park (see listing) and through Vancouver Island retailers
285 Reynolds Road
Saltspring Island, V8K 1Y2
Tel: (250) 653-2304
David and Nancy Wood

Saltspring Island Garlic Festival
food festival held in August • call for date
Farmers' Institute Grounds
351 Rainbow Road
Saltspring Island
Tel: (250) 537-1219
Kristie

Soya Nova Tofu
producer • product available for purchase on site and through Vancouver Island retailers
1200 Beddis Road
Saltspring Island, V8K 2C8
Tel: (250) 537-9651
www.soyanova.ca
soyanova@saltspring.com
Deborah Lauzon

Wave Hill Farm
farm not open to the public • produce and flowers available at Market-in-the-Park (see listing) • meat and poultry by special order — call ahead
340 Bridgeman Road
Saltspring Island, V8K 1W7
Tel/Fax: (250) 653-4121
Mark Whitear and Rosalie Beach

Pender Island
Iona Farm
farm not open to the public • produce available at Pender Island Farmers' Market (see listing)
3403 South Otter Bay Road
Pender Island, V0N 2M1
(250) 629-6700
iona@cablean.net
Rob and Ellen Willingham

Jane's Herb Garden
herb garden and farmgate sales • open March to October, daily, 11 a.m. to 3 p.m. or by appointment
3719 Rum Road
South Pender Island, V0N 2M2
Tel: (250) 629-6670
janesherbgarden@cablelan.net
Jane Gregory, owner

Morning Bay Farms
market gardens, vineyards and winery
open (hours of op — EL)
6621 Harbour Hill Drive
North Pender Island, V0N 2M1
Tel: (250) 629-8350
mrngby@netscape.net
Keith Watt and Barbara Reid,
owners

Pacific Shoreline
fishers • seasonal • call for days and times of dockside sales
Pender Island
Tel: (250) 629-9950
Bonnie and Cal

Pender Island Bakery Café
bakery and café
1105 Stanley Point Drive
Pender Island, V0N 2M1
Tel: (250) 629-6453 or
(250) 629-3877
Fax: (250) 629-3879
dmurdoch@gulfislands.com
Dorothy Murdoch

Poets Cove Resort and Spa
resort, restaurant, lounge, spa, marina • open year round
9801 Spalding Road
South Pender Island, V0N 2M3
Tel: 1-888-512-7638
www.poetscove.com
Martin De Board, Executive Chef

Saturna Island
Haggis Farm Bakery
bakery not open to the public • product available at Saturna General Store and through Vancouver Island retailers
110 Narvaez Bay Road
Saturna Island, V0N 2Y0
Tel: (250) 539-2591
Jon Guy and Priscilla Ewbank

Saturna General Store and Café
grocery, wine store and café
101 Narvaez Bay Road
Saturna Island, V0N 2Y0
Tel: (250) 539-2936
Fax: (250) 539-5136
Jon Guy, Priscilla Ewbank and
Hubertus Surm

Saturna Herbs
farm open to the public • no set times • product available at Saturna General Store and through online mail order
Breezy Bay Farm
131 Payne Road
Saturna Island, V0N 2Y0
Tel: (250) 539-5200
Fax: (250) 539-5201
www.saturnaherbs.com
saturnaherbs@canada.com
Flora House

Saturna Island Vineyards
vineyard, winery, tasting room and café open to the public year-round
8 Quarry Trail
Saturna Island, V0N 2Y0
Toll free: 877-918-3388
Tel: (250) 539-5139
Fax: (250) 539-5157
www.saturnavineyards.com
wine@saturnavineyards.com
Rebecca Page, general manager
Eric von Krosigk, winemaker

Mayne Island
Deacon Vale Farm
not open to the public • produce available at Mayne Island Farmers' Market (see listing) • sauces and preserves available through Vancouver Island retailers
380 Campbell Bay Road
Mayne Island, V0N 2J0
Tel/Fax: (250) 539-5456
www.deaconvalefarm.com
dvf@gulfislands.com
Don and Shanti McDougall

Mayne Island Farmers' Market
farmers' market Saturdays, 10 a.m. to 1 p.m., May long weekend to Thanksgiving
Agricultural Hall Grounds
Miners Bay
Mayne Island
Tel: (250) 539-5456
Shanti McDougall

Oceanwood Country Inn
restaurant and inn • closed November through February
630 Dinner Bay Road
Mayne Island, V0N 2J0
Tel: (250) 539-5074
www.oceanwood.com
oceanwood@gulfislands.com
Jonathan Chilvers, owner
David Kruse, chef de cuisine

Galiano Island
Daystar Market and Market Café
open Monday to Wednesday, 10 a.m. to 5 p.m.; Friday, 9 a.m. to 6 p.m.; Saturday, 10 a.m. to 6 p.m.; Sunday, 10:30 a.m. to 5 p.m.
96 Georgeson Bay Road
Galiano, V0N 1P0
Tel: (250) 539-2505
www.galianoisland.com/eating
places
Lony Rockafella, owner

Max & Moritz
Spicy Island Food House
*seasonal food kiosk at the Sturdies Bay
ferry terminal Galiano Island*
Tel: (250) 539-5888
Christian and Lucy Banski, owners

WINE ROUTE

Alderlea Vineyards
*vineyard, winery and tasting room open
year-round • hours vary • call ahead*
1751 Stamps Road
Duncan, V9L 5W2
Tel/Fax: (250) 746-7122
Roger and Nancy Dosman

Blue Grouse Vineyards
*vineyard, winery and tasting room open
Wednesday to Saturday, 11 a.m. to 5
p.m., October to March • Wednesday to
Sunday, 11 a.m. to 5 p.m., April to
September*
4365 Blue Grouse Road
Cobble Hill, V9L 6M3
Tel: (250) 743-3834
Fax: (250) 743-9305
www.bluegrousevineyards.com
skiltz@islandnet.com
Dr. Hans Kiltz, Evangeline Kiltz
and Sandrina Kiltz

Cherry Point Vineyards
*vineyard, winery, tasting room, tours
• picnic patio and gift shop open daily
year-round • call for dates of summer
outdoor concerts*
840 Cherry Point Road
Cobble Hill, V0R 1L0
Tel: (250) 743-1272
Fax: (250) 743-1059
www.cherrypointvineyards.com
Wayne and Helena Ulrich

Glenterra Vineyards
*vineyard, winery and tasting room open
daily year-round, 11 a.m. to 6 p.m.*
3897 Cobble Hill Road
Cobble Hill, V0R 1L0
Tel: (250) 743-2330
glenterravineyards@shaw.ca
John Kelly and Ruth Luxton

Venturi Schulze Vineyards
*vineyard, winery, vinegary and tasting
room open by appointment only*
4235 Trans Canada Highway
Cobble Hill, V0R 1L0
Tel: (250) 743-5630
Fax: (250) 743-5638
www.venturischulze.com
info@venturischulze.com
Giordano Venturi, Marilyn and
Michelle Schulze

Vigneti Zanatta and Vinoteca
Restaurant
*vineyard, winery, tasting room and
restaurant open March to December*
5039 Marshall Road
Duncan, V9L 6S3
Tel: vineyard: (250) 748-2338
Tel: restaurant: (250) 709-2279
Fax: (250) 748-2347
www.zanatta.ca
Loretta Zanatta and Jim Moody
and family, owners
Fatima da Silva, chef

Château Wolff
*vineyard, winery open daily year-round
• tasting room open Saturday and
Sunday year-round*
2534 Maxey Road
Nanaimo, V9S 5V6
Tel: (250) 753-4613
Fax: (250) 753-0614
Harry von Wolff

MID-ISLAND
Shawnigan Lake

Steeples
*restaurant • daily dinner and weekend
brunch*
2744 East Shawnigan Lake Road
Shawnigan Lake, V0R 2W0
Tel: (250) 743-1887
www.steeplesrestaurant.ca
darren@steeplesrestaurant.ca
Darren Cole, chef/co-owner

The Malahat

The Aerie Resort
*restaurant and inn • seasonal tours of
local farms*
600 Ebadora Lane
The Malahat, V0R 2L0
Tel: (250) 743-7115
Fax: (250) 743-4766
www.aerie.bc.ca
resort@aerie.bc.ca
James Kendal, general manager
Christophe Letard, chef de cuisine

Maple Bay

Grapevine on the Bay
6701 Beaumont Avenue
Maple Bay, V9L 5X8
Tel: (250) 746-0797
Daniel and Ruth van den
Wildenberg, owners

Duncan

The Community Farm Store and
Corfield's Coffee Shop
330 Duncan Street
Duncan, V9L 3W4
Tel: (250) 715-1383
Susan Minette, owner and baker

Cowichan Valley

The Asparagus Farm
farmgate open to the public in season
• call ahead for dates and times
1550 Robson Lane
Cobble Hill
Tel/Fax: (250) 743-5073
www.islandnet.com/~cford/
Charles and Carole Ford

Black Coffee and Other Delights
café
4705 E Trans-Canada Highway
Whippletree Junction,
Duncan, V9L 6E1
(250) 746-9973
cleveland@cvnet.net
Corrine Wilson, Andrew Simonson
and Morris Cleveland

Broken Briar Fallow Deer Farm
farm/restaurant supplier • some venison
sales on site
2692 Mt. Siker Road
Chemainus, V0R 1K0
Tel: (250) 246-9749
tdgroves@island.net
David Groves

Cowichan Bay Farm
farm store open daily year-round
• products also available through
Vancouver Island retailers
1560 Cowichan Bay Road, RR #1
Cowichan Bay, V0R 1N0
Tel/Fax: (250) 746-7884
farmer@cowichanbayfarm.com
www.cowichanbayfarm.com
Lyle and Fiona Young

Deerholme Farm and Cottage
email or call for appointment or for
schedule of workshops
4830 Stelfox Road
Duncan, V9L 6S9
Tel: (250) 748-7450
www.magnorth.bc.ca
bill@magnorth.bc.ca
Bill and Lynn Jones, owners

**Fairburn Farm Culinary Retreat
and Guesthouse**
bed & breakfast • farmers' market tours
• cooking classes • Sunday lunches •
buffalo tours • call ahead for meat orders
3310 Jackson Road
Duncan, V9L 6N7
Tel: (250) 746-4637
Fax: (250) 746-4317
www.fairburnfarm.bc.ca
info@fairburnfarm.bc.ca
Darrel and Anthea Archer
Mara Jernigan

Feast of Fields
food festival held at a different farm every
September • call for date and venue
Tel: (250) 746-4637
Mara Jernigan

Merridale Ciderworks
cidery and tasting room •
open daily, 10:30 a.m. to 5:30 p.m. •
guided and VIP tours, booked in advance
1230 Merridale Road
Cobble Hill, V0R 1L0
Tel: (250) 743-4293
Toll free: 1-800-998-9908
www.merridalecider.com
Rick Pipes and Janet Doherty,
owners

The Mushroom Guy
mushroom foraging tours and dinners
• call to reserve
Magnetic North Cuisine
4830 Stelfox Road
Duncan
Tel: (250) 748-7450
www.magnorth.bc.ca
bill@magnorth.bc.ca
Bill Jones

Saskatoon Berry Farm
orchard u-pick and farm store open in
season • call for dates and times
1245 Fisher Road
Cobble Hill, V0R 1L0
Tel: (250) 743-1189
toonfarm@yahoo.com
Alwin and Connie Dyrland

Cowichan Bay

Hilary's Cheese Company
Cowichan Bay Shop
(located inside True Grain Bread) • open
Wednesday to Sunday, 10 a.m. to 5 p.m.
1725 Cowichan Bay Road
Cowichan Bay, V0R 1N0
Tel: (250) 715-0563
Farm Shop
open Thursday to Sunday, 11:30 a.m. to
4 p.m. • hours may vary at the farm •
call ahead for group tours
1282 Cherry Point Road
Cowichan Bay, V0R 1N2
Tel: (250) 715-0563
hilarys@cowichan.com
Hilary and Patty Abbott, owners

The Mellow Side Arts Lounge & Café
arts lounge and café • open Wednesday to Sunday, 11 a.m. to 11 p.m. • closed Monday and Tuesday, but can be booked for special functions
1737 Cowichan Bay Road
Cowichan Bay, V0R 1N0
Tel: (250) 701-0448
www.mellowside.com
John Androsky, owner

True Grain Bread
bakery • open Wednesday to Friday, 8 a.m. to 6 p.m., Saturday and Sunday, 8 a.m. to 4 p.m.
1725 Cowichan Bay Road
Cowichan Bay, V0R 1N0
Tel: (250) 746-7664
Jonathan Knight, owner

Cedar

Cedar Farmers' Market
farmers' market Sundays, 10 a.m. to 1 p.m., mid-May to early October
Crow and Gate Pub, off Cedar Road
Tel/Fax: (250) 722-3526
George Benson

Mahle House Restaurant
dinner Wednesday to Sunday year-round
2104 Hemer Road
Nanaimo, V9X 1L8
Tel: (250) 722-3621
Fax (250) 722-3302
www.mahlehouse.com
info@mahlehouse.com
Maureen Loucks, chef/owner
Delbert Horrocks, sommelier/owner

Ladysmith

Barton Leier Gallery*
gallery of cover artist Grant Leier and his wife, artist Nixie Barton • open to the public
3140 Decourcey Road
Ladysmith, V9G 1E2
Tel: (250) 722-7140
bartonleiergallery@shaw.ca
Grant Leier and Nixie Barton
*Their paintings are food for the soul!

Hazelwood Herb Farm
farm • herb plants, gift shop and self-guided tours daily, 11 a.m. to 5 p.m., April to September • 11 a.m. to 5 p.m. Friday to Sunday, October to Christmas Eve • call for dates of annual festivals
13576 Adshead Road
Ladysmith, V9G 1H6
Tel: (250) 245-8007
www.hazelwoodherbfarm.com
info@hazelwoodherbfarm.com
Richard Wright and Jacynthe Dugas

Kiwi Cove Lodge
farm and bed & breakfast
5130 Brenton Page Road
Ladysmith, V9G 1L6
Tel: (250) 245-8051
Fax: (250) 245-8010
www.kiwicovelodge.com
kiwicove@shaw.ca
Peggy and Doug Kolosoff

Page Point Inn
restaurant and inn
4760 Brenton-Page Road
Ladysmith, V9G 1L7
Tel: (250) 245-2312
Toll free: 1-877-860-6866
Fax: (250) 245-7546
www.pagepointinn.com
info@pagepointinn.com
Lawrence and Lexie Lambert, owners
John Grove, chef

Nanaimo

Carrot on the Run and 24 Carrot Catering
deli and catering company
6560 Metral Drive
Nanaimo, V9T 2L9
Tel: (250) 390-0008
www.24carrotcatering.bc.ca
carrot@direct.ca
Alexandra Berlingette and Melissa Hamilton, owners

Glow World Cuisine
restaurant • lunch and dinner daily • weekend brunch
7 Victoria Road
Nanaimo, V9R 4N9
Tel: (250) 741-8858
Eric and Larry Lim, owners
Luke Griffin, chef

Island Natural Markets
grocery store
6560 Metral Drive
Nanaimo, V9T 2L9
Tel: (250) 390-1955
islandnatural@shaw.ca
Rhonda Lambert and Casey Mitchell

McLean's Specialty Foods
specialty food store, delicatessen and café
426 Fitzwilliam Street
Nanaimo, V9R 3B1
Tel: (250) 754-0100
Fax: (250) 754-0161
www.mcleansfoods.com
mcleans@nisa.net
Eric and Sandy McLean

Shady Mile Farm Market
grocery store and café
3452 Jingle Pot Road
Nanaimo, V9R 6W9
Tel: (250) 729-3801
Bill and Sharon Earthy

The Wesley Street
restaurant • lunch and dinner
1 – 321 Wesley Street
Nanaimo, V9R 2T5
Tel: (250) 753-6057
Gaetan and Linda Brousseau

Gabriola Island
Gabriola Gourmet Garlic
studio open daily year-round
1025 Horseshoe Road
Gabriola Island, V0R 1X0
Tel/Fax: (250) 247-0132
www.gabriolagourmetgarlic.com
gabriolagourmetgarlic@shaw.ca
Ken Stefanson and Llie Brotherton

Gabriola Agricultural Association
Farmers' Market
*farmers' market Saturdays, 10 a.m. to 2
p.m., beginning of May to Thanksgiving*
Agi Hall
465 South Road (top of the hill
from the ferry)
Gabriola Island
Tel: (250) 247-8216
ebus87@island.net
Tannie Meyer

Heavenly Flowers and the
Good Earth Market Garden
*farm not open to the public • farmgate
open in season • call for dates and times*
600 South Road
Gabriola Island, V0R 1X0
Tel: (250) 668-0670
Rosheen Holland and Bob Shields

Lantzville/Nanoose Bay
The Book Worm Café
café • breakfast and lunch
7221 Lantzville Road
Lantzville, V0R 2H0
Tel: (250) 390-4541
Chris Thomas and Vicky Adamson

Harvest Bounty Festival
*food festival held at a different farm every
August • call for date and venue*
Tel: (250) 248-8207
Debbie Schug

Nanoose Edibles
*farm • farmgate hours vary • call for
dates and hours*
1960A Stewart Road
Nanoose Bay, V9P 9E7
Tel: (250) 468-2332
Fax: (250) 468-2324
Barbara and Lorne Ebell

Parksville
Little Qualicum Cheeseworks
*dairy farm and farm store • open Monday
to Saturday, 9 a.m. to 3 p.m.*
403 Lowry's Road
Parksville, V9P 2B5
Tel: (250) 954-3931
cheese@island.net
Clarke and Nancy Gourlay, owners

Qualicum Beach
Creekmore Coffee
*coffee roastery • not open to the public
• coffee available through Vancouver
Island retailers*
P.O. Box 555
Qualicum Beach, V9K 1T1
Tel: (250) 752-0158
Fax: (250) 752-0138
coffeecreek@shaw.ca
David and Elaine Creekmore

Fore & Aft Foods
*caterers • by appointment • condiments
sold through Vancouver Island retailers*
5390 Island Highway
Qualicum Beach, V9K 2E8
Tel: (250) 757-8682
Beverley Child and Patrick
Brownrigg

La Boulange Organic Breads
*bakery • retail sales on site • product
also sold through Vancouver Island retailers*
692 Bennett Road
Qualicum Beach
Tel: (250) 752-0077
Fax: (250) 752-0078
laboulange@home.com
John Taraynor and Jean Wilson

Qualicum Beach Farmers' Market
*farmers' market Saturdays, 9 a.m. to
noon, mid-May to September*
Fir Street at Memorial Avenue
Qualicum Beach
Tel: (250) 752-2857
Bea

RainBarrel Farm
*farm • not open to the public • produce
and flowers available at Qualicum Beach
Farmers' Market (see listing) and
Qualicum Beach Thrifty Foods*
599 Garden Road East
Qualicum Beach, V9K 1M5
Tel: (250) 752-0424
lmant@shaw.ca
Marilyn Mant and Tami Treit

Denman Island

Bien Tostado Custom Coffee Roasting
coffee roastery • not open to the public • online orders through website
3711 East Road
Denman Island, VOR 1TO
Toll free: 1-877-334-4433
Tel: (250) 335-1864
www.bientostado.ca
coffee@island.net
Elaine Head and Steven Carballeira

Cowppuccino Café
café • open in summer only • call for dates and times
5590 East Road
Denman Island, VOR 1TO
Tel: (250) 335-2195
Evelyn Martins

Denman Island Chocolate
factory not open to the public • chocolate available though Vancouver Island retailers
Site 136, C5
Denman Island, VOR 1TO
Tel: (250) 335-2418
Fax: (250) 335-0112
www.denmanislandchocolate.com
info@denmanislandchocolate.com
Ruth and Daniel Terry

Denman Island Farmers' Market
May 24th long weekend to Thanksgiving Saturdays, 9:30 a.m. to 12:30 p.m.
Old School Centre
5277 Denman Central Road
Denman Island
Tel: (250) 335-2294
Anne de Cosson

East Cider Orchard
orchard • apple and cider sales on site in season and through Granville Island, East Vancouver and Courtenay Farmers' Markets
2831 East Road
Denman Island, VOR 1TO
Tel: (250) 335-2294
decosson@mars.ark.com
Anne de Cosson and Larry Berg

Jacquie's Ices
ice-cream stand • open in summer only • call for dates and times
Gravelly Bay
Denman Island
Tel: (250) 335-2199
Jacquie Barnett

Windy Marsh Farm
farm not open to the public • farmstand open daily in season
8700 Owl Crescent
Denman Island, VOR 1TO
Tel: (250) 335-1252
Bob and Velda Parsons

Hornby Island

The Flower Lady
flowers and produce available at the Hornby Island Farmers' Market (see listing)
Hornby Island
Tel: (250) 335-0987
Anna MacKay

Hornby Island Co-op
grocery store
Central Road
Hornby Island, VOR 1ZO
Tel: (250) 335-1121
Phoebe Long, manager

Hornby Island Farmers' Market
farmers' market Wednesdays and Saturdays in season, 11 a.m. to 2 p.m.
behind the Community Hall
Hornby Island

Savoie Farm
farm not open to the public • flowers and produce available at the Hornby Island Farmers' Market (see listing) • flowers also sold from a stand across from the Cardboard House Bakery
2-7 Carmichael Road
Hornby Island, VOR 1ZO
Tel: (250) 335-0276
Elaine and Mary Savoie

The Sushi Lady
sushi available at the Hornby Island Farmers' Market (see listing)
Hornby Island
Tel: (250) 335-0399
Tania Hale

NORTH ISLAND
Buckley Bay

Fanny Bay Oysters Seafood Shop
fresh and frozen seafood • Open 9 a.m. to 6 daily, 9 to 9 on Fridays
#1 – 6856 South Island Highway (19A)
Buckley Bay, VOR 3BO
Tel: (250) 335-1198
www.fannybayoysters.com
Glen and Sharon Hadden, owners
Debbie Prowse, manager

Cumberland

Cumberland Village Bakery
bakery • open Tuesday to Saturday, 8:30 a.m. to 5 p.m.
2747 Dunsmuir Avenue
Cumberland, VOR 1SO
David Murray and Megan Sommers
Tel: (250) 336-2411

Hazelmere Farms
farm • farmgate open in season • call ahead for dates and directions
3222 Grant Road
Cumberland, V0R 1S0
Tel: (250) 336-2308
Fax: (250) 339-6676
huawongs@telus.net
Lijen and Sherlene Hua

Courtenay/Black Creek
Edible Island Whole Foods Market
grocery store
477 6th Street
Courtenay, V9N 1M4
Tel: (250) 334-3116
Fax: (250) 334-0575
edible@island.net
Sue Tupper, Sue Clark and Jackie Somerville

Hot Chocolates
Chocolates, candies, gelati and coffee bar open Monday to Thursday and Saturdays, 9:30 a.m. to 5:30 p.m., Fridays, 9:30 a.m. to 6 p.m., Sundays, 12 noon to 4 p.m. • extended hours in summer
238 Fifth Street
Courtenay, V9N 1J6
Tel: (250) 338-8211
Toll free: 1-866-468-2462
www.hotchocolates.ca
Jorden Marshall and Sherry Marshall-Bruce

Natural Pastures Cheese Company
cheese factory not open to the public • on-site retail shop open weekday afternoons
635 McPhee Avenue
Courtenay, V9N 2Z7
Toll free tel: 1-866-244-4422
Tel: (250) 334-4422
Fax: (250) 334-2922
www.naturalpastures.com
naturalpasturescheese@telus.net
Mary Ann Hyndman Smith, Edgar Smith and Rick Adams

On Line Farms
farm stand open in season • call ahead for dates and times • produce sold at the Saturday Comox Valley Farmers' Market (see listing)
5660 Island Highway North
Black Creek, V9J 1T2
Tel: (250) 338-8342
Price Lang and Marjan de Jong

Seaview Game Farm
farm tours and farm shop open daily year-round • call for cooking class schedule
1392 Seaview Road
Black Creek, V9J 1J7
Tel: (250) 337-5182
Cell: (250) 287-6334
www.seaviewgamefarm.com
Michel Rabu, chef/manager

Tita's Mexican Restaurant
open daily from 4:30 p.m. to 9 p.m. (10 p.m. on Friday and Saturday)
536 Sixth Street
Courtenay, V9N 1M6
Tel: (250) 334-8033
www.tita.ca
Martin and Lisa Metz, owners

Comox
Martine's Bistro
Open Tuesday to Saturday for lunch from 11:30 p.m. • Open daily for dinner from 5 p.m.
1754 Beaufort Avenue
Comox, V9M 1R6
Tel: (250) 339-1199
Marcus Aartsen and Christine Cameron, owners

Portuguese Joe's Fish Market
fresh and frozen seafood • open Monday to Saturday, 8 a.m. to 6 p.m.
3025 Comox Road
Courtenay, V9N 3P7
Tel: (250) 339-2119
Nilda, Eddy, Cecil and Lito Veloso

Quadra Island
Topcliff Farm
farmgate in season • call for dates and times
1181 Topcliff Road
Quadra Island, V0P 1N0
Tel: (250) 285-2343
sitkasil@connected.bc.ca
Linda Lessard and John Kragen

Cortes Island
Cortes Café
café open during Cortes Island Farmers' Market (see listing)
Manson's Hall
corner of Sutil Point Road and Beasley Road

Cortes Island Farmers' Market
farmers' market Fridays, 12:30 to 3:30 p.m., year-round
Manson's Hall
corner of Sutil Point Road and Beasley Road

Hollyhock
educational retreat and restaurant
end of Highfield Road
Cortes Island
Box 127, Manson's Landing
Cortes Island, V0P 1K0
www.hollyhock.ca
Tel: 1-800-933-6339
Debra Fontaine, head chef

Reef Point Farm
bed & breakfast
end of Sutil Point Road
Cortes Island, V0P 1K0
Tel: (250) 935-6797
Ginnie and Bruce Ellingsen

The Tak
café
800 Sutil Point Road
Cortes, V0P 1K0
Tel: (250) 935-8555
scottkennedymercs@hotmail.com
Scott Mercs

WEST COAST
Ucluelet/Tofino
Chocolate Tofino
chocolate factory and shop • open daily, 11 a.m. to 6 p.m. (later closing in July, August and September), closed January
1180-A Pacific Rim Highway
Tofino, V0R 2Z0
Tel: (250) 725-2526
www.chocolatetofino.com
chocolate_tofino@alberni.net
Gordon Austin, owner and chocolatier

Clayoquot Organics
farm not open to the public • produce available at Salal's Co-op Grocery, Tofino
Tofino
Tel: (250) 725-3967
mmacleod@island.net
Melanie MacLeod

Festival of Oysters and the Sea
mid-November
various locations in Tofino
Tel: (250) 725-4222
www.oystergala.com

The Goat Lady
farm not open to the public • visit by prior appointment only
Westerly Wynds Farm
P.O. Box 1029
Ucluelet, V0R 3A0
Tel: (250) 726-2682
Jane Hunt

Oyster Jim
producer • oyster sales on site
P.O. Box 947
2480 Pacific Rim Highway
Ucluelet, V0R 3A0
Tel: (250) 726-7350
Jim Martin

Raincoast Café
restaurant • dinner year-round
101-120 Fourth Street
Tofino, V0R 2Z0
Tel: (250) 725-2215
www.raincoastcafe.com
raincafe@island.net
Lisa Henderson and Larry Nicolay

Shelter Restaurant
restaurant • open daily for dinner from 5:30 p.m.
601 Campbell Street
Tofino, V0R 2Z0
Tel: (250) 725-3353
www.shelterrestaurant.com
Jay Gildenhuys, owner
Marco Lilliu, manager
Jesse Blake, chef

Sobo in the Garden
in the Tofino Botanical Gardens
1084 Pacific Rim Highway
Tofino
Tel: (250) 725-2341
Artie and Lisa Ahier

Trilogy Fish Company
fish store
Box 327, 630 Campbell Street
Tofino, V0R 2Z0
Tel: (250) 725-2233
Fax: (250) 725-2234
www.trilogyfish.com
info@trilogyfish.com
John and Donna Fraser

The Wickaninnish Inn
restaurant and inn
Osprey Lane at Chesterman Beach
Tofino, V0R 2Z0
Tel: (250) 725-3100
Fax: (250) 725-3110
www.wickinn.com
info@wickinn.com
Charles McDiarmid, manager
Andrew Springett, chef de cuisine